The Book of Hindu
Festivals and Ceremonies

The Book of Hindu
Festivals and Ceremonies

(Second Revised and Enlarged Edition)

Om Lata Bahadur

UBS Publishers' Distributors Ltd.
New Delhi ● Bangalore ● Chennai ● Calcutta ●
Patna ● Kanpur ● London

UBS Publishers' Distributors Ltd.

5 Ansari Road, New Delhi-110 002
Phones : 3273601, 3266646 ☆ *Cable* : ALLBOOKS ☆ *Fax* : 3276593, 3274261
e-mail: ubspd.del@smy.sprintrpg.ems.vsnl.net.in
Internet: www.ubspd.com
10 First Main Road, Gandhi Nagar, Bangalore-560 009
Phones : 2263901, 2263902, 2253903 ☆ *Cable* : ALLBOOKS ☆ *Fax* : 2263904
6, Sivaganga Road, Nungambakkam, Chennai-600 034
Phones : 8276355, 8270189 ☆ *Cable* : UBSIPUB ☆ *Fax* : 8278920
8/1-B, Chowringhee Lane, Calcutta-700 016
Phones : 2441821, 2442910, 2449473 ☆ *Cable* : UBSIPUBS ☆ *Fax* : 2450027
5 A, Rajendra Nagar, Patna-800 016
Phones : 672856, 673973, 656170 ☆ *Cable* : UBSPUB ☆ *Fax* : 656169
80, Noronha Road, Cantonment, Kanpur-208 004
Phones : 369124, 362665, 357488 ☆ *Fax* : 315122

Overseas Contact
475 North Circular Road, Neasden, London NW2 7QG
Tele : 081-450-8667 ☆ *Fax* : 0181-452-6612 Attn: UBS

Distributors for Western India:
M/s Preface Books
Shivali Apartments, Plot No. 1, S. No. 25/4, Chintamani Society,
Karve Nagar, Pune 411052 ☆ Phone: 349491

© Om Lata Bahadur

First Published	**1994**
First Reprint	**1995**
Second Reprint	**1995**
Third Reprint	**1996**
Second Revised & Enlarged Edition	**1997**
Reprint	**1999**

Cover Design :   UBS art Studio
Cover Illustration: Vikas Bhargav

Designed & Typeset at UBSPD in 10 pt. New Century Schoolbook
Printed at Pauls Press, Okhla Industrial Area, New Delhi

To
my mother
Raj Rani Bahadur

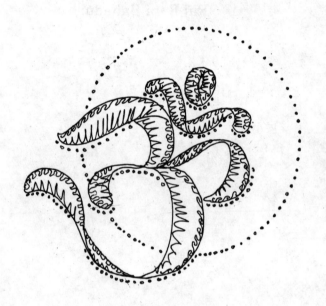

AUM — OM

The primeval sound. The only sound that envelopes the entire Brahmand (Cosmos) when all else is absolutely quiet. It is synonymous with the Holy 'Triad', 'Brahma-Vishnu-Mahesh', representing the union of the three Gods into 'The Supreme'. This sound remains for all times a mystic monosyllable as set forth as the object of profound religious meditation. The 'Abstract' translated into sound just as it is translated into a form 'Narayan'.

Acknowledgements

I WOULD LIKE TO ACKNOWLEDGE WITH GRATEFUL THANKS THE help given to me by my son Ashok who went out of his way to encourage and help me in every conceivable manner. I would also like to express my appreciation for my other son Harsh and his wife Monisha for their moral support.

I am grateful to Mrs. Promida Sapru and Mrs. Mohini Dayal without whom this book would not have seen the light of day.

I am also indebted to my sister Mrs. Sneh Lata Mathur for various nuggets of information regarding 'Tiths' and months of the festivals. My thanks to my niece Radhika and her husband Tilak for their help.

My thanks also to Pandit Narain Swami, Shankar Singh, Gopal Singh, Harbhajan Singh, late Mrs. Chandrawati Dayal, Mrs. Durgesh Dayal, Mrs. Amarjit Singh, Mrs. Zarina Begum, Mrs. Rama Chandra, Dr. Saini, Anil Mathur, Manisha Mathur, Mrs. Sharna Singh, Mrs. Umrao Singh, Mrs. Roop Dayal, Mrs. Vidya Shankar, Dr. S. Ramnath, Mrs. Anita Mathur, Mrs. Shahzad Bahadur, Mrs. Savitri Mathur, Mr. R. Vardharanjan, and Mrs. Kamalini Bahadur. Last but not least, to Mr. Kamla Prasad, Mrs. Sudha Prasad, Anamika and Shyam Bhargava, Vikas Bhargav, Mr. Sharna Singh, Mr. Umrao Singh, Mrs. Manjura Sarcar, Mrs. Devjani Chablia, Mrs. Bela Chandrani, Mrs. Sonia Tomar,

Dr. Harsh Kumar, Mrs. Anita Kumar, Mrs. Krishna Narani, Mrs. Ingla, Mr. Iqbal Singh, Mr. L.N. Misra, Mr. Rajan Tampi, Mr. A.V. Alex and all his staff at Orissa Bhavan and Mr. M.L. Mahapatra.

Preface

THIS BOOK IS INTENDED MAINLY FOR THE YOUNG HOUSEWIFE of today, who, as a student or as a working woman, has neither the time nor the inclination to find out the 'goings on' that once kept families together. After marriage, she suddenly realises that she has to make a 'home' in which family members of different age groups have to find common fields of interests and common topics of conversation. She has now entered the *grasth ashram*, the third stage of life, as described by the Indian *shastras*, and she has to be a good wife, a good daughter-in-law and a good mother, and later a good grandmother. She has to rise beyond her own self to carry on the multifarious activities of a household with tact, intelligence, common sense and practical, down-to-earth wisdom. She now has to make the home a 'heaven on earth' for all those who live there. This need not be tedious and tiresome, but could be a phase of life where one learns to make the joy of others a delight for oneself. The atmosphere in the house should be such that all its members make a beeline for home, and not wander around aimlessly looking for something exciting and interesting to do to kill their boredom, and in the process get entangled with alcohol, drugs or gambling and other crime-related activities. Therefore, I am writing down the age-old recipes for 'togetherness', which, if followed with wisdom, tact, persuasion and sanctity, will never fail but will create a sense of belonging to a great heritage and will anchor us securely to a given society.

By birth I am a Hindu and as such I know best the festivals that I have grown up with. Therefore, I describe them for those who follow my way of faith.

I am grateful to my mother to whose memory I dedicate this book, for she performed the rituals without fail and kept them alive for me. I am also indebted to my father, who kept up the spirit of festivity; to my grandparents who contributed so much to my knowledge of festivals when I was with them and made them such memorable occasions for the entire extended family; and last but not the least, to the memory of my husband, who shared the festivities with me for thirty-eight years, so much so that to this day we are in contact with over a hundred cousins on the paternal side, and over a hundred cousins on the maternal side (this is a conservative estimate). We are a unique family, where to this day, the youngsters find their best friends from amongst the family members.

This book is not meant to foster superstitious beliefs in *pujas* but to put them in the proper perspective. True to the Hindu way of life, events such as a change of season, welcoming a new bride, honouring a husband, or a daughter-in-law, or a daughter, or children or those who have departed from this earth, take on the significance of religious custom always revolving around a *devta*. This book seeks to capture the essence of such events.

One need not celebrate all the festivals, if it becomes cumbersome and difficult. One can leave out some, even if they have been celebrated every year, and I can assure you no harm will befall you. But one admirable quality that our mothers and grandmothers possessed was that despite all difficulties and hardships, they celebrated festivals in the traditional manner, following the rituals meticulously. *Pujas* generate sanctity and a feeling of complete pureness and 'goodness'. Festivals carry with them the wisdom of the ages which will reward everyone in the end.

In this book, I have described certain ways of celebration, if you know other ways, so be it! You are free to follow your own manner of celebrating. God in his heaven is the same for all, and the importance of 'togetherness' is the same for all. God be with you.

Om Lata Bahadur

Festivals and their Months

	Festival	Month
1.	Lohri	13 January
2.	Makar Sankranti	14 January
3.	Pongal	14 January
4.	Basant Panchami	January-February
5.	Mahashivratri	February-March
6.	Holi	February-March
7.	Bhai Dooj	February-March October-November
8.	Ram Navami	March-April
9.	Baisakhi	13 April
10.	Nirjala Ekathshi	May-June
11.	Festival of Jagannath Puri a) Chandan Yatra b) Snan Yatra c) Rath Yatra	May-June-July
12.	Sindhara	July-August
13.	Teej	July-August
14.	Raksha Bandhan	July-August
15.	Janam Ashtami	August-September
16.	Ganesh Chaturthi	August-September
17.	Onam	August-September
18.	Shraadh	September-October
19.	Durga Puja	September-October
20.	Dussehra	September-October
21.	Chaat	October-November
22.	Kati Bihu	October-14 (approx.)
23.	Karva Chouth	October-November
24.	Diwali	October-November

Contents

SRI GANESH

Pratham Sumer Sri Ganesh
Gauri Sur Priya Mahesh
Sakal Vighan Bhaya Kalesh
Dur Se Nivare
Pratham Sumer Sri Ganesh

Lambodar Bhuja Vishaal
Kar Thrishul Chandra Bhaal
Shobit Gale Pushp Haar
Rakt Vasan Dhare
Pratham Sumer Sri Ganesh

Ridhi Sidhi Dou Naar
Chavar Karat Baar Baar
Musak Vaahan Sawaar
Sakal Karaj Saare
Pratham Sumer Sri Ganesh

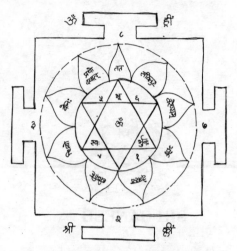

Gayatri Maha Mantra

Gayatri Mantra is above all other mantras.

"Om Bhoor Bhuvah Swah
Tat Savitur Varenyam
Bhargo Devasya Dhimahi
Diyo yo Nah Prachodayat"

Translation

Thou O Supreme Lord — The source of existence
Intelligence & Bliss!
The Creator of the Universe
May we prove worthy of thy choice &
acceptance!
May we meet thy glorious grace!
May Thou vouchsafe an unerring guidance
To our intellect and may we follow
The lead unto righteousness!

1

Lohri

LOHRI IS ONE OF THE MOST ZESTFUL FESTIVALS OF PUNJAB and always falls on the 13th day of January in the month of Paush or Magh, a day before Sankrant. Lohri is essentially a festival of the agriculturists and has been regularly celebrated for centuries by one of the most robust, tall, handsome and open-hearted people, i.e., the people of Punjab. The Punjabis are by nature cheerful, confident, outgoing, generous, and talkative, and are ambitious achievers in all fields of their choice, but mainly they are the sons of the soil. Their extreme hard work and endurance bring them bounty from mother earth. This particular region (Punjab) derives its name from the five rivers that flow

here. (*Punj Aab* literally means five waters.) These rivers
have rendered the soil fertile, which, in turn, has made
Punjab the 'granary of India'. Now, of course, some
sections of the rivers have gone to Pakistan, i.e., Indus,
Ravi, Jhelum and Chenab. Satluj and Beas still flow in
India. The waters of the rivers are shared wherever they
pass through each other's territory. The weather
fluctuates from extreme cold in winter to extreme heat
in summer, thus keeping the inhabitants very alert,
strong and active.

The Rabi crop (wheat) is normally sown in October
and the half-grown saplings show promising signs of a
good harvest when they are cut in March-April. The
delight of the farmers on seeing the fields coming up
with the promise of gold (the wheat fields look golden
in colour) knows no bounds and after the intense toil
and sweat that they have put in, they would definitely
like to celebrate, for there is plenty of time before work
in the fields again requires their attention. The people
celebrate with gay abandon. In January the weather is
very cold and what better way than to light a bonfire,
which forms the essence and the focal point of Lohri.
The menfolk gather round a bonfire in the *choupal* (the
village square) attired in *salwar kameez* and very
beautiful jackets embellished with small mirrors (or *gota
kinari*). Big colourful *paggers* (turban) decorate the
heads, with fringes hanging on the side and reaching
down to the chests or waists. The festivities include
dancing and the boisterous Bhangra dance (a typical
Punjabi group dance performed by men) which is ideally
suited to the occasion. On Lohri, dancers perform the
Bhangra in a ring round the fire. The fire is offered
chirva, *meva*, *til-gur-revri* and *gazak* (various kinds of
eatables) by each individual. The fire becomes the deity
of the day. No one is allowed to throw any leftovers or
anything that is *jutha* (touched by the mouth) into the
fire (in order to maintain its purity). While makin

offerings to the fire, each one says 'Aadar aye dilather jaye' (may honour come and poverty be banished). Everyone does the parikrama round the fire before starting to dance, and individuals who join the ceremonies in the middle must also perform it. Eatables such as meva (dry fruits), revri, til laddoos, gur, chirva and popcorn are served to everyone. People bring these items in plenty from their homes; or else they are collected or bought by the enthusiastic boys and girls of the locality who, earlier in the evening, go around to individual houses, seeking donation for the bonfire festival, and also singing special Lohri songs, much to the delight of the householders. On the roads, these children usually utter the cry: 'Aye mai de ke ja, daari mouch mul ke ja (O women give before you go). One special hero of Punjabi lore is Dhula Bhatti, who was really a dacoit (but on the lines of Robin Hood), and, to this day, many songs highlighting his heroic deeds are sung during Lohri celebrations.

Before and during Lohri, the women are invariably very busy and active. Well before the festival, the mothers and grandmothers are engrossed in drawing up lists of the materials required for Lohri. Each household stocks adequate quantities of (1) til, (2) gur, (3) revri, (4) dry fruit, (5) popcorn, (6) chirva (7) mumphali and (8) gazak. The women have to decide as to how much they would give to the children who come asking for donation both in kind and money, how much they would require for the men who may want to participate in the village celebration and how much has to be retained at home since the women celebrate Lohri in their own courtyards, where the holy bonfire is lit and they perform the Gidda (a kind of dance). The difference between the Bhangra and the Gidda is that Bhangra is performed by men to the rhythm of a dholak and the Gidda is performed by women. In the Bhangra, the main rhythmic movements involve the outstretched arms with hands also outstretched or kept up and constantly flailed; the shoulders are rhythmically jerked, and the steps are deliberate. The younger and more athletic indulge in a lot of acrobatics, but again to the graceful rhythm of the *dholak*. This dance can continue well into the night, with new people joining in and the tired ones stepping out to rest for some time and to partake of the delicious eatables.

The dance performed by women entails more play of the body and the arms in quick graceful movements. One or more of the women move centrestage while the rest clap to the beat of the *dholak* standing in a line. They catch hold of each other's hands and perform the *kikli* (going round and round with their own hands crossed and holding the crossed hands of a partner, and twirling very fast in a given space). A good deal of singing and 'making a racket' are the order of the day. The loud beating of the *dholak* with sticks invokes a festive mood in everyone. Of course, like the men, the women also do the *parikrama* of the 'fire god' and hand out their offerings. They recite: *'Aadar aye dilather jaye'*.

On the festive occasion of Lohri, the young women have a field day and get intricate *mehndi* patterns decorated on their hands and feet. They buy the most colourful bangles and *bindis*. Their garments are grand, especially the *chunni* which is very heavy with *zari* and *gota*, *salma* and *sitaras*. *Sindhoor* is applied in the parting of the hair (for married women). *Salwar kameez* or *ghaghras* are the favoured attires for this day. Everyone is invited to join in the fun and frolic; no one can resist doing so!

The first Lohri celebrated by a new bride represents a grand occasion and is comparable to the Sindhara of Rajasthan and Delhi. The mother-in-law presents heavy garments and jewellery to the new bride. Unlike Sindhara, in this case the bride remains in her in-laws' house where a grand feast is arranged and all sons and daughters of the house with their spouses and children and all their close friends and neighbours are

invited. Early in the evening, when the main people have
arrived, the new bride is dressed in her best *salwar* suit
or *ghaghra* and is made to sit, along with her husband,
in a central place where the father in-law and mother-
in-law perform the presentation of clothes and jewellery.
The close relatives and friends also join in and present
clothes or cash to the new bride.

The first Lohri of a new-born baby is equally
important and the immediate family members are
definitely invited. If the occasion is to be celebrated on
a big scale, then all close friends are also invited. The
mother attired in heavy clothes and wearing a lot of
jewellery with *mehndi* on her hands and feet sits with
the baby in her lap. The family does the presentations.
The mother-in-law and father-in-law of course give a
large quantity of presents in the form of clothes and cash
and others do so according to their relationship with
the couple as also their capability and desire. Lohri is
then celebrated with traditional dancing and singing
around the bonfire.

Food served during Lohri is non-vegetarian but no
hard drinks are served. Mostly, all the sons and daughters-
in-law of the house get together to celebrate the festival.
They eat together and dance the Bhangra and Gidda and
make merry with the children. Lohri is a great 'fun
festival' and a most enjoyable one at that. The festivities
keep everyone warm, hale and hearty.

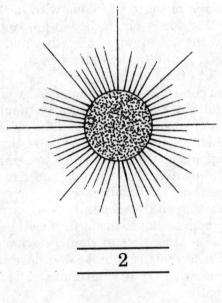

2

Pongal

PONGAL IS UNDOUBTEDLY THE MOST IMPORTANT FESTIVAL celebrated by Tamilians. This is a harvest festival honouring the sun god and the god of rain, Indra. Pongal represents a kind of thanksgiving for the plentiful paddy crop that the farmer has harvested during the mild winter months in the south of India. (Pongal literally means 'boiling over'; symbolically the boiling over of bounteous crops in the fields.) The festival is normally celebrated over a period of four days. The festival always starts on 13 January every year and coincides with Lohri of Punjab and Goopi of Andhra Pradesh. The calculations are done according to the solar calendar, therefore, the dates do not change. Since the same is the case with

Lohri, Makar Sankranti and Goopi, these festivals will always coincide. The actual day of Pongal celebration is 14 January. It is considered a very auspicious time when the sun enters the 'Makar Rasi' (northern hemisphere). The sun moves from the Tropic of Capricorn towards the Equator and then towards the Tropic of Cancer. This period beginning from 14 January lasts till 14 July and is known as 'Uttarayan'. Bhishma Pitamah, the grand sire of *Mahabharata*, in fact, waited on his bed of arrows in the open battlefield of Kurukshetra for Uttarayan in order to free his soul from mortal bondage and attain *moksha*.

Although Pongal festivities normally last for four days, some households celebrate it for three days only. There may be a slight difference in the rituals and rites between Brahmin households and the other castes. Nevertheless, all farmers intermingle with other members of the neighbouring families. Each farmer contributes his share, in one way or the other, during the six months preceding the festival, called the period of 'Dakshinayan'. This is the time for sowing of seeds and saplings and also for cultivating short-term crops. A rich and abundant harvest of paddy and other crops is dependent on a required quantity of rainfall at the right time, as rivers in Tamil Nadu are not perennial. Consequently, the Sun God and Indra are devoutly worshipped.

A few days prior to the Pongal festival, every house is cleaned, whitewashed and dusted. All broken or dented utensils are exchanged for new ones. The *chattaies* (mats) on which people normally sleep (on the floor), get frayed and decay as they are made from reeds. They are replaced by new ones, which are neatly stacked in corners. Rugs are taken out and beaten with sticks to get the dust out, or they are drycleaned or washed at home. The houses in South India are generally kept spotlessly clean, with the minimum of furniture. Everyone takes off his or her footwear before entering a home, thereby ensuring complete cleanliness inside. The utensils in the kitchen are usually made of steel, sometimes they are made of brass. They are kept regularly shining by the housewife, therefore, there is not so much cleaning required as in the north during Diwali, when summer gives way to winter. During summer the heat and the duststorms, which seem to constantly penetrate into every nook and corner, leave behind a lot of dust that needs to be cleaned up. Still, in the south, there is much to do and a housewife must make provisions for all the expenses that become unavoidable. The modern housewife can go in for new furniture and decorations -- more in keeping with a cosmopolitan way of life. New clothes for a festival are an Indian heritage and the shops go all out to lure the customer before and during Pongal. The temptation -- for new *saris* for the women and a new *langha* and half *sari* (known as *dhavini)* for the young girls and *lungi* and *angavastram* (a cotton or silk shawl, white or off-white, with *zari* border thrown over one shoulder, or round the neck with both *zari pallus* hanging down to the waist or even a little lower) for the men and young boys -- is hard to resist. The wise housewife should be well aware of the family's enthusiasm for wearing new clothes, which become the main topic of conversation days before the festival and keeps everyone in a happy and expectant mood. Wearing them on the days of the festival makes for brighter moods and lighter hearts, and that is what festivals are all about!

The first day (Bhogi pandigai): This day is dedicated to Indra, who is the one to bestow the much-needed rain. Indra is also called *'Bhogi'*, i.e., one who enjoys the good things of life.

The faithful believe that on this day Lord Krishna, who got annoyed with the erratic ways of Indra, directed the people not to pray to him but to Lord Narayan who was, in fact, Krishna himself. Indra lost his temper at this insult and sent down the rains in torrents. The people got scared and looked towards Krishna for succour. Krishna then lifted up the great Goverdhan mountain on one finger and provided shelter to human beings, animals and beasts, who gathered beneath this mountain. Everyone sang Krishna's praise and Indra realised that he could never get the better of Krishna, who was the reincarnation of Vishnu, the protector. Indra apologised profusely and asked for forgiveness, but pleaded that he be also prayed to since, in any case, he had always looked after the beings on earth as well. Krishna relented.

On Bhogi day everyone at home – old and young – rises early and has an oil bath; usually *til* oil is rubbed onto all parts of the body, including the head, which results in a satisfying massage, ensuring good blood circulation. Next, the persons take a good bath with water and *shikakai* or any other preparation that the mother or grandmother would have made to enrich the skin and give it suppleness. Everyone appears bright and ready to celebrate. In the countryside the farmers bring their yield to the place where it is stored before being utilised or sold. Both in the villages and towns everyone collects the old items that have outlived their use, such as mats, rugs, files and clothes, and burn them in a bonfire right in the courtyard or open space. The children dance round the bonfire, beating the drums specially made for this occasion, thus fulfilling their desire for making a noise and indulging in fun and frolic. Such a spontaneous release of pent-up energy helps throughout the year in curbing the children's natural desire for wild behaviour and creating a racket by promising them complete freedom on the first day of Pongal. A time for children to look forward to! Everyone enjoys the warmth of the fire. This is the last day of the month of 'Maargazhi', the ninth month of the lunar calendar. This month is considered very sacred. According to the *Bhagavad Gita*, Lord Krishna manifests himself the most during this month, beginning, according to the English calendar, on 13 December and ending on 13 January.

Lunch is grand on this day, but outsiders are not invited and only those who live under the same roof partake of the feast. Several dishes are prepared on this occasion; for instance, sweets such as *poli* and salty dishes such as *vadai* and different kinds of rice.

The housewife will be well advised to make arrangements to keep the following items ready for the actual day of Pongal:

(1) Sandalwood paste.
(2) *Kumkum* (vermilion).
(3) Mango leaves and saplings.
(4) Coconut fronds.
(5) Sugarcane leaves and saplings.
(6) Banana leaves and plants.
(7) Ginger pieces.
(8) White flour and other colours to make different coloured powders.
(9) New vessels of brass (known as '*vengalapanai*') or mud.
(10) *Haldi* powder.
(11) A *thaali* or metal plate in which the sun is viewed.

The second day: The first day of the next month – known as 'Thai', equivalent to the North Indian lunar month of Magh – always falls on 14 January. This day is celebrated as Makar Sankranti in the northern regions of Karnataka, and also in Andhra Pradesh, Maharashtra, Punjab, Rajasthan, Haryana and Delhi, and some other parts of India. Actually, the whole of India celebrates this festival in one way or another under different names.

On this day, the outside of the house is decorated with strings of mango leaves tied neatly with the stems tucked inwards to form a loop, creating a beautiful green chain. Such mango-leaf strings are tied across all doorways or around pillars. The banana and sugarcane plants and coconut fronds are stood against gateways, large doorways and some pillars to form green archways. Marigolds strung up in threads are tied alongside this greenery and lend colour and freshness to the decoration. Fresh *rangoli* (known as *kolam*) patterns are drawn on the floor of the verandah and rooms by the women of the house. These patterns virtually convert the home into an art gallery. Such an art form inspires the young ones to learn this beautiful skill of decorating the floors with white and coloured flour and fresh flowers.

The *rangoli* is always prepared with the outline in white flour deftly traced by holding it between the thumb and index finger and letting it go to form a geometrical or floral design as desired by the person doing it. Later, the outlines are filled with coloured powder in accordance with the design, delighting the eye of the beholder. The floral decoration is done by removing the stems entirely and letting the colour of the flowers to guide the pattern. *Rangoli* is an everyday feature in South Indian homes, at least at the entrance. The material used need not be rice flour but white finely ground chalk, available in the market, can also be used.

New clothes are donned on this day after an early bath, and there is, naturally, a lot of good-natured hubbub in the house, with a lot of activities going on at the same time. New items are set in place if not already there. Everyone admires the new acquisitions and an atmosphere of gaiety and happiness prevails. The lady of the house must pay due attention to her kitchen so that the food items are ready in time. Only the people living in the house need be the ones partaking in the celebration, but visiting others could be done if time permits.

The special vessel of brass or mud is decorated with mango leaves, ginger saplings, fresh turmeric leaves with the pod/stalk and sugarcane pieces tied around its neck in a string. The vessel itself is decorated with *kumkum* and *haldi* dots. The vessel and its contents (see recipes) are placed on the fire in a very clean and neat kitchen by the daughter-in-law or the lady of the house and not by the servant or any visitor. The dishes prepared are special to this day. The salty one is known as *venpongal* while the one with jaggery is known as *chakkaraipongal*.

RECIPES FOR PONGAL

Rice	1/4 of any suitable vessel
Milk	1 glass
Water	1/2 of the vessel
Ghee	2 tablespoons or more or less according to the vessel size
Jaggery or salt	According to taste and the quantity of rice taken
	Jaggery is the brown unrefined juice of sugarcane (known as *gur* in North India)
Cashewnuts	As many as one desires
Crushed cardamom seeds (*elaichi*)	Small quantity

Method

Mix the water with the *ghee*, milk and rice and place the vessel containing them on the fire and cook. The cooked rice and the liquid boil and soon flow out from the vessel symbolising the overflowing fields, known as *Pongothal* (this may have become Pongal in the course of time as the term means to overflow). Take the vessel off the heat when cooked to the required strength, and add jaggery or salt as the case may be. Also, add the *elaichi*.

Next, the vessel containing the cooked food is taken outdoors along with some coconuts and other fruit. It is then kept in a clean place letting the rays of the sun fall on the foodstuff. The entire family chants: "I give to you what you had given to me." The *arti* is performed to the sun god amid chanting of Sanskrit *slokas* in praise of the 'sustainer of life'. *Surya namaskar* is done by raising the hands high above and folding them or lying down flat on the ground with head towards the sun, the hands out-stretched and palms joined, with the forehead touching the ground, the legs close together. Some people pour water in a symbolic gesture of giving water to the sun. A red flower is also the offering usually made to the sun god.

The sun is seen through the fingers entwined in a particular way so that the rays do not reach the eyes; or the sun is seen in a *thaali* full of water with *haldi* and *kumkum* mixed. *Pujan* is thus done to the sun god outdoors. Neither any image of any element, nor any planet is worshipped in the home. We do find the images of the *navagrahas* or planets in temples and people pray to them to ward off their evil effect, but *puja* is not done to them inside the house.

A grand lunch is the order of the day for the people of the household, with *idli, dosa* and rice cooked in different styles – boiled, salty or sweet. Rice can also be mixed with curd or *sambhar* or coconut chutney, and, of course, the special Pongal dish, is now taken as *prasad*.

The third day: This festival is known as Maatu Pongal. In Tamil *maatu* (or maadu) means cow or bull and also represents prosperity. Importance is therefore given to the cows or bulls which are of immense value to the farmer. The more the cattle the more the prosperity.

The horns of cows and bulls are decorated with *haldi* and *kumkum*. Small bells are tied around their necks. The cattle is then paraded along the streets. People offer fruit and other delicacies to them. Bull-fighting is indulged in with gusto where the young men pit their strength against the bull's, trying to catch its horns with their hands and making it back away in fright. More often, the young men get hurt, but not the bull. Such bravado makes heroes out of the young men, specially in the eyes of the young, beautiful damsels of the villages and towns, lending a lot of enthusiasm to these young men. Such an activity leads to betting and gambling which are allowed on this day, as the Indian recognises the need to give up prejudices for at least one day. There is a lot of dancing in groups, to the accompaniment of music. The lower classes take a holiday and go around in groups to visit temples, museums and aquariums and other places of interest and amusement and sing and dance to the beat of the *mridung* and *dhol* (drums of different kinds). The women wear colourful clothes and bunches of jasmine in their hair and make merry till late at night and carry on the festivities to the next day.

The fourth day: This day (17 January) is the last day of Pongal, and is known as Kaanum Pongal. It is a period for relaxation and, on this day, nothing new is started as it is believed to be *karinaal* (inauspicious). The people, therefore, prefer to indulge in sight-seeing and continue the merry-making of the earlier day. Some also go in for gambling.

The last day is also called Kanyapongal, when different preparations of rice and curd are kept on banana leaves or on leaves from the turmeric plant and left in the open so that the birds, squirrels and ants may also partake of the newly harvested rice. This also teaches the children to think of all the other living beings as members of the universal family and teaches them to share with the latter our prosperity and goodwill, as the latter, in their turn, give us so much pleasure and prove useful in several ways.

The married women along with their families are invited by their parents or brothers on this day for a meal in the afternoon. The women pray to the Almighty for the long lives and prosperity of their parents, brothers and children. They are given presents of cash from Rs 5 to Rs 500 (or so) by each brother. The mother can give in kind. (This day is treated like Raksha Bandhan celebrated in the northern regions.)

The festival of Pongal was celebrated mainly by the farmers and rural folk earlier on, but has now become a national festival and people living in towns not only in South India but also in North India are getting enthusiastic about Pongal. The excitement generated by this festival is becoming infectious, just as the South Indians celebrate some of the North Indian festivals. Thus, these festivals foster a feeling of togetherness not only within the family or neighbourhood but also in the whole of India.

Here are the recipes for a few of the tasty eatables.

STUFFED DOSA

Rice	9 oz
Husked black gram dal (dhuli urad dal)	3 oz
Salt	1 tsp
Green chillies	3-4
Ghee for frying	Suitable quantity

Method

Soak the rice and *urad dal* separately for about 8 hours and grind separately to a smooth fine paste. Also, grind three to four green chillies, and squeeze out the liquid. Add this ground stuff and salt to the *dosa* mixture; stir well and leave the mixture (batter) covered overnight.

Before frying the batter for making the *dosas*, heat the mixture well. Add 1/4 oz of wheat flour, a pinch of bicarbonate of soda and 1/2 tsp sugar. If the mixture is thick, add a little water and again beat it well. It should be of pouring consistency. Keep a heavy frying pan or griddle on a source of moderate heat. Smear it with a little *ghee* and when quite hot, pour a ladleful of the mixture. Spread out the dough uniformly in a circle (this calls for a good deal of skill) and add *ghee* or oil along the circular shape and cook for about two-three minutes, then overturn the *dosas*. Cook again for about two-three minutes, then remove from the fire. Add a tablespoon of the mixture in the centre, fold over and serve immediately with chutney.

FILLING

Potatoes	8 oz
Ghee or oil	2 oz
Urad dal	1½ tsp
Chana dal	1 tsp
Rough cut onions	8-10 oz
Red pepper	1/2 tsp
Coriander	1 level tsp
Green chillies	4 (cut)
Grated coconut	1/2 oz
Thinly sliced ginger	1/2 oz
Pepper corns	8
Salt	1½ tsp

Method

Boil and peel the potatoes and allow them to cool; cut into small bits and crush a few; scrape the coconut and grind along with green chillies, coriander, ginger and pepper-corns to a soft paste with a little water. Add this paste to the potato bits. Heat the *ghee* or oil. Fry in it *chana dal, urad dal,* mustard seeds, *zeera, hing* and *karipattas*. Then, add the seasoning and the onions. Keep the vessel containing these items on a heat source till the onions are cooked. Lastly, add potatoes and masala and cook on moderate heat for 10 minutes or till the potatoes get blended with the masala. Add 4 oz water and simmer for 5 minutes.

DOSA CHUTNEY

Coconut (grated)	1 oz
Green chillies	4
Urad dal (optional)	1 tsp
Ginger	1/4 oz
Tamarind	3/4 oz
Chana dal	1 tsp
Mustard seeds	1/2 tsp
Oil or *ghee*	1 tsp
Onion bits	1/4 oz
Coriander leaves	1/2 oz
Karipattas	2-3
Salt	1 tsp
Curd	2 drops

Method

Grind the grated coconut along with green chillies, coriander leaves (or *dhania* powder), onions, ginger, fried *dal*, tamarind, *karipattas*, and salt, with a little water, to a smooth paste. Heat oil or *ghee*, season with

1/2 tsp of mustard seeds and *urad dal* (if preferred); then add to this the ground mixture. Add beaten curd and seasoning. Serve with the *dosa*.

SAMBHAR

Arhar dal	4 oz
Carrot	1
Potato	1
Garlic cloves	2-4
Salt	1 tsp
Haldi (turmeric)	1/2 tsp
Water	1 lb
Tomatoes	4 oz
Pepper corns	6
White *zeera*	1 tsp
Ghee	1 oz
Mustard seeds	1 tsp
Methi seeds	1/2 tsp
Hing	a pinch
Karipattas	2-3
Red chillies	a few bits
Tamarind pulp	1/2 oz

Method

Boil *dal* with carrots, potatoes, garlic, salt, turmeric and water. When cooked, remove the carrots and potatoes and mash well. Add tomato puree and cook a little longer. If preferred, you can add any vegetable bits and heat till the vegetables are cooked. Lightly fry *dhania, zeera, methi* seeds, pepper corns and after that grind these in the dry form. Squeeze out tamarind pulp and add this to the boiled *dal*. Wait till the mixture boils once or twice. Next, heat the *ghee*, fry mustard seeds, *hing,* red pepper, finely cut green chillies and *karipattas*. Season the *dal* with the mixture and serve hot and sprinkle with dry ground masala.

3

Makar Sankranti

MAKAR SANKRANTI FESTIVAL FALLS ON THE DAY OF THE YEAR when the sun – considered the king of all *grahas* (planets) – is in the *rasi* (zodiac sign) known as Makar (Capricorn). This is considered the most beneficial *rasi* of the sun, and it is very auspicious. The calculations for determining Makar Sankranti are done according to the solar calendar. Therefore, Makar Sankranti always falls on 14 January according to the English calendar. It is usually the month of Magh of the Hindu calendar; the 'Tith' or the position of the moon keeps shifting because of the difference in calculations.

Although Sankrant comes every month, the position of the 'sun in Makar' bestows the most *punn* (merit) for those who abide by the rules of the festival – by bathing in the rivers or tanks, offering water to the sun god and giving *thaan* (charity). Such deeds earn special and lasting merit and assure one a place in heaven.

The faithful flock to the water sources (such as rivers, tanks or lakes) in all towns and villages. As the water levels in the rivers are low at this time of the year, the urchins of the town have a rollicking time. A *mela* is held on the banks of the rivers and tanks. *Chaatwalas* and 'icecream walas' display and sell their stuff, much to the delight of the kids. People from the upper classes usually avoid this type of bathing because of the fear of polluted waters, but the very religious do take the chance, because for them, the *punn* earned from the bath is greater than the danger of disease.

Makar Sankranti is a day of *thaan* (giving) to the poor and needy. There are two festivals, Makar Sankranti and Nirjala Ekadashi (or Ekathshi), where the focus is on those persons who may be suffering hardships and cannot afford to celebrate. It is good to teach the children from the very beginning that a thought for the less fortunate should always be there and should be translated into action at least some time in the year religiously. Therefore Makar Sankranti and Nirjala Ekadashi are the two days ordained for such *thaan*. It of course does not absolve one from being kind and charitable all through the year, whenever the occasion or situation demands! A bit of compulsory goodness does not harm anyone.

On this festival day the *thaan* consists of the following :

(1) Raw *khichri* (rice and *moong dal*
    mixed)   — 500 gm
                                        at least
(2) *Ghee* or cooking oil   — 1 *katori*
(3) Salt   — 250 gm
(4) *Papad*   — 4 pieces
(5) *Til ke laddoo*   — 4 pieces
(6) Some rice and water in a small *lota* for *manasna*.

All the items should be in the raw form except for the *laddoos*. The aforementioned list is for one individual only and portions must be made for everyone in the house.

The *puja* is performed in the morning. It need not be arranged in the *puja* room. No deity is required to be seated where the items for the *thaan* are kept. Since everyone in the house will be doing the *thaan*, it is best to arrange the required items in a big room or a verandah. The *thaan* can be done by each member separately and all need not sit together; the children can do it after they return from school. For the grown-ups even breakfast should be taken after the *thaan* has been done. The lady of the house supervising the *thaan* should be the one who eats only after the family members going for work have finished doing the *thaan*. As the arrangements are not very elaborate, no decoration or ornamentation need be done and no *pujan* of gods is necessary for an individual. Nevertheless, the *puja* room should be cleaned earlier on, some essence burnt and a lamp lit in front of the gods. This ritual should be carried out as it is done every day by the housewife.

Each individual is asked to sit in front of the portion set aside for him or her and the lady of the house or an elderly lady who knows the chant gives some water and rice in the cupped right palm of the individual who puts his or her first finger of the left hand into the water. The lady chants *Addey, addey, paksha var* – day of the week – *Tith Makar Sankrant* – name of the person – *mansa ha khichri, laddoo, ghee, papad, namak, apne sukh chain ke liye Sri Krishna nimant*. The water is taken round the relevant portion and dropped gracefully on the side (clockwise). The water is thus taken and dropped once more, this time without the chant. Then, the stuff is put aside to be given to the person for whom it is meant. One portion should be kept for the pandit who performs all the ceremonies of the household in times of need, i.e., *katha*, marriages, and so on.

In times gone by, when the households were joint and large, people derived immense pleasure by celebrating the festival at home, especially the women. They celebrated Makar Sankranti with greater enthusiasm and more elaborate rituals than at present. A newly married girl would bring what they called *vrat* for her in-laws – not only for her father-in-law and mother-in-law, but for all the elder married couples of her husband's family. All these *vrats* were not brought at one time. Two, three or four *vrats* were brought in one year. This would continue for years, till she gave every couple in her husband's family a *vrat*. This *vrat* included any *mithai*, fruit, *meva*, salty snacks, a big *rawe ka laddoo*, and *jalebis*. Cosmetics were also brought for the younger sisters-in-law, all decorated beautifully in a *thaal*. A beautiful couplet specially composed for that particular couple, written on a hand-painted card, added to the sentiment of the occasion. Everyone in the family became emotionally charged and much blessings and love were bestowed on the bride.

The *manasna* was done to one set only because after a thing is *mansood* (given away) the one doing it cannot partake of it. The second was for the girl herself. The chant for the *manasna* is the same as is done for the *khichri*, etc., except that another line is added as to the Paksh and Tith. On Makar Sankrant it could be either Krishna Paksh (dark fortnight) or Sukul Paksh (moonlit fortnight) and the chant is accordingly changed. With water and rice in the right hand and the first finger of the left hand in it, wearing the auspicious *chunni* and *chonp* on the forehead, the girl *mansos* with someone chanting '*Addey addey – Paksha, Var .... Tith Makar Sankrant* name (hers) and of the husband – *ki bahu* (wife of) *mansan hain, Mandhi or Til-ke-laddoo apne raj suhag ke liye, rani ka sa raj dena, Gaur ka sa suhag dena, Sri Krishna nimant.*' Then dropping the water after circling with it round the said items it is dropped gracefully on one side of the *thaal*. After touching the feet of the mother-in-law, the *baya* is given to her. The feet of all elder members are touched and blessings received. If someone would like to follow the old customs and make it a big occasion for the family, this would enliven the atmosphere as well as the people and bring them together.

Makar Sankranti is celebrated all over India, north, south, east and west; the manner of celebration may differ, but the sanctity of the occasion is accepted by all the Hindus as the Surya (sun) moves into the Northern hemisphere known as "Uttrayan" a most auspicious time.

4

Basant Panchami

'**A**YA BASANT PALA URANT' [COME BASANT (SPRING) AND winter flies] runs a popular saying in North India. This is one of the first festivals of the year. The cold, miserable days usually give way to warmer ones and the fields become very beautiful with the swaying of yellow *sarson* (mustard). The cold is normally replaced by balmy, soft, lingering breezes and everyone comes out to enjoy and make merry. Basant falls on Panchami of the Sukul Paksh (waxing moon) in the month of Magh sometime at the end of January or the beginning of February. People are still a little cautious about discarding winter clothes and keep light woollen sweaters on – in fact, sometimes, it can be quite cold and one is advised not to be too quick in packing the woollens away. During the morning and evening, one has to be very careful and children must be protected against the cold.

On Basant Panchami day the *puja* is devoted to Saraswati, the goddess of learning and wife of Brahma, the creator. She bestows the greatest wealth to humanity, i.e., the wealth of knowledge and she must not be neglected. Another goddess, namely Durga Ma, is worshipped very often, but Saraswati is normally worshipped only once a year.

The *puja* room, as usual, must be clean and neat and a picture or statue of Saraswati, the main deity of the day, is adorned and decked with yellow flowers. Some people provide garments for the idols and cloth covers for the pictures, leaving the face and figure of the deity uncovered. These dresses are yellow on the festival day and the cover for the table where the deity is seated, along with an idol or picture of Ganesh, is also yellow with *gota kinari* (fringes) attached all round. Of course, all these decorations are made earlier and must be ready for Basant Panchami. The family should be ready for the ceremonies and everyone should wear yellow if possible. The women should drape themselves in *zari saris* or in *salwar kameez* with some *zari* or *gota* attached to make the occasion festive and gay. Usually, it is not a holiday; so, before going to office or to the place of work, one must be ready and the children should do *pranam* before they step out for school, since *puja* is not possible that early in the morning but when they come back home they should worship the idol or picture and be given the *prasad*.

The *prasad* on Basant is very different from any other. On this day *ber* and *sangari* form the main *prasad*. *Ber* is the fruit of the *ber* tree which grows in abundance in North India. *Bers* used to be available freely and very cheaply once upon a time. Now they are really expensive and one cannot find them easily in the market. *Sangaris* are the beans that bear the seed of the *mooli* (white radish) and are found in plenty during this time of the year, when the *mooli* is becoming ripe and throws up its seeds. These two items are placed in a *thaali* along with some yellow *barfi* or *laddoos* made of *besan* or *nukthi*, and some *paans*. A *nariyal* of course is a must and a few sheafs of *sarson* (if one can get them). Another *thaali* with *puja* items of water, *aipun*, *roli*, rice and yellow flowers is made ready and a little coloured powder, usually red, is also kept with these items.

The lady of the house dressed in yellow with *zari* and *gota* on the dress, looking like Lakshmi, the wife of Vishnu (a housewife is always alluded to as Lakshmi and no other goddess) with the *chonp*, *bindi* on the forehead and yellow and red bangles on the arms, sets the trend for everyone to become festive.

The *puja* is begun by the youngest girl present by applying the *teeka* on everyone's forehead and then, by turns, everyone sprinkling water, *aipun* and *roli* by the third finger of the right hand dipped in each liquid, by turn, holding the finger each time by the thumb loosely and then letting it go with a light jerk, so as to sprinkle the attached liquid onto the deity. This is done three times with each liquid. The rice and flowers are picked up by the fingers and thumb and showered on to the gods. Everyone puts a little colour onto the gods. The heralding of summer begins with a bit of colour sprinkled even today (before Holi) on the gods. The lady of the house then takes a few *bers*, some *sangaris* and a *laddoo* and a *paan* (the same *paan* along with the *nariyal* can be given to everyone since *paan* is now a very expensive item) and gives them to each member present. This activity can be done in two instalments as it is difficult to hold all these items at one time. The receiver takes the offerings in both hands and touches them to his or her forehead and returns these items to the giver, but from the second instalment, he or she must take one

or two items at least and eat them in the *puja* room.
There is never any objection to eating *prasad* in the *puja*
room at any function or festival.

On Basant Panchami children have a wonderful
time. They are freely allowed to fly *patang* or *guddi* (kites)
and are seen on rooftops and on the maidans or any open
space they can find carrying their *huchkas* (the big reel on
which the string used to fly the kite is rolled). The high
point of this joyful pastime is when two 'high fliers' cross
their threads in midair and, by deft handling, cut away
the string of the opponent's *patang*, which then goes flying
with the wind. The loser of the game is left quickly pulling
the *dor* (the string) back into his territory, before someone
grabs at it and makes it his own. The free flying kite is
chased by all the urchins of the locality. Even those who
can well afford a brand new *patang* can be seen running
on the roads with a one-track mind. Those driving cars or
other vehicles must be very careful to avoid such diehard
patang fliers, because the flying of kites is an addiction
with kids and even some grown-ups. While the grown-
ups do not normally run after the free flying kites, the
kids can think of nothing else except how to grab it. In
times gone by when we lived in the main city, where the
houses were two to four storeys high, with only a narrow
lane running in between, the children were to be found
on roof- tops, days before and after Basant; they really
didn't mind jumping from their roof to another's and
actually ran the whole length of the lane; jumping from
their roof on to the neighbour's, and then on to the next.
It was very dangerous and the elders were forever
shouting to get them to come down and stop flying kites,
admonishing them and telling them in no uncertain
terms that only the rifraff flew kites and the children of
good families kept away from such rowdy games! Only
on Basant Panchami were they officially allowed to fly
kites in a dignified manner, which was a most unwelcome
proposition. So when the older men went out to work

and women were busy in the kitchen, the kids climbed up and even braved the presence of many monkeys that ran around freely in most North Indian towns. They were scolded and their ears got pulled in the evening as the mothers and aunts complained to the male members who returned from work. This was akin to today's coming home late from a 'disco' or an evening party. The reaction of the youngsters today and then was quite quite different. The youngsters of yesteryear did not open their mouths before an elder of the family as they could be soundly slapped by a *chacha* or a *tau* (uncles on the father's side). But Basant Panchami was a different day and greetings and *patangs* were freely given by even the most harsh parent or uncle.

There is no ceremonial lunch or dinner on this day. The concentration is focussed on outdoor activities, but visiting the temple and relatives is the done thing. Of course, the entertainment and refreshments served to visitors are festive. The clothes worn by men and women are usually yellow. They need not be totally yellow, but some part of the attire should be yellow. Yellow represents an auspicious colour in the Hindu way of life. The food prepared on Basant Panchami is tinged with yellow as far as possible. A speciality of this day is sweet rice with almonds, *kismis* and *kaju* added to it. *Karhi chawal* is a must in the afternoon. Yellow *barfi* is served to the visitors and family. *Kheer* with *zafran* (saffron) is a great attraction for children and elders alike; the rest of the menu can be varied according to one's choice.

In schools and colleges Basant Panchami is a great day of celebration in honour of the goddess of learning and knowledge and is celebrated accordingly, for Saraswati is the patron of all schools and places of learning.

MEETHA CHAWAL

Sela Basmati rice	1/2 kg
Badam (almonds)	20 pods
Pista	25 gm
Kaju	25 gm
Kismis	50 gm
Khoya	200 gm
Lavang	9 + 4 pieces
Elaichi (small, whole)	9 + 4 pieces
Yellow colour in powder form	1/4 teaspoonful
Kewra	400 gm
Sugar	100 gm
Pure *ghee*	100 gm
Water	7 glasses

Method

Wash the rice very well in fresh water at least 6 times. Soak for one hour. Soak the *badam* and *kaju*. Soak the colour in 7 glasses of water and boil. Take out the soaked rice and add to the boiling liquid on fire (coloured liquid) put 4 *lavang* pieces and 4 small *elaichis* whole. Boil for 5 minutes or till it is done (in a *dekchi*). When the rice is done (a little hard) put it through a big sieve and drain water out. Put two glasses of water on the hot rice while still in the sieve. Put 9 more *lavang* pieces and 9 small *elaichis* in the *ghee* in a heavy-bottomed pan leaving a tablespoon of *ghee* in the pan for later use. Cook the *ghee* and *elaichi* and *lavang* in this pan for 2 minutes; pour half the rice into the heavy-bottomed *dekchi* or pressure cooker. Then put half the sugar and add the rest of the rice. Cook over a low fire, covering the pot. Break the *badam* into two parts and the *kajus* in the same manner and take out the soaked *kismis* (take the stems of the *kismis* out). Add the remaining *ghee*. Stir the rice occasionally, put on a low fire and cover the vessel. Cook for 20 minutes. Mix all the dry fruits; the mixture should be well steamed. Cook again on a low fire. Add 3 desert-spoonsful of *kewra*. Cover the pot with a cloth-wrapped lid for very good results. To hold the cloth in position, place a stone on it. Add *khoya* after the water has dried. Cook for another 15 minutes and take the vessel off the fire. Put a silver *varak* on it.

Cooking time: 45 minutes.

5

Bihu

Bihu anondia Bihu binondia
Bihur mou mitha hat
Bihur ba lagi bihua kokair e
Deu dhoni laguse gat

Bihu is full of joy, Bihu is beautiful,
Bihu songs are very sweet, when the winds
of Bihu flow, one's body
becomes possessed by the dancing spirit.

BIHU COMES THREE TIMES IN THE YEAR, AND MARKS THE
change of seasons in the lush green hills and the
valleys at the foothills of the Himalayas in Assam.

31

April comes with great colour to this fertile and beautiful land of India. Flowers and foliage cover the landscape and *kopoful* (orchids) of exotic shape and colour hang from the trees in their splendour. The one found most commonly is the purple *kopoful* which adorns the young maidens' hair at Bihu. The creeper *bhebel* also bursts into flower around the time of the first of the three Bihus' which falls on the Sankranti of Chait or Baisak, which falls on 13, 14 and 15 April every year. The calculation of this festival is according to the solar calendar coinciding with Baisakhi of Punjab. The new year for the Assamese, likewise, starts on 14 April.

On Bihag Bihu or Rangoli Bihu as it is also called, the young men and women of Assam look colourful. The farmers celebrate it with song and dance lasting for a week at least, although it could be for a whole month (as in days gone by). Historically, these festivals and the dances associated with them are of pre-Aryan origin – the dances were the fertility rites of the primitive people who inhabited the north-eastern hills of India. The farmer believed that songs with evident erotic content would lead to a strong sexual arousal in the body of the earth which would result in an increased crop production. The dances are performed exclusively by men with no holds barred to erotic manifestations. In upper Assam the men dance all night long in open fields.

Nowadays, boys and girls from different localities form groups and invite veterans to teach and lead them. They dance in the main centre of the town or village and in different localities too. The Assamese have always been fun-loving and have evolved many ways to express their *joie de vivre*. Rangoli Bihu is the most festive of all the Bihus.

Every home in Assam used to have a loom. The women wove their own cloth and one of the special weaves is the *gomacha*, a decorated towel with intricate designs woven in. They are a prized possession, given as *any Bihu* (Bihu presents), especially by a mother to her son, a wife to her husband, a girl to her father, brother or a special boyfriend. These *gomachas* are worn by the men around their waists over their white *dhoti* or *lungi* or as head bands, especially during festivity. They are also used to cover the special places reserved for *tamul* (*paans* or betel leaves) to be offered to the 'Bihu Dals' that come visiting and dancing all through the week with their musical instruments – *dhool* (drum), *pepa* (an instrument made from bufffalo horn) and *gagana* (an instrument made from bamboo and held between the teeth), with small cymbals keeping rhythm. They sing devotional songs, in a style known as *hosari*, invoking Lord Krishna to bless their households with health, wealth and happiness. They sing :

Chotote chakori bohagot bogari
    Jhetothe aamona dhan
Garur bihu dinakhon sharai aagloraba
    Tehe paba baikunthat dhaam

In Chait thread spinning,
In Baisak plums,
In Jaath the fields are full of red-coloured paddy.
On the day of 'cow-bihu'
Offer the 'sharai' platter
Filled with prasad.
Then you will reach Baikunt Dhaam [heaven presided over by Lord Krishna].

The 'Bihu Dals' complete the rounds of the neighbourhood and then gather in open grounds called 'Bihu *toli*' where teams from other neighbourhoods also come. Each group tries to outshine the other in the dancing competitions and beauty pageants that are held. The winners are announced in the local papers within the seven days of the festival.

Each day of Bihu has a specific name. The first one, Garur Bihu, is the actual day of Sankranti, also known as Uraka: this is the Bihu of the cow. On this day the cows are taken to the river and bathed with great love and care. Cows are one of the greatest assets of a farmer. Besides giving milk, which in itself is a complete food and yields butter, buttermilk and *ghee,* the cow also provides cow-dung which is made into *uplas* for fuel. The male calf also ploughs the fields and bullock-carts act as transport for men, crops and baggage. Cows have always been revered in India. Sri Krishna was a cowherd, and he taught everyone to revere the cow as a mother. The Hindus bestow upon the cow the status of a deity.

On this day of Garur Bihu cows are made much of and, after a thorough bath in the river or pond, they are brushed and their hooves and horns cleaned with whisks made from the twigs of the *deegloti* or *makheatr* (*Lilsoca salocrfolea*) to remove parasites and to disinfect. Turmeric paste, mixed with black *moong dal* paste is applied on their horns and hooves (turmeric is a very good disinfectant).

The livestock is brought into an open space and everyone throws small pieces of gourd and brinjal as food to them, singing and fanning the cows with new fans.

The song goes like this:

Deegloti deegotpat, makhi maru jat jat
Lau ka begena ka, bosore bahija
Mar khoru bapes khow toi habi bor.

I kill the flies by the flock with the leaves of *deegloti,* you feed on gourd and eggplant and grow every year. Your father is small, your mother is small but you became a big cow.

After feeding the cows, vermilion is put on their foreheads and they are then led back to their sheds. The sheds have been also thoroughly cleaned and disinfected, new ropes are put on the pegs where the cows will be tied when so needed. A lamp is lit and incense burnt in the cowshed. The Assamese are mainly farmers and this 'worship' ensures the health of the cows and bullocks and keeps them fit for the heavy work of the new sowing season.

For the household, special food is prepared. Rice is not made in the usual manner but flat rice *(chirwa)* is cooked in different ways. Many kinds of sweets are made and families and friends enjoy each other's hospitality.

The second day of Bihu is also the first day of the Assamese new year and is known as Manuhor Bihu or the Bihu of the human being. This falls on 14 April. Friends and close relatives are invited along with the daughters of the house and their husbands and families to a feast known as *Bihu Kabo Loi*. The daughters-in-law are allowed to go to their parents' house, but if the daughters and guests are coming for dinner, the daughter-in-law could go to their house for lunch. Since the celebrations last for at least a week, these feasts are arranged at everyone's convenience making them joyous affairs. Everyone wears new clothes and presentations of *gomachas* are done on this day, first to the elders of the house and then the others. The women wear the *mekhele chadar* made from the golden-coloured *muga* silk which is unique to Assam. They wear the *gumkham* bracelets which are made from an alloy of silver and gold nuggets, found in the rivers of Assam.

The food for this feast is *pitha*, made from ground rice, *narikel*, *laddoo* made from shredded coconut, and *til laddoo* (made from sesame seeds). Households make preparations well in advance. (The recipes are at the end of the chapter.)

The third day is the day of young women and is known as Gabhori Bihu. Men have no access, nonetheless the girls dress in their *muga* silks and *gumkham* bracelets and, with orchids in their hair, they sing and dance in the fields and under the banyan trees all through the night. Banyan trees are held holy by the Hindus because in the summer or rainy season vast numbers of cattle, men and women can take shelter under 'nature's tent'. The instruments which accompany the singing are indigenous: *toka* and *gogona*. Bihu songs are composed spontaneously in couplets. They are sung in slow tempo in the beginning but gather momentum as they progress. Those who are dancing join in the rhythmic clapping and sway to the music.

A song which is very popular goes like this:

Ati kai chenchar mugare mohura
Ati kai chenchar mako
Talokari chenchar bohagar bihooti
Nepali kene koi thako

Very dear is my *muga* bobbin,
Very dear is my shuttle,
Dearer is my Bohag Bihu
How can I not celebrate it.

When the dancing and singing stops, the ladies of each household where the dancers are performing offer the dancers fermented *tamul* (betel leaves). These are again presented in a tray or *thaal* on which a *gomacha* is spread, or a platform is made on which the *thaal* of fermented betel leaves is kept.

On the last day of the festivity each household writes the following *mantra* on the leaves of the Indian iron-wood tree (known as *Nahar pat*).

Deva deva mahadeva nee lag riva jatadhara
Vaata vrishti haran deva mahadeva namasutate

The leaves are strung together and tied across the main door of each house. This *mantra* is a prayer to Lord Shiva asking him to protect them from disease, storms and rain in the new year and to let peace and prosperity prevail therein.

The second Bihu is known as Kati Bihu or Kangali Bihu and is usually held in the month of Kartik or Sankranti (falling in October according to the English calendar). This Bihu is not celebrated with gaiety; this is a Bihu of prayer and meditation. During the month of October people are preparing for the winter crop; there is no harvest – the seeds are being sown and consequently there is no money to splurge on fun. People practise the art of being thrifty and the young ones also learn that money is not just for the asking and that they must refrain from too much spending even on festivity.

Kati Bihu is celebrated at the time of sowing the crop. Goddess Lakshmi is invoked by lighting an oil lamp (*deep*) every night in the paddy fields, where the people have toiled all day for a month. At home, after a good day's work, the old and the young gather and pray to the goddess and ask her to bless their land with a bountiful crop, and the home and family and livestock with health, wealth and strength.

Tulsi (basil), a plant revered by Hindus, is planted or pruned, as the case may be, in the courtyard of every home and watered by all members with great care and piety. The lady of the house waters it after doing *puja* to it every day. It is believed that this plant has great healing powers and a few leaves taken with a few pods of black pepper and *misri* (sugar in crystal form) every day, will keep one healthy.

The third Bihu or the Magh Bihu falls on 14 January on the Sankranti of the month and in the month of Magh according to the lunar calendar. The Tith will differ due to the difference in calculations (even the solar calendar of the Hindus is not completely tuned to the English calendar, and a difference of a day or two occurs in the Sankranti of every month).

The emphasis during Magh Bihu is on eating. In winter, the harvest is gathered when the granaries are full and the people are free; they celebrate a Bihu again and this time there is feasting for seven days. The pattern is almost the same as in Rangoli Bihu or the spring festival but in Magh Bihu, the main function is a community feast on the night of 'Uruka', the first day of the festival (it is the Sankranti day). The feast is known as Bhog, meaning a great feast.

Another significant feature of this Bihu is *khel dhemali*, meaning play and fun. Fights between buffaloes, cocks and other animals along with other sports are held in every village to entertain spectators. Bonfires are also an important part of the festival and people gather around them rather than in the fields where it is very cold and dance just like they do at Lohri in Punjab and Pongal in Tamil Nadu. Magh Bihu coincides with both these festivals as well as Goopi of Andhra Pradesh and Makar Sankranti of North India. This is a very auspicious time and this Sankranti is celebrated all over India in one form or another with bonfires.

RECIPES FOR BIHU

TIL PITHA

Ingredients	
Bora rice (Bora is a type of glutinous rice)	2 cups
Black sesame seeds	80 gm
Jaggery or molasses	100 gm

Method

Clean and soak the rice overnight. The next morning strain the rice and leave it in the strainer. Cover the strainer with a cloth and keep for 2 hours. This allows the water on the surface of the grains to evaporate. After 2 hours pour the rice into a mortar and pound it till the grains are crushed fine. At this stage it is very crucial that the pounded rice not be exposed otherwise it will lose its stickiness. Keep it tightly wrapped in Saran Wrap or tightly packed in an airtight container; this is essential otherwise when the *pitha* is made it will crumble. The rice can be ground in a food processor instead of a mortar and pestle but take care not to overgrind.

Clean the sesame seeds. Heat a frying-pan or a *tawa* and lightly roast the seeds. Pour the seeds into a mortar and pound them so as to break the outer shell. This allows the aroma and flavour to be released.

Next, slice the jaggery into small chips. Pour the sesame seeds into the jaggery and mix well (like you mix dough) while crushing the jaggery chips with your fingers.

Traditionally, a *pai choru*, a flat-bottomed earthenware pot or wok, is used to make the *pitha*, and one or two bamboo *shala* (bamboo chopsticks for frying), are placed on one side to become a rack to keep the *pitha* after it is removed from the direct heat. This allows the *pitha* to firm up and prevents it from crumbling. The slow heat transmission of the earthenware is well suited for making the *pitha*. However, an iron *tawa* or griddle will also do as long as the heat is kept under control. Heat the *tawa* on low to medium heat. Usually one fistful of pounded rice is taken and placed on the bottom of the wok and the back of the fisted hand is used to spread it. However, a large tablespoon or small ladle could be used to scoop the pounded rice batter and spread it on the heated *tawa* to the size of a small *puri*. While it is being roasted, place the stuffing of jaggery and seasame mix in the centre. Check that the rice batter is firm, then fold over both sides so as to cover the stuffing, one side on top of the other, and turn over. Lightly heat and remove and place on the rack. Once the rack is full, remove the earlier ones and place in an open platter till they cool to an ambient temperature. The trick is to see that after the *pitha* is stuffed and folded, the jaggery does not melt or run. The *pitha* is not allowed to brown; it should be white. Store in a covered container. It will keep for about a week at room temperature.

TIL LADDU

Ingredients	
Sesame seeds (black/brown)	40 gm
Jaggery	55 gm
Ghee	1 tablespoon

Method

Clean and lightly roast the sesame seeds. Heat the jaggery in a wok or frying pan until it melts into a consistent fluid. Add the roasted *til* and stir well until the two mix thoroughly. After some time the jaggery will start to firm up. Remove from heat. Lightly grease your fingers and palm with the *ghee* and with a tablespoon scoop up the mixture, take it on the palm and roll into a ball. The key to making the *laddoo* is not to allow the jaggery to cool before it is shaped into a ball. Be careful as hot jaggery can cause burns.

NARIKEL LADDOO

Ingredients

Narikel or *nariyal* (coconuts)   2
Sugar   2 cups
Some powdered camphor

Method

Traditionally, the *nariyal* is cracked, the water inside
allowed to seep into a receptacle, and then it is broken
into two halves. There is a special implement called
rukoni which is used to grate *nariyal*. Canned coconut
may be used, but some care has to be taken to select the
right type as it may be too dry.

Pour the grated coconut and sugar into a saucepan
and mix well. Place over low to medium heat and stir
continuously. The water from the grated coconut will
begin to form lumps. Remove from heat, add a pinch of
camphor to the mixture and mix well. In order to ensure
the *laddoos* are of good quality, the following precautions
should be taken:

(1)   The mixture should not be overheated as it will
       fluff up and will not lend itself to the formation of
       laddoos.
(2)   It should also not be allowed to cool down as it
       will not form *laddoos* then.

Usually, to form *laddoos* with hot ingredients the
palms and fingers are wet with cold water and the
mixture scooped and rolled between the palms and
compressed into *laddoos*. However, care must be taken
to prevent palms from getting burnt.

6

Mahashivratri

O N THE 'THRATHSHI' OR THE THIRTEENTH DAY OF THE waning moon in the month of Phagun falls the festival of Mahashivratri, symbolising the wedding day of Shiv and Parvati. This festival comes some time in February or March according to the English calendar (14-15 days before Holi).

Shivratri is a very auspicious day. The married and the unmarried girls perform *puja* with great faith, fervour and feeling, since Parvati is considered 'Gaura' the giver of '*suhag*' – married bliss and a long and prosperous married life. The unmarried girls pray to 'Gaura' to give them handsome husbands with wealth, knowledge and talent.

Shivji is reputed to be of frightening aspect with ash smeared all over his body and wearing garlands of human skulls, live snakes and *malas* (necklaces) of *rudraksh* round his neck and arms. He has matted hair piled up on his head (*jatta*) with the new moon stuck in front of the *jatta* and the Ganga (river) coming from heaven and falling into his locks, so as to find a soft spot to fall upon (or else she would have gone into the earth due to the impact of the fall). From his hair Ganga gently finds her way on to the plains of 'Bharatvarsh'. Shivji's neck is blue, because he was the one who consumed the poison when the sea was churned and out came the various things that are relevant to life. The *devtas* eagerly wanted the good things, but none would take the poison, so Shivji took it and drank it, retaining it in his throat, thereby giving the neck the blue colour. It is said that the bird 'Neel Kanth' with its blue neck is specially dear to Shiv and will take your message straight to him, if you tell it to do so.

Shivji is easily pleased and grants boons and wishes to his *bhakts* without going into the pros and cons of the situation or the consequences thereof, usually landing everyone in a mess! Shiv was specially close to Ravan whose '*isht devta*' (family god) he was and always helped him although Ravan was an Asur. Shiv came to Ravan's side during the great war with Ram, but was disenchanted due to the arrogance of the king of Lanka, and took refuge in the fact that although Brahma had granted Ravan near immortality and given him the knowledge of ten heads, he had still witheld one which enabled Ram to kill him. Shiv did not then interfere, or else the fight would never have ended.

There was another Asur named Banasur, the grandson of Prahlad, who was a great *bhakt* of Shiv. Banasur ruled the mountain kingdom of Shonita (now known as Sarahan, about 200 km from Shimla). Banasur had a beautiful daughter named Usha, who fell in love in her dreams with Anirudh the grandson of Krishna and

Rukhmini and, as usual, wanted to marry him in real life. She got Anirudh kidnapped from Dwarka through her friend Chitralekha who could fly. There was a great war between Krishna and Banasur and Shiv came to fight on the side of Banasur. The two indestructible aspects of the Almighty – Vishnu and Shiv – could not lose to each other nor could be slain! All the other gods beseeched Shiv and Vishnu to reach a compromise or else the world would have been destroyed.

Shiv is as much in the hearts of the Hindus as Vishnu and most of the Hindus pray to both with equal devotion.

The Hindus believe the 'Supreme' to be unmanifest, but to visualise and understand such a phenomenon, the Hindu has projected it into the forms of 'Brahma', 'Vishnu' and 'Mahesh', i.e., Brahma the creator, Vishnu the preserver, and Mahesh or Shiv the destroyer (all facets of the Supreme Power equal in strength and knowledge, never born, never destroyed). Brahma, after creating leaves the work of the world in the hands of Vishnu and Shiv. That is why those that live on this earth pray to them. The devtas are not 'supreme' but only ministering angels, and a Hindu never mixes the two.

Vishnu comes down to earth as an avtar (incarnation) whenever the people stray away from the path of righteousness, whereas Brahma and Shiv do not come down to earth in human form. While Brahma washes his hands off after creating, Shiv has a lot to do with the world. He does a lot himself, or through his doots (emissaries). The chief of the doots is Yum, who takes away those that have finished their span on this earth.

Mahashivratri is the most revered festival of the Kashmiri pandits. It is celebrated for full sixteen days, from Parva of the waning moon to Parva of the waxing moon (i.e., to the day after Amavas). The wedding of Shiv and Parvati is usually celebrated for four days continuously – Thrathshi, Choutash, Amavas (of the waxing moon) and Parva (of the waxing moon).

Mahashivratri normally comes just fourteen or fifteen days before Holi. The preparation for this festival begins 10 days earlier and it is treated like Diwali as far as house cleaning and related activities are concerned. The house is generally whitewashed or the *kuchcha* houses made of mud have cowdung applied on them, a custom now slowly disappearing. New beddings, utensils and other household items that are required are bought. Everyone in the family purchases new clothes – as many as they can afford, but one set definitely for the main *pujan*. When one gets down to the nitty-gritty, the activity motivates everyone; there is a lot of excitement and a good deal of work for the whole fortnight and much interaction between the members of the family results. Both young and old alike are involved. Food becomes a great attraction and special dishes of mutton, fish and chicken are prepared. The Kashmiri pandit is not necessarily a vegetarian and, for every meal, everyone is given a chance to learn to cook the dishes. Meat is not taboo during the Shivratri week, but on the main days it is not cooked or eaten.

The whole of the 16-day period is devoted to gambling. The old custom of playing with *kauri* (a type of sea shell) is still prevalent, and no one forbids it. The elders also join in the evenings. Nowadays, of course, cards have taken the place of *kauri* and flash is played in most homes.

The Kashmiri Hindu buys earthen pots (*gaggar*) as symbols for Ganesh, Shiv and Parvati and the other gods and the *baratis*. *Dhatura, aak, aak* flowers and camphor are bought for *pujan*. Also, about 50 walnuts form an essential part of the *prasad*. In Kashmir itself all the items, except the walnuts, are available in dry powder form because it is cold and wintry and not much can be grown in the valley during this time. This is known as '*vatuk*' *masala*, since the *puja* is known as '*vatuk puja*'.

On the eleventh day the *puja* room is decorated with the images or pictures of gods and *devtas*. Floral decoration is usually not done because the carpets and other related items cannot be removed. Everything pertaining to the clothing of the gods or the *puja* is new.

Next comes the twelfth day or the day of Ganesh *puja*. One earthen pot (*gaggar*) is placed in the centre, filled with water, a little Ganga *jal* (Ganga water) and some walnuts. This symbolises Ganesh. *Pujan* is done to this *gaggar* with water, *roli*, *aipun*, rice and flowers so that the marriage of Shiv and Parvati is blessed. Although Ganesh is their son, still it is decreed that he must be worshipped first and anything coming after that decree must be adhered to in all *pujas*.

The thirteenth day, Thrathshi or Terash commemorates the great marriage day and is the actual day of Mahashivratri. Decorated earthen pots filled with walnuts are placed on the *puja* pedestal symbolising Shiv, Parvati, Ganesh, and the *baratis*, *rishis* and *munis* of great repute. Mutton and fish are offered to the *baratis* as *prasad* and many types of eatables are made. Only milk sweets made of *khoya* and fruits are placed for the *rishis* and *munis* and the *devtas* as *prasad*, other than Shiv himself who is offered *bhang*, *dhatura*, *belpatra*, *aak*, etc. The *katha* (story) of Shiv and Parvati is read from a booklet. A small *havan kund* is set in front of the gods and the head of the family performs a small *havan*, after performing *agni puja* (prayer to the fire), with the help of the family priest if the head of the family does not know the *mantras*. Of course, the head of the family keeps a fast and only takes *phalar* during the day. The *havan* ends with the ringing of bells and the sounding of the conch shell when the *arti* to Shiv and Parvati is sung.

On the fourteenth day or 'Chauthas', the daughters and sons-in-law are invited for a special meal by the father and mother or the brothers and sisters-in-law. The meal is sumptuous and consists of meat, fish, chicken and vegetables, prepared in the manner that the family decides. The day is treated like Diwali and gambling is the order of the day. Children are given money to go and

buy anything that catches their fancy, according to what
the grandparents and parents can afford. As the Muslim
culture has had a lot of impact on the Hindus of Kashmir,
this day is known as 'Salaam'. People greet each other
and send sweets and *prasad*. Great rejoicing marks this
occasion. Girls receive money from their parents and so
do the children. The sons-in-law are given the *pyala*
(money in lieu of a drink) and at the end everyone is tired
but content.

The fifteenth day or 'Amavas' heralds the end of the
wedding celebrations. All the earthen pots are collected
and immersed in the nearest river or lake and things are
cleared up. On this day, *rotis* made of rice *atta* and the
soaked walnuts are distributed as *prasad* to the members
of the community living nearby. Thus the Kashmiris
honour Lord Shiv and his consort Parvati.

A little further down, in the plains of North India,
Mahashivratri celebrations are confined to the temples,
and not much is done in the house and no arrangement
for *puja* needs to be done at home. Those who keep the
vrat naturally prepare the *phalar* which is taken as the
main meal during the 36 hours of *vrat* in this case.

In any case, the family prepares for the festival from
the early morning of 'Terash'. Every member takes a bath
and dresses up in clean clothes. The *puja* room is naturally
cleaned up and the images of Ganesh, Shiv and Parvati
cleaned and placed in the centre of the room. A *jyot* (lamp)
is lit in front of the images and *agarbattis* are also lit.

The persons who go to the temple take a vessel
(usually made of copper) filled with water with a little
Ganga *jal* and milk mixed. They also take along some
belpatra (leaves of the *bel* tree), a *bel* fruit (available with
the people who sit around temples selling flowers),
dhatura, *bhang*, *aak* and bits of flowers, fruit, *aipun*, *roli*
and rice and a small *katori* with oil and a wick of cotton
all nicely set in a *thaali* which can be carried easily. Shiv
bhakts are allowed to drink *bhang*. The *aak* flower can be

cooked as a vegetable or *achar* (pickles) can be made but *dhatura*, etc., are poisonous. Such *prasad* of Shiv is not consumed.

In the temple, the devotees bathe the Shiv *ling* with the water mixed with milk, by pouring the liquid slowly on top of the *ling*. The *puja* is then done with water, *roli*, *aipun* and rice and then flowers are showered on the *ling*. Fruits and other stuff are then offered to the deity and the small *jyot* is lit and *arti* performed by circling with the *thaali* three to four times in front of the *ling*. *Parikrama* is then performed three times. In the case of a Shiv *ling* the *parikrama* is half only, one returns from where the water falls away from the *ling*. This water is given as *charnamrit* to the devotees but the *prasad* is not eaten as it contains poisonous and intoxicating items.

In homes, the persons who have observed the fast prepare the *palahar* (or *phalar*) which is taken during mid-day and consists of non-cereal food such as boiled potatoes made into *chaat* or made into a curry without garlic, onion, *adrak* or *haldi* but with *zeera*, salt and a little chilli if required; *arvi* in any form is eaten. *Kuttu singhare ki puri* or *pakori* is also prepared. Fruit, *mithai* made from milk — like *barfi* (without lentils) — is taken and so is curd. Tea, coffee or milk is allowed, but should be restricted. Water can be taken. No meal is taken at night and the next meal can be taken only in the morning of Amavas or the third day, after a special alms-giving. This consists of giving cooked rice and *khari* to the *sadhus* who are *bhakts* of Shiv with ash smeared on their body and faces. These *sadhus* also wear *rudraksh* and other beads and *malas* round their necks and arms. They have long plaited hair full of ash, looking as fearsome as the god they worship. These *sadhus* carry a *kamandal* (a kind of pot) and get it filled with the rice and *khari*. The stuff is cooked the next morning after Shivratri and only when it is given away the *vrat* can be broken and a normal meal taken by the *vratis*. This will be around 10.30 or 11 a.m.

One has to be prepared for this type of fasting, if one wants to keep the sanctity of the *vrat*. (The *vrat* lasts for more than 36 hours.)

The real celebration of Shivratri takes place in the temples on the night of 'Chauthas' or 'Choudesh' (fourteenth day of the waxing moon) and lasts till the morning of Amavas (dark night) although the wedding starts from Terash (thirteenth day of the waxing moon) and singing continues throughout the night in the temples. On Choudesh night everyone who wants to take part in the *pujan* is individually given a Shiv *ling* by the temple management – this *ling* is placed in front of the person. A medium-sized vessel with a narrow neck known as *kalsa* is also placed near that person and is filled with water mixed with milk, and also leaves of the *bel* tree, flowers and fruit. *Roli, aipun* and rice along with water for *pujan* are kept individually. The *puja* is directed by a priest (pandit) of the temple who sits on a platform and performs the rituals with chanting of *mantras*, and everyone follows his actions even if they cannot chant the *mantras* verbatim. The *puja* is done four times during the night. The directions are given by the learned pandit; therefore one need not know the rituals oneself and should merely follow him. On the next day (Amavas) the alms-giving to the *sadhus* – *bhakts* of Shiv – is done and only then the *vrat* kept is broken, after the last meal of 'Thrathshi' has been taken.

It is believed that Shiv and Sati (later Parvati or Uma) fly on their *vahan* (vehicle), i.e., the bullock, around the world every 24 hours and keep a watch on the inhabitants of the earth. At one such time in the 'Treta Yug' when Ram *avtar* had taken place Shivji spotted Ram when he was hurt and crying, while looking for his wife Sita who had been carried away by Ravan. Shivji at once recognised him as 'Vishnu' in the form of Ram on earth and saying 'O! Ram *avtar* has taken place on earth', he bowed and performed '*namaskar*' to Ram from above. Now, it is a fact that the three manifest aspects of the 'Supreme', whenever they meet each other, bow and worship the other as the 'Supreme' and so Shivji did just that. The whole incident intrigued Sati who asked: 'My Lord, who is that you bow to?' 'It is Lord Vishnu who has, at last, taken a human form and has come down to earth to rid it of all its sins,' replied Shiv. 'If it is so why does he lament? He knows all, for he is the "Supreme". So why is he crying for his wife, he should know where she is?' asked Parvati.

Shivji laughed and let this comment pass. Sati was not satisfied and she quietly took the form of Sita and stood in the path of Ram. On seeing her, Ram bowed with folded hands and said: 'Mother, how come you are alone, where is Shivji?' Sati was very ashamed and promptly went back to her husband, who was sitting in a *samadhi* by now. She went to sit on his left side as usual, the place always reserved for a wife, but he told her to sit in front of him and not by his side. She protested and asked him for the reason. He replied: 'You took the form of Sita who is like a mother to me so you cannot be my wife any more and shall henceforth take the place that is meant for a mother – only in front of me. Also you did not trust me; I am your husband, there should be absolute trust between a husband and wife, instead you wanted to test if I had told you the truth. I now forsake you as a wife.'

Sati was very upset but sat down in front of Shivji, who straightaway went into *samadhi* again. Sati looked up and saw a lot of *uran khatolas* (flying objects) going past towards the north, and asked her husband where the *devtas* were going. He replied: 'They are going to your father's house; he is conducting a big *yagya* and has not invited us.' This angered Sati very much; still she wanted to go. Shivji told her that one should never go anywhere without an invitation, but she insisted saying that a daughter could surely go to her father's house without being invited. Shivji couldn't refuse anything to Sati and told her that although she would be sorry to do so, he would not stop her.

So, Sati went to her father's house where no one came forward to receive her except her mother. Her father spurned her and did not speak to her, and the rest of the people kept their distance. When the *yagya* was over, food as a special potion, was taken out in the names of all the gods and *devtas* but no *havis* (potion) was taken out for Shivji. Sati was furious at this insult to her husband, and also at all that had befallen her lately. She threw herself in the *havan kund* and burnt herself.

Sati was reborn to the king of the mountains 'Himalaya' and his wife Maina as Parvati and was again married to Shiv on Shivratri. They are believed to be living blissfully together even now and it is said that Parvati can get anything done by Shivji even if he is not doing it on his own.

There is a belief that when Shiv and Parvati travel round the world on their *vahan* – the bullock – even today, they visit every nook and corner, looking down on the inhabitants with great benevolence. If at the precise moment when they are right above you, you wish for something, that wish will come true. That is why sometimes when one wishes even for a silly thing it comes true! Well, anyway try it, but you have to keep wishing for 24 hours (all the time) for Shiv and Parvati's time of visiting is never the same.

7

Holi

HOLI, THE GRAND FESTIVAL MARKED BY COLOURED WATER, gaiety and real gay abandon, comes when the cold winter months give way to summer. The crops have been cut, threshed, and stored or sold away. The farmer and his wife are free, and money is in hand. This festival falls on the full moon during the month of Phagun some time in February or March, which is conducive to getting out and about. Everyone is generally full of cheer.

Holi is associated to a great extent with Lord Krishna, who in his childhood and youth, ran around with his band of cowherds and maidens of the village, completely captivating everyone. He loved festivity, and the hamlets of Brindavan, Gokul and Barsana were full of fun and frolic. Lord Krishna played Holi with so much gusto that even today the songs sung during Holi are full of the pranks that he played on the Gopis and the Gopis played on him, especially those on his childhood sweetheart Radhika, who lived in Barsana. She remained his heartthrob and none of his eight wives could ever take her place.

Krishna played Holi with a *pichkari* (a brass syringe which squirts water in a spray or even in a straight line). Therefore, it is the done thing during Holi to buy *pichkaris* for the children of the house. A variety of *pichkaris* are available nowadays, in plastic, aluminium, and of course brass. Just before Holi, a special shopping spree must be arranged for the kids. *Gulal* made up of numerous colours such as pink, magenta, red, yellow and green, along with *abeer* (small crystals or paper-like chips of mica) is bought. *Abeer* and *gulal* are an essential part of all Holi folk songs. *Abeer* adds a good deal of shine and richness to the dry colours of *gulal*, but seems to have been banned recently due to its being a solid material which can hurt the eyes (and also due to spurious, adulterated material being sold). Of course, one must not forget the *tesu* (flower of the Palash tree otherwise known as the 'flame of the forest'). The flowers are dried and sold in the market. On being mixed in water, they leave a beautiful saffron-reddish colour. They can be boiled to make a rich decoction, which is then mixed with cold water in different tubs and buckets, strategically placed in the courtyard, verandah or even on the rooftops. This water is supposedly good for health. The dry colour or *gulal* should be chosen with great care, since, nowadays, there is a lot of spurious stuff mixed up with it, which can be very injurious to the skin, lungs and eyes. Buying from recognised dealers is strongly recommended. The *gulals* look beautiful, heaped up in cone shapes, in gunny bags all around the shops. There are also soluble colours available for colouring water in different hues.

The festival of Holi begins on Duwadashi, three days earlier to Puno – on the 12th day of the waxing moon of

Phagun. The children may have started festivities even earlier, with everyone shouting at them not to get wet and fall sick! They are seen running amok on roads and rooftops with syringes filled with water. Every prank is taken in one's stride and tolerated (to a certain extent, of course!). Nothing which can injure or hurt, or throwing colour or balloons on people going to their places of work, is to be allowed, but laxity and smiles are well writ on the faces of even those who usually wear forbidding expressions.

Holi is a festival when new clothes are made for a married daughter and her children. There is a special *sari* made for the daughter known as *dandia* (described at the end of this chapter) which is a must for a married girl. The sons-in-law need not be given any clothes for Holi and the children also forfeit the right to get clothes from their *nansal* (mother's house) once they get married, but a *dandia* is a must for the daughter.

'Rang Pashi', falling three days earlier to the full moon, heralds Holi into the household when all members of the family get together in the evening. The gathering can be in one single house, or the families can go around to each other's homes to perform the formal sprinkling of colour. In olden times the household *purohit* (priest) was invited to start the function, but now since there are very few *purohits*, the eldest male member takes the *thaali*, already decorated with *gulals* and *tesu* water in a small *lota*. The men, women and children all assemble together in the sitting room. All women wear their *dandias* – the men take out their handkerchiefs and put them on their laps. Beginning with the eldest male member, each male member goes round and sprinkles some *gulal* and coloured water onto each individual. The women take that on the *pallu* of their *dandias* but, if they want to safeguard their *dandias*, they can also take it on their handkerchief. Children put colour on the elders and enjoy the liberty of the occasion. Some naughty elders will colour the face of a new bride even on this day, but it is a subdued celebration. A dinner can be arranged on this day by any member of the family, otherwise only the special eatables like *gujia*, *papri* and *kanji-ke-bare* are served along with some meat dish like *kofta* (meat balls) or *kaleji* (liver) which can easily be picked up with one's fingers. Hard drinks can be served if the people are not teetotallers. In households where hard drinks are not served, *bara* water is substituted. There is a lot of comparing and discussion about the way 'eats' have turned out in different households. The *dandias* are admired and the festival becomes infectious and the atmosphere of Holi invades the house from this day onwards.

Then comes the day of Puno, when Holi is 'burnt' in the evening. Usually, it is a community celebration and bonfires are lit on crossroads. People do *pujan* and bring green sheafs of gram known as '*boot*', to be roasted black with shells on; wheat sheafs are also roasted likewise. They are then taken out of shells and eaten right there. One gets quite black in the face and the hands, but it is very enjoyable nonetheless, and the stuff is quite tasty.

Bonfires date back to the days of Hiranyakashyap, when he ordered his son Prahlad (the great *bhakt* of Lord Narayan) to be burnt alive, because Hiranyakashyap was an Asur and hated Lord Narayan. He asked his sister Holika, to wear the set of clothes she possessed which could not catch fire. She was told to hold Prahlad on her lap tightly, so that he could not escape while in flames. Holika was a very good soul; she quietly transferred the clothes onto Prahlad and got burnt herself, thus saving Prahlad to grow up and be the greatest *bhakt* of Lord Vishnu. To celebrate this great event the bonfire is still lit.

The next day is the real day of Holi. This day is called Parva. From the morning onwards, people gather and play Holi. They visit each other's houses, carrying colour and water, drenching each other as they visit different places. Some get on to two-wheelers, cars and trucks and visit people living far away; others choose to play with their neighbours. Some just go driving around in town in coloured clothes singing at the top of their voices.

While people are indulging in the fun and frolic, foodstuffs like *papri, kanji-ke-bare, gujia*, preparations of meat, boiled sliced eggs, tea, coffee and, of course, hard drinks are freely served to known groups. There is much dancing and singing, the old and young join in the merry-making. Lunchtime heralds the closing of the festival and everyone is tired and sleepy. A good scrub and shampoo are now needed to wash off the colour as much as possible and it is time to see oneself in the mirror, clean again.

During Holi, Diwali, Dussehra and Saluno (Raksha Bandhan), it is a custom to invite the daughters, sons-in-law and their families for a meal on any day during the festivals. Actually, all the daughters of the house (including aunts) and their husbands are entitled to be invited. On completion of the meal, all sons-in-law and nephews of the house are given what we call a *pyala* – a crisp note of any denomination from Rs. 5.00 to Rs. 50.00. Previously, it used to be one rupee only, gradually 'graduating' to two rupees, but now it is up to the father or the brother, to do as he thinks fit. This is supposed to be offered with a glass of whisky. The married daughters, aunts and nieces are given some money known as *kothli*. This is a quaint custom and is always given by the mother-in-law or sister-in-law. It is generally handed over by the receiver to the mother-in-law, or the eldest lady in the in-laws' house. The mother-in-law of the girl also gives her some money when she is going to her *maika* (mother's house). It ensures that a girl, while travelling, always has money in her pocket. In olden times all the money was with the eldest lady of the house, and the younger women did not keep any – not even a paisa. The young women travelled in a *doli* (palanquin) to and fro even in the city, as the custom of *parda* (the face of a woman not to be seen by men) was prevalent in North India. Therefore, it was essential that a young woman travelling alone with her small children be given some cash to be able to pay the *doliwala* at the other end, if no one else was present to do so. Another bit of fun during the Holi week is to somehow get elder married couples locked in a room of the house, by a new bride. The new bride then demands a present for setting them free, and she is supposed to sing a song especially composed for the occasion in which she demands an expensive piece of jewellery or a *sari*, as ransom. The children of the house help her in getting the couple together. The mother-in-law and father-in-law are the prime targets for the new bride. Fun is derived by all members present. Of course, the couples are very alert, but usually they fall into the trap, as husbands and wives have much to do with each other alone and can be lured into a room, the moment they are not on their guard.

College and university students make merry in their campuses and the festival of Holi 'rolls on' in full steam, with people being dumped in tubs full of water, or buckets of water being dumped on them! We see boys and girls giving mudbaths to their friends wherever water has collected on the ground. All through Holi, there is no holding back the children who chase each other with mugs full of water or take hold of a hosepipe attached to a tap and squirt water all around. *Gulal* is freely sprinkled on the wet hair and faces. New brides create a special gold and silver colour from a powder available in the market especially for this event. This colour is mixed with a little coconut oil and kept in a broad bottle and is applied in tiny quantities on the coloured faces of all the near and dear ones. Everyone is pleased to get a *teeka* put on the forehead by a young bride. This gold and silver paste brightens up the dirtiest face.

There is no *puja* associated with Holi, except putting a little colour on the faces of the gods, at the beginning of the festival.

A description of the *dandia* would be appropriate at this stage.

The *dandia* is a white cotton *sari*, preferably of voile or *mulmul*, the edges of which are coloured with a non-fast colour known as Indian pink. The *dandia* is made by dipping the gathered sides (all four) and letting the colour catch on to 2 to 3 inches of cloth, on all sides. All the sides are done in turn. The colour spreads in uneven splendour and makes inroads into the cloth in the middle to a limited extent. When this cloth is dried, the middle can also be designed making small paisley designs or anything else that one likes. After it is dried, a full length of *gota* (gold or silver border about 2 to 3 inches in width) is stitched on to the *dandia*. The portion covering the head and the *pallu* end also has a *kiran* attached to it, thus giving it more shimmer. (*Kiran* means finely cut edges of a silver or gold border, a must for a bride.) *Dandia* is usually accompanied by another *sari*, blouse and petticoat when given to a married daughter of the house. *Dandias* are also made for the unmarried daughters. Making a *dandia* is difficult these days, so this problem is solved by getting a *sari* printed in pink and attaching *gota kinari* to it. This *dandia* is worn for playing Holi and gets into quite a bad state, especially on a new bride, but it is a must for her. The older ones prefer to wear it only for Rang Pashi.

RECIPES FOR HOLI

KANJI-KE-BARE (VADA)

These *vadas* are made eight days before Holi-ki-Parva, on the day known as Baro-ki-atthan. These are made like ordinary *urad dal baras*, but are thinner. We now list the ingredients needed for making approximately one kilogram of *bara*:

Ingredients and other items

Urad dal	1 kg
Hing (asafoetida)	2 small pieces
Salt	6 heaped dessertspoons
Finely ground rai (mustard)	8 heaped dessertspoons
Pounded red chillies	3-5 heaped dessertspoons
Matka / Martban	1 (medium size)
Oil/Cooking medium	for deep frying
Water	6 jugs (1 jug=6 glasses)
Karahi (skillet)	medium size, preferably with a thick bottom
Whole red chillies	handful (for decoration of kanji)

Method

Soak the *urad dal* overnight and grind it to a fine paste next morning, in a mixie or on a *sil*. When its consistency is that of a cake mix (it should be able to form flat round shapes), put it in a vessel and whisk it very well with the hand so that it fluffs up, and there is plenty of air mixed in it. Heat the cooking medium in a *karahi* and check the heat by dropping a little piece of the dough into it – if it comes up and starts getting cooked, it is ready. Take a piece of wet cloth or a piece of plastic and hold it on the palm of the left hand (this lets the *bara* slide off easily), put some dough onto it and flatten it, shaping it into round quarter-inch flat *baras* and deep fry it at once. Two or three *baras* can be fried at one time. Take one out and see if it is fried through and through – it should be a very light brown in colour, more the colour of the *dal* itself. The *baras* should not be very thick.

Keep a *tawa* (griddle) on the fire and put the *hing* crystals on it – break them up and let them heat up and, as soon as they emit an aroma, put the *matka* upside down on the *tawa* and let the aroma saturate the inside of the vessel. Take it off the fire and fill it with warm water, and mix the salt, mustard (*rai*), chilli powder and red whole chillies (the last mentioned are decorative and as many as one likes should be added and mixed well). The *baras* or *vadas*, which have been just taken out on a piece of paper (so as to get the extra oil out) and then soaked in clear water, to take away any extra grease, are now put into this mixture. Cover the top of the vessel with a piece of cloth and tie it securely and leave it in the sun during the day (if possible) for eight days so that the *baras* will be ready even for Rang Pashi.

If, however, you have forgotten to make the *baras* on Baro-ki-atthan, then it is advisable to put very hot water in the vessel, instead of warm water. The *baras* will be pungent within four days. They can be easily digested and are very tasty. Make them in such a quantity that they can last till the end of Holi.

If one is residing in a very hot place, one need not keep the *baras* in the sun, since the tang subsides and the *baras* and the water lose their taste. Do not touch the *baras* with any other spoon except a very clean one and do not mix up any water or *bara* that has been once taken out (from the main ones). The main ones will become mouldy even with a slight touch of *atta* or any other foodstuff that may find its way into the *matka*.

PAPRI

Ingredients and other items

Besan	1/2 kg
Sarson oil	2 dessertspoons
Salt	1 heaped teaspoon
Ground chilli powder	1 teaspoonful (neither heaped nor level)
Water	1 cup
Methi leaves (cut into bits by a knife)	2 dessertspoons
Karahi	1/2 full (about 1/2 to 3/4 litre oil as cooking medium)
Maida	for *parothan*, 1/4 kg

If *lehsun* (crushed garlic) or onion is required, put 1/2 teaspoon of each or if *ajwain* is required, add 1 teaspoonful.

Method

Mix well the *besan*, salt, red chilli powder and oil. Add one cup of water in two or three instalments and then knead well so as to form a dough. Knead for about 5 minutes. Mix the *methi* leaves. Knead for another three minutes, every time scraping the *thaal* to pick up the scrapings stuck to the *thaal*. Make the dough into a big round ball, throwing it on to the *parothan*, now and then, scraping the *besan* stuck on the utensil; this should be done for about 7 minutes. If you are making over a kilo of *papri* then take the dough and beat it up with a grinding stone for another 7 or 8 minutes, since you cannot beat it properly with your hands. Heat the cooking medium to very high heat. When the frying is done the oil should be brought to medium fire. Take some oil (in the cold state) in the hand and roll out the dough into a long roll of 1 inch thickness, then cut the roll into 1 inch pieces, all the time taking oil in the palm and wetting the pieces with it. Flatten each piece into a round shape so as to roll it out into 6-inch *chappatis* (they will be thinner than normal *chappatis*). Use dry *maida* as *parothan* (on both sides of the *papri*) while rolling, using it lightly so that it does not stick to the *papri* and spoil the cooking medium. Fry very lightly, turning the flame to medium now and then. Do not let them turn red or brown; a yellowish finish should be ensured. You can roll out all the *papris* first putting them one by one on a clean sheet spread on a bed or a divan and later fry them one by one.

GUJIA

Ingredients and other items	
Maida	500 gm
Khoya	1 kg
Oil	6 tablespoons + a little more for deep frying
Water	200 ml or 7 oz
Kismis	3 tablespoons
Almonds	200 grams cut into long thin strips

Method

Mix the 6 tablespoons of cooking oil with the *maida* and using the fingers mix them so that the mixture takes the form of bread crumbs and binds to a certain extent. Now add water and knead it into a soft dough by adding more water, as required. Set this dough aside and cover it with a damp cloth.

Put the *khoya* in a dry *karahi* (a deep frying pan) and fry it to a light brown shade. Add the sugar mixing it well into the *khoya* and add the almonds and *kismis*. Fry for a few minutes more and remove from the fire. Let it cool. Roll out the kneaded dough into a *chappati*-type round shape, thicker than a normal *chappati* and smaller, depending on the size of the finished *gujias* that one requires. Fill half the round with the *khoya* mixture and seal the other half, twisting the edges inwards, taking small portions at a time and making a neat edging so that the filling does not ooze out of the *gujia*. Make all the *gujias* together or a few at a time and deep fry to golden brown on a slow fire, making them full if required so that they cook well and do not get overfried before being cooked right through. Drain the oil completely by using a sieve-type ladle, and transfer the *gujias* onto a brown paper or even onto a newspaper, so that all the grease is soaked up by the paper. Store for use later.

If one wants to store *gujias* for a longer period, they can be dropped into a thin hot sugar syrup, which leaves a thin coat on the *gujias* and will preserve them better. The ingredients taken here should make about 40 *gujias* of medium size.

8

Bhai Dooj

ALL FESTIVALS IN THE HINDU WAY OF LIFE ALWAYS HAVE something to do with relatives. Family ties are paramount – these ties keep the family unit together, throughout a lifetime. Generally, the girl of the house is given presents of clothes, utensils, and lots of *mithai* and fruits at festivals, but there are two festivals where the girl (after marriage) gives presents to her brothers – she sends *mithai* and *fruit* to her mother's house. These two festivals are Raksha Bandhan and Bhai Dooj.

Bhai Dooj comes twice a year – once after Holi and again after Diwali. The name itself denotes the day of the festival, i.e., it falls on Dooj, the second day after the full moon. Since Holi is played on Parva, the day after the full moon, i.e., the day following Holi, is celebrated as Bhai

Dooj. Since Diwali falls on the absolutely dark night of Amavasya (new moon), Dooj comes two days after Diwali. For a married girl, it is also a good time for a get-together with her own family, as she can discuss the events of the big festivals that have preceded Bhai Dooj, especially so for the newly wed, who is keen to tell her mother, sisters and brothers, what all she received during Diwali and Holi celebrations. She brings home the jewellery and clothes that she has acquired, and talks about the excitement of having 'shut up' her in-laws during Holi, how she had to sing to get her *neg* (present), or how everyone made a beeline for her and her husband with the *pichkaris*, and how she was dumped in the tub, and how the different foodstuffs tasted in different homes and so many other things!

In any case, the show of affection for her brother is always paramount in a sister's mind. She takes a *teeka* for her brother on both the occasions, consisting of the very auspicious items of *puja*, namely:

  (i)   Coconut.
 (ii)   *Batashas*.
(iii)   *Mithai*.
 (iv)   Fruits.
  (v)   Seven *paans*.
 (vi)   *Roli*.
(vii)   A little rice.

On Bhai Dooj, the *teeka* is applied on the brother's forehead but no presents of money need necessarily be given by the brother. The sister usually goes in the morning and does the *puja* in the mother's house, before the brothers leave for their places of study or work. However, the *puja* can always be arranged in the evening, because distances are nowadays very great, even if one tries to reach early. Also, the *teeka* can be sent to the brother's house, if the sister is unable to go herself. Later in life, money can be given to sisters-in-law to buy the necessary items on behalf of the sister, especially if the brother lives in a different town. A little *roli* and rice can be sent in an envelope by post.

The *puja* itself is carried out in the *puja* room, or on the same *chowk* that had been decorated for Diwali. There is no special deity for this *puja*. The Diwali *chowk* should not be cleaned up until the Dooj *puja*. At the time of Holi, one is generally too tired to decorate a *chowk*, as Dooj comes on the very next day. So, it is best to do the *puja* in the regular *puja* room. The sister decorates the *mithai*, *batashas*, *roli* and rice along with the coconut on a *thaali*. The *puja* lamp is lit; everyone does the *puja*, and the sister applies the *teeka* on the forehead of the brother, and gives him a few of the eatables along with the coconut. The brother takes some portion to eat, and he is then free to move out, while the women and children sit around, to hear the story behind Bhai Dooj from someone who knows it. The story goes as follows:

Once upon a time there was an only brother and an only sister, living in a village along with their widowed mother. As is the custom in villages, the girls were married young, and so was this sister. The sister had to go and live in another village. The brother was much younger to her, and was only about five years old when his sister got married. He grew up and slowly the image of his sister faded from his memory. He was not even sure whether he really had a sister.

The festival of Bhai Dooj used to come and go every year and he would watch sisters and brothers make merry. Every one of his friends boasted of a *teeka* on his forehead applied by his sister. Of course, he also had a *teeka* on his forehead, but his mother had put it. On one Bhai Dooj, he asked his mother, 'Ma, have I not a sister, to put a *teeka* on my forehead? All the boys in the village receive *thaals* full of *mithai* and good things for the festival, but I have to make do with what is in the house, or what you buy for me!'

The mother replied with a sigh: 'Son, you have a sister alright. You were too young when she got married, and was taken away to another village.' The boy asked: 'But then, why does she not come and visit us? I have never seen her.'

The mother replied: 'You may not remember, but you were there as a small child, during the marriage. She does not come because there is a big forest between this village and the one in which she lives and there is a big river flowing in between. One has to cross the river by boat and then there are wild animals which fill people with so much terror, that many people do not travel through the forest.' The boy was not satisfied and was very keen to visit his sister's house. He declared: 'If she cannot come then I will go there, on the next Bhai Dooj, and get a *teeka* put by her, and nobody else.' The mother reminded him again of the dangers, but he did not listen, and so it was decided that he would go and visit her.

The mother was naturally worried, but decided that it was best that he went. When the time came she told him to tell his sister that she should now come over and choose a suitable bride for him.

The boy set off, with just a bag of food for the journey. He was not afraid, although there was no one else going that way. Soon he came to the river, which had very little water at that time. He decided to cross it on foot, and as he reached halfway, he saw the water rising. He told the river not to drown him, since he was going to meet his only sister, for Bhai Dooj; on his way back the river could do so. The river agreed and went down and the boy crossed it easily. As he went further into the forest, there came a snake which wanted to bite him. He asked the snake not to do so since he wanted to meet his only sister, but the snake could bite him on his return journey. The snake agreed, and the boy proceeded. Now, he came to a mountain, which started to throw big stones on him, and he again pleaded with it to let him go. The mountain also agreed. When the boy was near his sister's village, a big tiger appeared and decided to eat him up: 'Please, please, dear tiger, do not eat me up, I am on my way to my sister's house. I have not seen her since I was a boy, and now I want to be with her for this Bhai Dooj. You can eat me up when I am on my way back.' The tiger also agreed, and went back into the dense forest. The poor boy knew now that his days were numbered. Still, he eagerly went along to meet his only sister. He reached the village, and enquired as to where his sister lived, and soon found her house. He entered the house, and saw that she was doing the Bhai Dooj *puja*.

Now there is a unique feature in this *puja*. The sister takes a chunk of cottonwool, and spreads it out from the middle, making a sort of round garland, without any break in the circle, rolls the edges smooth, and makes a necklace. This is known as an *aaun*. Then, dipping the first finger in *roli* and then *aipun*, she applies them alternately around this necklace with the help of the thumb, leaving a little space in between. One keeps silent while doing this, as one takes the name of each brother or cousin brother, with each application. Finally, a little garland is formed with red and yellow spots. Then taking the *aaun* in the left hand and rolling it to fit the palm, a *batasha* is placed in the middle. Next, the *puja* with *roli*, *aipun* and rice is performed for this *aaun*. The *aaun* is then placed near the deity, and later immersed in a river or a lake. Since one is meditating and praying for the good of the brother, one is completely devoted to the task and must not turn away or speak to anyone.

Now, it was exactly at this time that the young boy entered the house of his sister. She did not speak to him, nor did she look at him, which made him very very sad and he thought to himself: 'I made this long and terrible journey for no reason! My sister does not recognise me, nor is she prepared to talk to me. I was foolish in insisting on visiting her.' Still, he was tired and hungry, and he thought that he would go out into the village and find some food. At this moment the sister finished her *puja* and got up with a smile and embraced him. When he asked her if she knew who he was, she said: 'You are my only brother. Although I have not seen you for ever so long, how can I ever forget you. You are always in my thoughts and in my heart.' And she at once brought lovely fruits and sweetmeats to eat. She set about preparing *kheer*, *puri*, *kachori*, and lots of other tasty items. When her husband came after work, both of them provided a very enjoyable and memorable time to the young lad, so that he was full of joy. Both exchanged news of every member of the family. He was happy to see his sister so well married and living like a queen.

Days passed, and it was time for the brother to take leave of his sister and brother-in-law. One day he told her that he had to go back to his own village. The sister got up very early in the morning and made some *laddoos* for her brother to carry with him on the journey. It was very dark and she could not see much while she was grinding the lentils: unwittingly, the skin of a snake got mixed up with the lentils. She made a bundle of the *laddoos* and gave them to her brother, who started off on his journey. After some time, a stray dog arrived at her doorstep and she threw a *laddoo* for him. On eating it the dog suddenly died. The sister was terrified and knew that some poison had got mixed up with the *laddoos*. She was frantic with fear and rushed out to find her brother.

The brother had gone only a little distance, when she found him. She quickly took the bundle from his hand and threw it far away. She then told him about the poison that was in the *laddoos*. The brother then sadly told her: 'Sister dear, how much can you help me? I think my time has come. You have saved me this once, but do you know what all happened to me on my way to your village?' He narrated the whole story, about how the river, the snake, the mountain and the tiger had all wanted to finish him off. The sister was shocked, but said: 'Brother, I will also accompany you. After all, our mother wants to get you married, and has asked me to come and choose a bride for you.' She made him come back to her village, where she packed her things, and informed her husband of her plans. She also secretly packed some meat for the tiger, some milk for the snake, flowers of silver and gold for the mountain, and some *roli* and rice for the river.

Soon they were on their way and, of course, the tiger came first to eat up the brother. The sister gave him the meat and he went his way. Then came the mountain, which wanted to fall on her brother. She quickly performed *puja* with the gold and silver flowers and the mountain was very pleased with the offerings and stopped falling. Then it was the turn of the snake, and it was given the milk, and went away satisfied. They now reached the river and as was expected, it started to rise, but the sister subdued it by doing *puja* with *roli* and rice, and the river went down.

She was now tired and thirsty. Soon she saw some gypsies working far away. She wanted to ask them for water, so the brother sat down under a tree – happy to be alive – and she went to the gypsies and got some water. After drinking it she looked up and was puzzled by the work that the gypsies were doing. So she asked them why they were carrying large slabs of stones and sticking them onto the mountainside. They replied: 'You know, ours is a sad tale: there is an only brother and an only sister, and a very sad thing is going to happen to them. The brother's days are finished in this world and he will surely die. Hence we are putting these stones against the hearts of the mother and the sister, so that their hearts become hard like stones and they do not feel too much the pain of parting.'

The sister knew at once that they were talking of her brother. She asked them to tell her some way by which this calamity could be averted. The gypsies looked at each other and shook their heads, and started to do their work again. The girl pleaded with them and begged them to tell her of some method, since they seemed to know more than ordinary people. Soon one old woman came forward. She was very thin and grizzled: 'I can tell you the method, but you have to pay me for it, as we are really very poor and you look so rich,' she remarked. The sister agreed and quickly took off all her jewels and gave them to the old woman and her companions. The old woman took her aside, and said: 'The boy is to be married very soon. If his sister goes on cursing him, right from now on and continues to curse him all through the wedding and also insists on getting all rituals done to her first, this boy can be saved. But how will you convey this to his sister?' The girl did not wait to explain but rushed to her brother, and as soon as she reached him, she started to curse him and to abuse him. The poor fellow was taken by surprise, and said: 'Dear sister, have you eaten something to be so agitated?' She replied: 'No, you scoundrel, it is you who is wishing me ill, you fit-for-nothing. You made me do all the hard work at my home and unnecessarily came to visit me. Now I will definitely go to our village and tell our mother what a bad boy you are.' She made him get up and they started to walk towards their mother's village, and all the while she called him bad names, so nasty that the brother was in tears. He could do nothing about it though, he could not send her back and did not know what else to do. Soon, they reached the village and he thanked god for the safe return.

When they entered the house, everyone was very happy to see the sister, but as soon as she entered, she flung curses around and everyone ran helter-skelter. The mother came forward and pacified her. She told everyone that perhaps her daughter was very tired and should rest a while. The sister was sent to take rest, and all became peaceful. When she woke up, she was still mumbling curses, but was more sullen than loud. The mother informed her that she would like her brother to be married in her presence. It was decided to hold the wedding very soon. A beautiful girl was chosen. Still the sister went on cursing on any pretext. Everyone wanted the wedding to be over as soon as possible and the sister to be sent back to her village. The wedding day arrived and the time came for the *sehra* (a kind of head decoration made of flowers) to be worn by the young man. The sister insisted that they tie the *sehra* on her forehead first. She said such nasty things that everyone exclaimed: 'Let her tie the *sehra* first; how does it matter?' So it was tied on her forehead first. She found a small snake in the *sehra* instead of a string and as if touching her forehead she pulled the snake out and put it in a small bag she was carrying, and stuck a needle to hold the *sehra* together. Next, the sister insisted that the *barat* (marriage procession) should go from the back door and not from the front door and no decorations be made. When the *barat* was to start, somehow the sister had fallen asleep and none woke her up, as they were fed up with her and wanted the *barat* to go from the beautiful front porch – and so it did. But lo behold! The whole porch fell down, and narrowly missed the groom! The sister woke up and started shouting: 'Whoever let the *barat* go before I woke up? I will get even with everybody,' and she raved and ranted on and on. Well, people were quite startled with the turn of events and did not say anything, as they were still recovering from the shock of the near disaster.

Now the time for the *pheras* (going round the fire) arrived and the sister had again gone to sleep. The *pheras* were to be done late at night. Again, nobody woke her up, for they feared that she would create a rumpus. And do you know what happened? As soon as the first round of the *pheras* was done, the boy fell down in a dead faint, because of the evil spirits who had come to take him away. The sister woke up on hearing the noise and came cursing into the courtyard. Hearing the abuses and seeing her blazing eyes, the evil spirits fled.

Everyone decided that there was something happening which they could not understand, and therefore from then on they would let everything happen as the sister desired. It was now time for the boy and the girl to give *kheer* to each other. They let the sister have the first morsel from which she took out a hedgehog's spiked needle and quickly put it in her tiny bag as well.

The wedding was finally over and everyone including the mother and brother were keen to see the sister leave. The mother gave her daughter her dues for the wedding, and bade her farewell with tears in her eyes. The sister's eyes also filled with tears and looking at her brother, she said: 'Dear brother, when I started out with you, did I not look grand and beautiful with jewellery and lovely clothes?' The brother said: 'Yes, dear sister, you had so much jewellery and I wondered what happened to you on the way.' 'Well, you remember that I went to drink water? Right there the gypsies I met told me about the danger that was looming upon you and it was there that they told me to curse you and curse at every point to avoid any tragedy.' It was then that she told them all the details. Everyone had tears in their eyes and they hugged and kissed her. Her brother and sister-in-law touched her feet, and all present said with one voice: 'Let everyone have a sister like this, who is willing to be talked ill of, and will go about looking wild and angry even during a wedding, although it was to be the only wedding in the family – all this just to save her brother and family from disaster.' Everybody again hugged and kissed the sister. The mother gave her a lot of jewellery and clothes and asked her to stay back a few more days, so that people could make a fuss over her. The new bride was so thankful to her sister-in-law that the latter declared that none should underestimate the power of a sister's love for the brother and was forever very good to her husband's sister.

Now the custom prevalent is that a brother does not go to his sister's house for the *teeka*; instead the sisters bring or send the *teeka* to the brother, as danger may lurk on the way. Anyway, there may be more than one sister and more than one brother, so the brothers or sisters cannot go from one house to another. Therefore, all the brothers can invite the sisters to the place where they assemble.

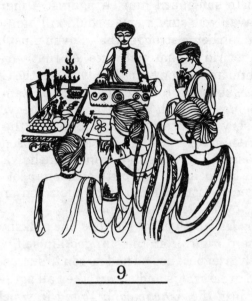

9

Ram Navami

ON THE NINTH DAY OF THE DURGA PUJA OF CHAIT [THE NINTH day after the new moon in the Sukul Paksh (the waxing moon)] some time in the month of April, Lord Vishnu took the seventh *avtar*, and Sri Ram was born to rid the world of Ravan who was creating havoc. Lord Brahma had granted so many boons to Ravan in the past, that he had become almost invincible and so became extremely arrogant. He was destroying *dharma* on earth and in *devlok* without a single thought for the future. The *devtas* ran to Lord Brahma. Brahmaji told them that he was well aware of the atrocities committed by Ravan, but he himself could do nothing about it. He had to depend on a human being to do something. Ravan could not be killed by any god or *devta*, but, in his arrogance, Ravan had forgotten to safeguard himself against a mere human being! Ravan was sure no man could kill him, therefore, only a human being stronger than Ravan must be born on earth to get rid of that evil force. At that very moment Lord Vishnu arrived on his *vahan* (vehicle) the Garud, and Brahma asked him to take the *avtar* of Ram. All the human beings on earth and the *devtas* in heaven were in utter misery because of the atrocities of the *rakshas*, Ravan. Vishnu agreed as he had also promised to be the son of Dasarath (or Dashrath) and Kaushalya in 'Treta Yug'. (The two in a previous birth had done a lot of *tapasya* and prayed to Lord Vishnu to be their son and he had agreed.) Now the time had come.

King Dasarath of the glorious line of Ikshwaku who traced their origin from the sun god himself was bowed down with grief because he had no son to succeed him. He consulted great *rishis* and *munis*; they all agreed that he must perform the *Ashvamedha Yagna* in which a horse is let loose. It roams in every town and country and anyone who dared to stop it had to fight the performer of the *Yagna*. When the horse returned unharmed, it was sacrificed with great pomp and show. Well, just when the *yagna* was about to come to a close, Dasarath asked the gurus to perform the *Putrakama Yagna*, which would grant him a son, the greatest desire of his heart.

That great *yagna* was being performed when from out of the fire came a divine (male) form. He was dark and he was clad in crimson. He was wearing the most beautiful gold ornaments around his neck and arms and he smiled softly and charmingly. The divine being had a bowl in his hand and he gave it to King Dasarath and asked him to distribute the contents to his wives, saying, 'I have been commanded by the gods to give this *kheer* to you to give to your wives to eat and they will bear you the sons you crave for.' Dasarath took the bowl in his hands and the divine being vanished.

The king went to Kaushalya (the eldest wife) and asked her to take half the contents. He then gave half of what was left to his second wife Sumitra and then he went to the third, Kaikeyi, who took some, but a little was left over, which the king again gave to Sumitra. And so were born Ram the eldest to Kaushalya; twins, Lakshman and Shatrughan, to Sumitra and Bharat to Kaikeyi. They were all the *amsha* (part) of 'Vishnu' (all living beings according to Hindu belief are in essence a part of the manifest 'Supreme'). They loved each other and were the most perfect of brothers, but Ram and Lakshman along with Ram's wife Sita were to lead a life that became the essence of the great epic *Ramayana*, which is the guiding light of virtually every Hindu household and moulds the Hindu character to such an extent that many people fail to understand its full implications. It is held in such high esteem even in the south-eastern Asian countries such as Indonesia and Malaysia (which have now turned mainly Muslim) that to this day the traditions of the *Ramayana* are rooted deep in their lives and their plays and dramas and even their names are based on the epic.

So, in Ayodhya, on the banks of the Sarayu river, in the kingdom of Kusala, was born Ram who grew up to be the most righteous of men, truthful, courageous, full of valour, firm of mind, handsome – with a very attractive personality – unruffled by emotions, powerful, highly intelligent and charming. Dark in complexion, broad shouldered with long arms and a wide chest, he had a large and beautiful forehead, liquid eyes and a very attractive gait. He was a great archer. He was noble and good and spoke softly. All the great qualities that one could ever aspire to were in this son of Kaushalya.

Ram was the perfect man and in the words of Swami Vivekananda, he was 'the ideal son, the ideal husband, the ideal father and above all the ideal king'. Ram was a man who grew into perfection as he faced the turmoils of life. His life and the life of his wife Sita have become the role models for married couples, and the lives of his brothers, the role models for the younger brothers. By adhering to these ideals, one can get guidance as to the right or wrong of a situation when one is confronted with a dilemma in human relationships. Ram's and Sita's life story serves as a strength-giving narration and Ram Rajya is the ideal rule of a king or the one in power. This is what Gandhiji aspired for our India, and we are ever striving for Ram Rajya.

We must honour such a man with great love and sanctity and his birth is celebrated with piety and devotion.

The *puja* is simple and is done in the morning. Some people as usual would like to keep a fast and only eat *phalar* which is taken in the afternoon. *Phalar* consists of a sweet made of *khoya*; potatoes made in any form without *haldi* (turmeric), garlic, *adrak* (ginger) or onion. In *phalar*, all root vegetables are allowed to be consumed, but no green vegetables are permitted. Fruit of every kind is allowed. *Puri* is made with *kuttu-singhare-ka-atta*. These are two different types of root vegetables which have been dried and ground into flour and mixed, and used instead of wheat flour; they don't hold very well, therefore, boiled *arvi* is mashed and mixed with the dry *atta*. It is then mixed in water to form a pliable dough to make *puri* or *pakori* as one likes. Curd is allowed and, of course, tea, coffee or milk, but not taken more than twice or thrice in the day. Of course, water can be taken.

Ram was born at noon and therefore the *puja* is performed in the afternoon. *Prasad* consists of:

(1) *Kasaar* (recipe given in chapter on Janam Ashtami).
(2) *Charnamrit* (recipe given in chapter on Janam Ashtami).
(3) Fruit, which can be cut into pieces.
(4) *Mithai* – *barfi* or any *mithai* which is dry and can be easily placed in a *thona* or plate along with the *kasaar*, etc.

The *puja* should be arranged in a fairly large room, since several people are invited from early morning onwards to sing *bhajans* in praise of Ram, Sita and Lakshman. Usually the sitting room is used. A sturdy *chowki* or table, on which the pictures of Ram, Sita, Lakshman and Hanuman are kept, is placed in the centre. Of course, Ganeshji must always be there first. Any other deity is not usually worshipped that day and need not be brought out of the *puja* room. Of course, the *puja* room itself is cleaned and spruced up and a *jyot* lit there; or else, some incense like *agarbatti* or *gugal* is ignited, and some flowers decorated in front of the family deities. The main decoration is of course where the Ram Navami *puja* is to be performed. Garlands must be bought for all images or pictures, failing which fresh flowers should be decorated or put in vases to make the place delightful to the viewer. A smaller table to keep the *thaali* of water, *roli*, *aipun*, rice and flowers, the bell and the conch shell is placed in front. The *thaal* containing the *prasad* is placed on the side on a *chowki* if that is big enough. *Charnamrit* can be kept on the cleaned floor in a big *dekchi* or an earthen pot.

The youngest girl of the household takes the *roli* and rice and applies *teeka* on the forehead of all male members. She applies the *roli* with her thumb, pulling it a little up while applying so as to form an elongated red mark on the middle of the forehead, more like a flame, and then putting a little rice on the wet *teeka* which holds a few rice grains (two or three) and letting the rest fall. The persons getting the *teeka* applied must cover their heads as a mark of respect, either with a handkerchief or with just the right hand, just at the time of the *teeka* application if not for the full duration of the *puja*. A round *bindi* is applied, with the third finger, on the forehead of the married or unmarried women; the widows usually apply it at the base of the throat. Nowadays, however, the taboo on widows not applying *teeka* on their forehead or the parting of their hair is fast disappearing. All women are taking full part in life and are entitled to be as much of individuals in their own right as their counterparts. Everyone is then asked to do the *pujan*, first with water and then with *roli* and *aipun*. Lastly, rice is showered on the gods. The *pujan* is done by dipping the third finger of the right hand in the liquids (one liquid at a time) three times and each time sprinkling it on the gods, with the help of the thumb which holds the finger and then jerking the finger loose. Everyone sits down and the time of birth is heralded by singing the *arti* of Lord Ram. Everyone is given flowers, distributed by youngsters generally during the singing amid the ringing of the bell; if anyone can blow the conch shell, this deep sound adds to the grandeur of the occasion. The *arti* is always done standing up and everyone does so. One person can perform the *arti* or people desirous of honouring Lord Ram, take the *arti* in turns. The *arti* finally reaches the hands of the householder. If the singing continues beyond the people thus being honoured with the *arti*, the lady or the gent who is the main host, must be right there to take hold if necessary. *Karpur* or camphor is put in the lighted flame and the appropriate chant is recited:

> *Karpur gauram karuna astharam samsar sarum*
> *bhugrendra haram*
> *Sada vasantam hardey arvinda bhawan bhawani*
> *sahtam namami.*

Then, any other *sloka* that the householder would like to be included in praise of Lord Ram is sung, but it should be short and sweet. A little Ganga *jal* (if available) mixed with plain water or plain water alone is then taken in the hand by the one conducting the *puja* and thrown with a little force (so as to reach everybody) over the whole gathering, moving a little and throwing it twice or thrice to reach everyone in case the first attempt does not succeed. All elder persons, in low tones, and the children, in high tones, together recite: 'Chittan para neer ka, dukh gaya shareer ka' (a drop of water on me and all the illness and sickness of the body are driven away). More singing could continue, but those who want to leave can do so after taking the charnamrit and the prasad. For the prasad special arrangements must be made for thonas, and small kullars for the charnamrit, or else pieces of paper can be cut in appropriate sizes so as to contain all the items of the prasad. Small spoons should be given alongside so as to enable a person to eat the kasaar. If you have enough small glasses or cups, kullars are not required. These arrangements must be made earlier, or there is an unnecessary hassle at the last moment.

To come to a very pertinent question which does rack the minds of people who have paid attention to it is: 'How come that Treta Yug came after Sat Yug or Sat Yug and Duapar Yug after Treta? The order should be Sat Yug, Duapar Yug, Treta Yug and Kal Yug. Yet it isn't so. Let me tell you why. Do you know that in Sat Yug there was a great rishi by the name of Gautam who had a very beautiful wife, Ahilya. She was really very good looking and Indra devta fell in love with her and wanted her. He decided to somehow get Gautam rishi out of the way for even a few hours. Gautam rishi used to rise at 4 o'clock in the morning and go to the river bank for his ablutions, etc., and then enter his hut and do his puja, taking quite some time at the river to have a bath and pray to the sun god also. Heralding of the morning was the cocks' crowing at 4 o'clock without fail. Now, on a particular day Indra devta first took the form of a cock and crowed loudly at 2 a.m. Gautam rishi without thinking took his kamandal and went to the river. Indra devta took the form of Gautam rishi and entered the hut. Ahilya was surprised, but like a good wife allowed him to make love to her. At that moment the real Gautam *rishi* came back and seeing his wife and Indra together became so furious that he cursed his wife to become a stone. The curse of true *rishis* never can be dispelled. Ahilya was very agitated and upset for she had done no wrong and told her husband so; he realised the situation a little later and calmed down, but he couldn't take the curse away. To provide her solace, he told her that now only when Ram *avtar* would take place on this earth and Ram would go with Guru Vishvamitra to Mithila, the kingdom of Raja Janak, to attend the 'Swayamvara' of his daughter Sita would he touch the stone (that Ahilya would become) after the curse commenced. She was not pleased and pointed out that Ram *avtar* would take ages to come – first would come Duapar and then would come Treta and it was very unfair indeed to let her be a stone for so long! Gautam *rishi* then said, 'Then I decree that Treta Yug will come first, the rest I cannot change.' And so it was that Treta came before Duapar. Perhaps Krishna had to come first, to break the rigidity that had been built up in society during Sat Yug and then would have come Ram to again give humans the norms to follow and lead an ideal life before the disastrous Kal Yug set in, in which we find ourselves. But the Almighty has ordained otherwise.

SRI RAM CHANDRA KRIPALU...

Sri Ram Chander Kripalu bhug mun hridya bhavbhaya daarunum

Nav kanch lochan kanch mukh kar kanch padh kandarunum

Kandeep aganit amit chabbi, navneel - neerath sunderam

Pat peet manuh theneet ruchii suchi naumi janak sathavanam

Bhaju theen bandhu thenash thanav - thaathyavansh nikantham

Raghu nath aanathkanth kaushalchand thesherath nanthanam

Ser mukut kundal thelak charu tharu ang vibhushnam

Ajanubhuj sher-shaap-dhar sungram jeet kharthushanum

Iti vanditi Tulsidas shankar-shesh-muni-ranjanum

Mum hridya nivas kuri kamadi khul dal ganjanum

Manu jaahi rachaoo milihi so baru sahaj sunder sanvaru

Karunanidhan sujaan sillu snehoo jaanatv raavroo

ahe bhunti gauri aseer suni siye sahit hiya harshit ali

Tulsi bhavani puji puni puni mundit mun mandir chati

***

Jaani gauri anukul siya heya harshu na aaee kahi

Munjul angal mul bam aug pharkan lage

Sijaver Ramchander ki jai

10

Baisakhi

BAISAKHI, LIKE LOHRI, IS AGAIN A FESTIVAL OF NORTH INDIA and a very prominent one for Punjab. This festival is also agriculture-based, celebrated with gusto and gaiety by the hardy and hardworking farmers of Punjab after the harvest.

Baisakhi always falls on 14 April and marks the beginning of the solar year. If one follows the lunar calendar, then Baisakhi usually comes in the month of Chait and not in Baisakh as the name indicates. However, once in four years, when the extra month (Purshottam or the Longth) is added (in the middle of the year, thus making a year of 13 months), Baisakhi falls in Baisakh. Just before Baisakhi, the first crop of the year, the Rabi crop, has been harvested and sold. Consequently, the farmer has ample money in his pocket and is free from worry till he again goes to plough the fields. He is extremely happy and has time for family and friends, but first he must thank the Almighty, i.e., by celebrating Baisakhi.

In the morning of Baisakhi, people take part in a big *nahan* (bath) at all the rivers and tanks. From early morning there is a great rush of people. Dressed in festive attire, people go to temples and gurdwaras with *mithai* and money (which is supposed to be one-tenth of the total produce or whatever they are capable of donating). They give 'thanks' for their fortune and pray for a better crop the next year. The day is considered very auspicious and big *melas* (fairs) of cows and buffaloes are organised in the village grounds, where many financial transactions take place. Also, fun *melas* enliven the landscape in every town and village. Here the old and the young in colourful clothes and turbans come to enjoy the *mela*. The giant wheels and the merry-go-rounds (set up in virtually no time since they are portable and every village has hand-manoeuvred contraptions) provide great entertainment and joy. Eating is the order of the day, and *chaat*, ice-cream, flossy sugar lollipops and other delicacies are in great demand. Balloons and all varieties of wooden and clay toys are displayed for sale. People take other household or daily requirement articles like pots and pans to sell and buy and the hustle and bustle attracts almost everyone to the fair.

Sometimes, a new-born baby is taken to the temple or gurdwara and the first drink of water is given to it with a rose petal. (Of course, if the baby is a few days old, one is not supposed to deny water to a baby for long.)

For the Sikhs, Baisakhi represents a very sanctified day. It is on this day that Guru Gobind Singh initiated the 'Panch Piyara' (the five loved ones). He decorated the Khalsa (*Khalsa-Sajaya*) at Anandpur Sahib near Chandigarh and gave these five people (all from the scheduled castes, and from different provinces of India, e.g., from Punjab, from Uttar Pradesh, from Andhra Pradesh and from Bihar) the first sermon on being a true Sikh. He made them promise not to cut their hair or beard; to always keep a comb; always wear an iron bangle on one arm; always wear an underwear; and always carry a *kirpan* (a small sword so as to be ever-ready for battle). (Guru Gobind Singh was then fighting the invading Muslims.) Baisakhi becomes a really sacred and pious day for the Sikh community and a true 'Khalsa' rejoices in it.

One of the most sacred pilgrimage centres for the Punjabis, especially for the Sikhs, is Amritsar, where the Golden Temple is situated. This temple is known as 'Hari Mandir'. It has a huge tank all round the temple and anyone bathing in it is purified, and his or her sins are washed away. On Baisakhi day, water is brought from all the sacred rivers of India and poured into this *sarovar* (mini-ocean).

Every household teaches its children to give *thaan* on Baisakhi day which is the first day of the solar calendar, so that throughout the year the feeling of charity remains in the heart.

Baisakhi involves a lot of socialising. Friends and relatives are invited for dinner or lunch. Hard drinks and meat are allowed to be served and people really enjoy themselves at home. There is no *puja* to be performed at home, except of course the necessary cleaning up that should be done during all festivals. Lots of fruit like *ber* and *lookat,* and *mithai* are sent to the houses of the daughters as gifts for the entire family, as the father and brothers would have earned a lot of money and must share it with their daughters and sisters. The whole community celebrates Baisakhi together but, at home, Baisakhi must also become a festive occasion with everyone sharing in the giving and taking. Visitors are welcomed, and offered *lassi* and *mithai*, and also other foodstuffs. On the whole, the festival leads to contentment and offers bright hopes for the future.

11

Nirjala Ekathshi

E KATHSHI COMES TWICE IN A MONTH ACCORDING TO THE Hindu calendar. It falls on the eleventh day of the waxing moon (Sukul Paksh) and again on the eleventh day of the waning moon (Krishna Paksh).

Ekathshi is very significant for a Hindu, as the observance of rituals connected with this occasion is said to take away any sin that he or she may have accumulated during the fortnight. To be able to absolve oneself from sin every fifteen days is very helpful to the mind, and, in any case, it focusses the memory on the wrongs done during that fortnight, thereby acknowledging a wrong behaviour or deed, and cleansing one's mind for the future. It is similar to the Christians going to their priest for 'confession'.

The very religious observe a fast on both the Ekathshis of the month. The fast regulations are not very strict as fruit, milk, sweets, tea and coffee are allowed and anything made of root vegetables can be taken once in a day. There is no restriction on drinking water at any time. A full meal (vegetarian) is taken at night. Still, even for the very religious there is a way out. A visit to the sacred *dhaam* (pilgrimage town) of Jagannath Puri in Orissa will absolve one from keeping the fast. According to folklore, Sri Krishna (who has his abode in Jagannath Puri during Kal Yug) got fed up with 'Ekathshi' turning up every fifteen days and hung her upside down and declared that those who saw her in this condition need not ever keep the *vrat* (fast) again.

The foregoing form of Ekathshi with the special name of 'Nirjala Ekathshi' falls in the Hindu month of Jaath, the 11th day of 'Sukul Paksh' and comes some time in June. The origin of the festival can be traced to Bhim, the son of Kunti, who was a great gourmet. He loved food and just could not resist it, and the idea of 'Ekathshi *vrat*' every fifteen days was absolutely unthinkable. His mentors felt that he should absolve himself of his sins at least once a year, since once in a year it was decreed that it be a total *vrat*. He had to give up even drinking water on that day. That settled the day for all of us to do likewise in case we want to get rid of a guilty conscience. It is psychologically a very potent idea. Anyway, Nirjala Ekathshi has a social function as well, just like Sankranti. Even if one does not keep the fast, it is a day for showing charity and kindness to the less fortunate. The wise have decided that on this day householders must think of the less fortunate of their brethren, and give in charity those items which are needed badly during the hot summer months.

In the morning, after a bath and cleaning up, the entire household collects in a room (which need not be the *puja* room). The *puja* has to be arranged in a covered space which will accommodate the entire family and all the

material stuff which is to be given in charity. The day is
bound to be hot from the very morning; hence a covered
space is necessary. A higher place is prepared for the
family deity and Ganeshji. A *diya* (lamp) is lit; a *gugal*
or *agarbatti* is also lit. There is no great formal dressing
up required on this day; it is a day of meditation. A bath
is of course required. As just stated, there is no elaborate
dressing up needed for the members of the family; they
can wear any clothes that they desire. It is not a festive
occasion but a sober one, where one is supposed to think
of the poor and the humble. Everyone does the *pujan* –
first with water then with *aipun* and *roli* and lastly with
rice, worshipping Ganesh and the appropriate deity
(Ganesh must always be worshipped before any other
god or goddess). Everyone sits in a semicircle around
the gods, and for each member of the family, a *surai*, a
reed fan, one or two *kharbuja* (yellow melon), other fruit
like *kakri*, mangoes and, anything else one desires to
give, are apportioned. *Laddoos* made out of ground sugar
(known as *'holas'*) are distributed but, if not available,
some sugar (about 100 gm for each member) is set apart
for each one. The ceremonies begin with the eldest
member present -- one who knows the chant comes
forward and puts some water and rice in the cupped
right palm of the person performing the *thaan*, he
keeps the left hand first finger in the water – and chants:
'*Addey addey Sukul Paksh Var* (the day); *Tith Nirjala
Ekathshi* — name of the person — *manse ha* — *surai,
kharbuja, pankha, aam* (mango)*, kakri apne sukh aur
parivar ke sukh chain ke liye Sri Krishna nimant.*' The
water is taken round (clockwise) the entire stuff that
each person has in front of him or her; once again water
and rice are given (in the cupped palm of the right hand
and the first finger of the left hand dipped in the water).
This again is taken around and then dropped gracefully
on to the side of the *surai*. After everyone has done the
needful, the stuff (in the form of sets) is kept aside to be

given to the poor later. The family pandit (even though he need not be poor) is given one such set. He represents the teacher. He is the person who always provides guidance in spiritual matters of the home. The other recipients can be just anyone — people serving in the house are entitled to receive these items. The distribution can be done in two days' time and the receiver should be requested to take these items away as soon as he or she can.

On this day the good Samaritans set up 'piyaos' (places where drinking water is distributed free to all and sundry). Huge earthen or metal pots are especially placed on tables with iced water or even sherbet in crowded markets or any strategic place much used by pedestrians. People can just send in bottles of sherbet, or ice, to be mixed with the water. The contribution can be as little as one or two bottles but since a large number of people join in, there is plenty of sherbet available to the passers-by. Of course, plastic glasses are the most useful and these are also contributed by more than one person. The distribution is done with great enthusiasm, people on foot and people in vehicles are stopped and offered these cold and welcome drinks with a great deal of respect. This philanthropic endeavour represents a very good form of celebration and could be adopted if it is not being done already. It makes the heart feel really good and is definitely beneficial to the receiver. The mind must be trained to think of the less fortunate, and it is good to teach it to the young from the very beginning.

12

Rath Yatra

RATH YATRA IS NOT A FESTIVAL OF THE HOME BUT A community affair. In fact, it is an affair where the entire state awakens to a great happening. The festivities connected with the Rath Yatra begin from mid-April which is the beginning of the Hindu solar calendar and summer therefore becomes the season for this great *yatra*, which spreads over the entire summer and monsoon months. It involves everybody and is therefore a great force which brings not only families but all of Orissa together.

Lord Krishna declared that in Kal Yug he would dwell in the seaside town of Puri. Therefore Puri is accepted as the abode of Jagannath, the Lord of the Universe.

This land of plenty, with rain and sunshine is one of the most picturesque in the eastern coast. Blue, white and maroon lotus grows wild in the *pokries* (natural ponds) that naturally abound in the countryside fed by the monsoon rain during May, June and July which comes early to Orissa. The beach of Jaganpuri is the longest in the world. The sand is grey and coconut palms, *thari* palm and the *kadly* plant (small bananas) grow in plenty. Paddy is their agricultural crop and rice is eaten morning, noon and night, except when one is ill; then *chappati* is prescribed by the village doctor.

The men and women are dusky; the women look beautiful in their *kaptas* – a four-and-a-half yard thick sari, with checks and flowers of bright colours and intricate designs of fish, shells and animals woven into a bright background. It barely covers their knees when worn tightly around the waist at one end, and the rest is taken again round and then over the left shoulder, gracefully covering the bosom. They wear no blouse or petticoat with the *kapta*, yet they look demure and modest. The hair is tied in a bun at the back of the head and a flower is stuck into it. Every morning they thread their way to the village *pokri* to bathe and wash their clothes and bring water for the household. Most of them know how to swim; they learn in the ponds. Little children frolic in the water while the mothers work. This was quite the scene some forty years back, but now the urban influence is felt in every village, and one sees women wearing blouses and petticoats and mill-made *saris*. Still, one can spot tribals even now in this beautiful attire.

Adi (first) Shankaracharya chose Puri as one of the four sacred *dhaams*. A visit to the four would bestow *moksa* on the person. The other three are Badrinarayan in the Himalayas in the north; Rameshwaram in the extreme south, and Dwarka on the west coast: the four *dhaams* are situated in the four extreme corners of India and anyone going to all four traverses the entire length and breadth of our country, experiencing the different cultures, customs and even laws.

Adi Shankaracharya, a thousand years ago, wanted the people of India to understand that everything was admissible in Hindu society; if done in keeping with the environment, social conditions and the codes of conduct of the society of the particular region. He felt that people who experienced the differences would be enlightened.

Jagannath Puri is visited by thousands of pilgrims all the year round, but to be there at the time of the Rath Yatra is regarded as holy as a visit to Hardwar or Kashi. Elaborate arrangements are made by the state government and the local people. There are numerous *dharamshalas* and small hotels for the pilgrims, as well as five-star hotels.

The beach is filled with people, especially during the evenings, and many enjoy the sea for the very first time in their lives. Catamarans and fishermen's boats coming in with the day's catch attract crowds and fish can be bought cheap at such a time — in most seaside towns even Brahmins eat fish without any qualms on the grounds that fish is *jal thori* (water marions). Orissa is famous for its handicrafts, miniature sculptures, stone carvings, shell items, *patta* paintings on canvas and colourful applique work.

The temple of Puri is dedicated to Lord Krishna, his elder brother Balabhadra and their sister Subhadra. The Sudershan Chakra also becomes a deity in its own right here. The temple is a majestic structure, 65 metres high and stands on an elevated platform in the heart of the city. It was built during the twelfth century A.D. in the Kalinga style. The images in the temple are unlike those in any other. They are not carved out of stone but are made of wood, and do not replicate the human form. They are very large and the faces are more or less square with a protruding nose and straight body. The faces are painted with bold strokes giving only an impression of a face with round eyes. The three deities, Krishna, Balabhadra and Subhadra, stand side by side with Subhadra in the middle, and the Sudershan Chakra on one side. There is an ancient legend describing how the images first came to the temple. The story goes that a long time ago, a few years after the great Mahabharat war, a king named Indradyumma lived in Avanti, the capital of Malwa of which he was the ruler. His chief minister Vidyapati had a dream where the god Nilamadhava was in a temple situated in a deep jungle jealously guarded by a tribal chief on an island known as Swarn Deep, in Udra Desi (Orissa), beckoning to him to come there. Vidyapati told the king about this dream and was soon dispatched to that town to find out why the good Lord had come in his dream! Vidyapati took two years to reach Nilakandara. To his dismay he found that the deity had vanished from the temple. This upset everyone, particularly Indradyumma. Still, he decided to perform the *Ashvamedha Yagna* on the shores of Udra Desi. During the *yagna* he heard the voice of Lord Nilamadhava asking him to look for a piece of wood with special divine specifications marked on it. When all the rituals of the *yagna* were completed they saw, to their amazement, a log of wood floating near the shore which they discovered was that of the *neem* tree. It had strange markings which convinced them that this was divine wood. At this very moment a man walked in and said he was a carpenter and would shape the wood, as he understood the sacred markings, but that he should not be disturbed while executing the task and no one should enter the chamber where he would work without eating or drinking or sleeping for eight full days and that he would himself open the door when the task was completed. The king agreed and the carpenter went inside the room with the log of wood and shut himself in. Four or five days passed without a sound coming from the room. The king got apprehensive and ordered the door to be opened and found, to his surprise, no one inside except the four idols, and those too half finished.

Even today everyone believes that it was Lord Krishna who had come as the carpenter and fashioned the idols. They remain so even when remade. They had no hands or feet and so they remain to this day. New ones are only made in a year which has two Ashaads and this happens every 12 to 19 years. This event is known as Nav Kalever. The idols are designed exactly as the original and painted also in the same manner. The chariots are mended every year since they lie out in the open.

Even now the idols are made of *neem* wood. It is believed that particular wood can be handled only by particular castes, but *neem* wood can be touched and shaped by every caste. The truth is that *neem* is a very strong disinfectant and repeller of all types of germs.

The main events of the Rath Yatra revolve around Lord Jagannath, the Lord of the Universe (in the form of Krishna), his elder brother Balabhadra and sister Subhadra. They are the main deities of the great and beautiful temple of Puri, but there are smaller temples inside the main one where Ganesh, Lakshmi, Saraswati and the other deities reside.

The Hindu believe that what is good for them is good for their gods and so they are anxious to see that the heat of the summer is mitigated for the gods too. From Akshya Tantiya (Teej), the third day of the bright fortnight of Baisakh which falls in mid-April, all the deities in temples are taken for boat rides in the afternoon for 21 days to a lovely tank, known as Narendra Tank. The boats are beautifully decorated each day, sandalwood water is sprinkled on the deities and flowers are showered on them. This is known as the Chandan Yatra. The *chalanti pratima* (moving images) give *darshan* to the thousands of devotees who throng Puri especially for these rituals. There are great celebrations and dancing and singing to the beat of drums and ceremonial music.

The gods are still not quite satisfied, nor are their devotees, so they are brought out in a colourful *pahaudi* (procession) from the sanctum sanctorum to the open *pandal* for a bath on the full-moon day in the month of Jaath (May-June). This is known as the Snan Purnima. The water is scented and poured 108 times over each deity. A form of Ganesh is then decorated on the deities since it is believed that Jagannath once gave *darshan* to a devotee of Ganesh, thereby accepting the Maratha as a true devotee who had reached the Supreme through Ganesh. This bath ceremony is witnessed by everyone, and crowds go to see it from every corner of our country. This ritual goes on till late in the night and then the gods are taken back to the sanctum sanctorum.

The paint on the wood gets washed off and has to be retouched. No one is allowed inside the sanctum sanctorum, and only special priests who have inherited rights carry this out. For 15 days the idols are treated with herbs and oils of different kind before being retouched with paint in the same style as before. They are reported as being ill because of the moonlight bath. There is no *darshan* of the deities during these 15 days. No one other than the chosen priests can see the rituals during this time.

The priests rest little during this 15-day period. They only eat fruit. After this period, idols are clothed in beautiful rich clothes and ornaments of the greatest value. These ornaments belong to the temple and some of them are only taken out for the great *yatra*. Clothes are made specially for this occasion by the temple trust. This trust is under the Raja of Puri, known as Thakur Raja and he is still regarded as the head of the temple.

The *puja* rituals incorporate tribal, Buddhist, tantric, Jain and Sanatam Dharam rites; this is even so during the daily *pujas* all through the year. Because Puri

came under the sway of different dynasties of differing
faiths, the temple accepted everyone, as Lord Krishna
is accepted by everyone (who follows any branch of
Hinduism) as the incarnation of Vishnu (the Supreme).
While the Lords 'convalesce' inside the sanctum
sanctorum, closed to the public view, the devotees have
to be satisfied with a *darshan* of the images or cloth
paintings (*pullachitra*) of the Lord, especially made for
this purpose. There is no *mahaprasad* made during this
time either. The devotees, who are not satisfied with
the *darshan* on cloth, go to a temple situated at
Brahmagiri to seek the *darshan* of Alarnath, another
manifestation of the Lord. Brahmagiri is 22 miles south
of Puri. There the priests await the arrival of devotees
during these fifteen days and special prayers are
conducted and offerings made just like in Jagannath Puri.

The gods came out in their *nava youban* (renewed
youth) on the new moon day of Ashaad, sometime during
the end of June. On the day of the Rath Yatra, which
falls on the Doadshi of Ashaad and is known as Gundicha
day, the idols are taken out for eight days to a garden
resort known as Gundacha Mandir. They came out in all
their finery in three palanquins early in the morning
amidst chants of Sanskrit *slokas* and other *bhajans*. The
procession is known as 'Pahandi Vijaya' in the local
dialect.

People take the deity in dancing positions to the
rhythm and beat of drums and bugles, escorted by the
Gajapati, the Maharaja of Puri. It is an inspiring sight;
thousands of devotees along with the king pray to the
God to ascend the *raths*. The three *raths* are:

(1)   Nandi Gosh for Lord Jagannath
(2)   Padmadhwaja or Darpadalan for Subhadra, and
(3)   Tala Dhawa for Balabhadra.

Lord Jagannath's *rath* is decorated with stripes of

dazzling red and yellow, Subhadra's with black and red, and Balabhadra's with green and red.

Throngs of people chant *Jai Jagannath, Jai Jagannath*. The name resounds in every nook and corner of Puri. The deities are brought in facing north-west after they step down from the newly erected 22 steps to the *rath*. Every year three huge chariots are renovated. Jagannath's chariot has 16 wheels, each 2.13 metres in diameter and 13.71 metres high. It has 4 wooden horses attached to it. Balabhadra's carriage has 14 wheels and is 13.2 metres high and has 4 wooden horses attached to it, Subhadra's carriage has 12 wheels and 4 wooden horses and is 12.9 metres high. Silk, satin and brocade, with decoration of gold and silver shimmer in the summer sun. The deities are seated in their different *raths*, except the Sudershan Chakra which is attached to Subhadra's *rath*.

As soon as they are seated, talismans of roots and leaves are tied onto them and to the *raths* to ward off evil. Songs and *slokas* continue as the Raja of Puri comes to sweep the path of the chariots for a little distance. He sprinkles sandalwood paste with a golden broom. The huge images are carried into the chariots to which a ramp of wooden beams is made. Many priests who even have the inherited right to do so, carry the idols. The chariots have ropes for pulling and people chosen from amongst the devotees are ready to give the first heave. The crowd jostles to hold the rope for even a few minutes, often getting bruised in the process. Sometimes there is a stampede and the police has to be very dextrous in dealing with such a situation. The chariots move and shouts of *Jai* rent the air.

The distance to the Gundacha Mandir, or the garden resort, which is 2-1/2 miles, is supposed to be covered in one day, with the journey breaking mid-way where the *Mausi-ma* – mother's sister – stays. Here deities do not go into the temple, but rituals are performed welcoming them right on the *raths* and *Mausi-ma* feeds them *poda pitha* (the recipe is at the end of the chapter), a *laddoo* made of cottage cheese, *suji*, sugar and *elaichi*. All through the way *prasad* is offered to the deities by worshippers individually. The *prasad* consists of coconut, betel leaves, banana, pineapple, mango and dates or any other fruit. The priests on the chariots have a busy time taking the different offerings from the people and giving them something in return as *prasad*.

Sometimes the procession gets late, and the deities have to stay the night at *Mausi-ma* before they can start again for the Gundacha Mandir. This rarely happens and the journey is usually completed in one day. The stay at Mandir Gundacha makes the total outing of an eight-day duration. The priests of this *mandir* look after the idols in the same manner as at Puri, changing their clothes every day. People can have *darshan* here during this time.

The gods have 'rested' and they now return to the Puri temple which has been scrubbed and cleaned as it is the only time when the temple is not filled with people. There is great rejoicing. The gods are dressed in finery – there is no dearth of devotees who offer their thanks for favours granted and others make offerings for the sheer love of Jagannath. It is said that if one gets a full *darshan* of the Lord during this time, dresed in jewels and fine clothes, one is sure to attain *moksha*. The sight is bewitching, and remains with one for a lifetime.

When the temple of Puri is reached and the beautiful palanquin fetches the idols, they first take them to the Singha Dwar and then the 22 steps of the temple are climbed to reach the sanctum sanctorum or the *garba ghariba*, the seat of the Lord. The idols rest for the night.

The next day starts with the full focus again on the temple of Puri, from where Lord Krishna watches the onslaught of Kal Yug and saves those who come to him for salvation. The actual Rath Yatra lasts for nine days and the last day is known as Bahuda. The *yatra* generally falls in the first week of July.

It must be mentioned that in Jagannath Puri there has been a great effort to assimilate all castes and there are several stories that bring this out so clearly that Jagannath Puri is perhaps the only place in India where the main idols are brought to give *darshan* to every creed. One of the stories that illustrates this aspect of Jagannath is as follows.

Once upon a time, the king of Puri, Purshottam Dev was fascinated by Padmavati, the daughter of the king of Kanchi of the South, and wanted to marry her. The father of the girl was unwilling. Therefore, the king went into battle but lost the war. This made him very angry. He prayed fervently to Lord Jagannath, and again went to war with the neighbouring state. This time, with the blessings of the Lord, he won the war but he was so incensed at the defeated foe that he declared that he would take Padmavati to his kingdom and marry her off to a *chandal* (the lowest of the low caste). But before he could find a *chandal* the festival of Rath Yatra came about and he made preparations to do the rituals that the king of Puri had to perform. He took a broom and began to sweep the path in front of the chariots. The head priest was a very intelligent and pragmatic person; he knew that the king's daughter must not be insulted and quickly declared that since the king was doing the work of a *chandal* he was now a *chandal* himself and as such could marry the daughter of the defeated king, and so the princess was married to the king of Puri.

Another story which illustrates the secular character of Jagannath Puri goes thus: Once upon a time

Goddess Lakshmi – who is the consort of Vishnu (Jagannath is none other than Vishnu) – had a small temple also in the premises of the Puri temple. On a certain day the women of Orissa keep a fast in honour of Lakshmi. On one such day Goddess Lakshmi decided to visit some of them and see for herself the adoration they had for her. As she visited she came across a Sudra (low caste) woman praying to her with such piety that Lakshmiji decided to eat the food offered by the woman. This came to the knowledge of Balabhadra, who called Jagannath in the form of Krishna and told him to reprimand his wife. Lord Jagannath stood outside the temple and as soon as Lakshmi came back he told her that although (if he had to decide the issue himself) he would not have said anything, his elder brother had commanded him to do so, and he had no choice but to scold her for her sinful lapse. Lakshmiji was very annoyed and left the temple. As soon as she was gone the temple became very poor, and Balabhadra, Krishna and Subhadra had nothing to eat, they went in search of food outside. In the meantime, Lakshmiji had made a beautiful palace of gold in which she lived in great style with the Sudra woman. When the two brothers saw the palace, they thought of asking the inmates for food. Lakshmiji knew who was at the door and soon made her presence known and told them that she still lived with a Sudra and would they eat the food she made? The gods didn't know what to do and Krishna looked at Balabhadra who was really very hungry. Still Balabhadra did not want to give in completely and said that they would accept the dry ingredients and cook the food themselves. That is what Lakshmiji did – she sent some *atta*, salt, vegetables and *ghee* and let them cook themselves. She did not let down her *bhakt* (worshipper) and the gods ate what the Sudra gave them. The good Lord of the Universe does not bind himself by any caste or creed and through the Rath Yatra he gives an audience to and blesses all, and is therefore known as 'Jagannath', the Lord of the Universe.

RECIPES

MAHAPRASAD

This *prasad* is made in a special chamber. The chamber is a very large one where the *mahaprasad* is made simultaneously (at least 10,000 people depend daily on the *mahaprasad* for their meals). The *kundua* (earthen pots) are placed one on top of another in pillars of nine each and spread over the grill which covers the entire chamber above the fire: they contain rice, *dal* and many different vegetables. The placing is so that the one containing the most water is placed lowest. The whole process starts very early in the morning. The priest, who is the main cook, gathers his helpers and after doing the *surya namaskar* starts the process of making the *mahaprasad*. The process also involves changing the placing of the vessels (untouched by hand but done with an iron rod or grip). The *kunduas* are changed from the lower portion to upper and vice versa. The entire food cooked at one time is ready for the afternoon meal. A portion is taken out as offering for the gods and hundreds of earthen pots are carried to the canopy popularly known as *bhog mandap*.

New earthen vessels are used for cooking *mahaprasad* twice a day and it is sold to the pilgrims on banana leaves. It is cooked every day of the year except on the eight days when the gods go to the garden resort, then the people can go and see the ingenious kitchen. The *mahaprasad* consists of *arhar dal*, rice, *saag, arvi*, curd and *kheer*. No tomato, garlic or potatoes, cabbage and cauliflower are given in the *prasad*, perhaps because it is presumed that the Jagannath temple is an ancient one and is not familiar with certain vegetables which have western origins. Pilgrims desirous of taking dry *mahaprasad* can buy small mud pots with plain (dry) *kisris* (some jaggery and different types of dry sweets) about 20 to 30 varieties, outside the temple at Khaja Patti.

Jagannath temple has been acclaimed as the biggest 'hotel' in the world, as its kitchen has the capacity to cook 72 quintals of rice daily and can feed one lakh people a day. There are 200 cooking places in the kitchen and 400 cooks who prepare a hundred different types of food daily.

PODA PITHA

Ingredients	
Chayna (cottage cheese)	1 kg
Sugar	300 gm
Elaichi small	6 (shelled)
Kewra	3 spoons

Method

Take fresh cottage cheese. Put the *ghee* in a *karahi* or any suitable cooking utensil, add powdered sugar and *chayna*, the *elaichidana* (shelled seeds) and saute, but do not let it get brown. Turn off the heat and add the powdered sugar. It should be of binding consistency. Make balls of whatever size you like and put aside to cool. Serve.

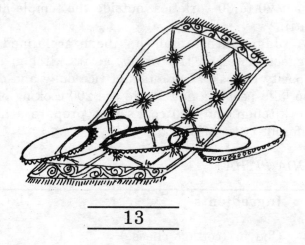

13

Sindhara

SINDHARA IS CELEBRATED ON THE DOOJ OF THE MOONLIT fortnight of the Sawan month (some time in July or August) just a day before Teej, when the rains fall on the sun-baked and parched plains of North India, thus ending summer. This festival generates waves of joy in the hearts of the people. The farmers have been working hard, sowing the summer crop known as Kharif. They have toiled together, woman and man, to put the seed in the good earth, which is expected to sprout with the coming of the monsoons. The hearts of poets are filled with ecstasy on observing the black clouds, spewing thunder and lightning and rain, sweeping the entire countryside. Kalidas wrote some of his most beautiful poems exalting this time of the year.

The common people are also gripped by the same feeling, and celebrate Sindhara with great pleasure by giving gifts to their loved ones. And who are the dear ones, but the women of the house, who now play and frolic in the rain. They string up swings on the big trees and sway merrily with the breeze. At last they can get out and enjoy the wide open spaces after the long hot summer months during which they were mainly confined to their homes. This special day, celebrated for the daughters-in-law, is known as Sindhara. Teej is for the daughters, and the two fall within a day of each other!

On both the days of Sindhara and Teej, the young women of the house decorate their hands and feet with *henna*. They get new clothes with *zari* and *gota*, and love to buy as many bangles as they can.

As mentioned earlier, swings are strung up on the big branches of the trees on the common grounds in the villages and towns. Mangoes are found in abundance in India; therefore, mango trees are the most commonly used trees for the swings. But any tree, with strong and spreading branches, providing a good oscillation to the swing, can be used. The swing gives a sense of freedom to the young girls soaring like birds! They seem to enjoy the dizzying heights that they achieve. They sing songs to the rain drops and the rain clouds in the form of Kajris and Malhars. Women are encouraged to do these things, and custom has it, that along with a heavy set of clothes and a heavy piece of jewellery, a new bride gets a *patri* and a rope for a swing. Sindhara is considered one of the major festivals of North India, and, as already stated, it is the festival of the daughters-in-law, and as such, the mother-in-law creates a lot of fuss during the first Sindhara of a new bride. Baskets of fruit, boxes of *mithai*, and cosmetics, perfumes, toys and games like *chaupar* (backgammon), depending on the capability and desire of the mother-in-law, are sent. Since many people do not know how to play *chaupar*, Ludo can be substituted.

Of course, one special item of *mithai* during this season is *antharse-ki-goli*, freely available with the *halwai* in Delhi and other North Indian cities.

The daughter-in-law goes to stay in her mother's house, or at any of her own relatives' houses, a day prior to the festival. There she receives the gifts from her mother-in-law and shows them to her own family. She returns to her in-laws' house in the evening for the *puja*. The mother now sends over the *baya* which consists of *kachori, khand, puri* (*maida-ki-puri* filled with *besan* and sugar), *antharse-ki-goli*, fruits and *mithai*.

As mentioned earlier, the *puja* is done in the mother-in-law's house, but in case this is not possible, it can be done wherever the girl is staying. The *puja* is done in the same manner as on Karva Chouth. *Baya manasna* is the chief ritual. Gaur Mata, who is none other than Parvati, is symbolised by placing an image or a picture of the Devi on a *patta*. This *patta* has been previously decorated and put on a *chowk*, made for the occasion, in the courtyard or verandah, or even in the *puja* room. If you want to go completely traditional, make a figurine of mud, and place it instead of a picture. A *diya* is lit in front of the goddess, the women wear their *chunri* and apply *chonp* on their foreheads, and then sit around Gaur Mata. *Pujan* is done first by sprinkling the water, then *aipun*, then *roli* and lastly the rice and flowers. Covering their heads, the *suhagans* put a corner of their *pallu* onto the *thaali* holding the *baya*, which is already there. No *karva* is required in this *baya*.

The *baya* consists of:

(1)   Four *kachoris*.
(2)   Two *khand-ki-puris* (*puris* dipped in thick sugar syrup).
(3)   Four *antharse-ki-golis*.
(4)   Four types of fruit.
(5)   Some money (Rs. 5 to Rs. 20).

An elderly lady of the house then chants the words as on Karva Chouth, substituting the term Karva Chouth with Sindhara: *'Adde adde Shukalpakshe, Var* (on whichever day it falls), *Tith Sindhare* (then the name of the person who is doing the ritual, followed by the husband's name) *bahu manse hai kachori, khand-puri, phal, mithai, nagdi, bartan* (optional) *apne suhag ke liye, rani ka sa raj dena, Gaur ka sa suhag dena, Sri Krishna nimant* (translation given in the chapter on Karva Chouth). This *baya* is given to the mother-in-law or any other elder member of the house, if the mother-in-law is not present. There is no fasting on this day.

14

Teej

THE TEEJ FESTIVAL FALLS ON THE THIRD DAY OF THE MOONLIT fortnight of Sawan month (in July or August), which is a day after Sindhara. Teej is the festival for the daughters of the house. Teej is much more talked about and more well known than Sindhara. On the occasion of Teej, Dandia dances are arranged by professionals and performed in courtyards at home and in public places. These dances are also performed by the young girls of the house who dress up in colourful *saris*, *lehangas* and *chunris*. Basically, Teej is a festival of Rajasthan and Gujarat, and as such the tie-and-dye *chunri* in green, red, and yellow with its *zari* and *gota* along with green, yellow and red bangles, becomes a feast for the eyes. The colourful *dandas* moving in rhythmic beats, with each swing of the hands and feet, hitting either at one's own *danda* held in the other hand, or at the one held by the other dancers, are really beautiful to watch. This dance has to be practised diligently earlier by all the participants. *Lehanga, choli* and *chunri* are the order of the day even for those who are not participating in the dance. Swings are set up in the open courtyards. Girls with *henna* on their hands and feet run about joyously. They are free of household chores on this day, and wait impatiently for the new clothes that their mothers would give, them.

On Teej, it is a must for the girls to receive clothes from their parents. A set of heavy clothes for the first year after marriage is given and then the gifts would depend on the economic status of the family. The children of the girls are also entitled to clothes from their maternal grandparents or maternal uncles. Sons-in-law are not given any clothes in most homes, but if some feel that he is the only one left out, a suit can be sent for him also.

The system of giving new clothes on all occasions to a daughter (and her children) was in lieu of her right to the family property and money, which was earlier denied to her by law, but was socially incumbent in the form of her right to get clothes and jewellery on festivals and other occasions. She was so entitled, that if anyone defaulted, it was considered inauspicious. Of course, as in cases when a custom becomes a social law, there is a reverse effect, where the maternal side being poor, cannot adhere to the custom, thus leaving a stigma on the family. Therefore, the law should be equal for sons as well as daughters (as it has become now). The distribution of whatever is in the father's or mother's side is done once and for all at the time of the death of any one of them, and the custom of giving can be dispensed with, but this is only possible if the entire property and assets have been equally distributed.

On Teej, just as on Karva Chouth, a *baya* is sent by the mother. The girl can be in her mother's house or in her in-laws' house. The *puja* is the same for both a daughter-in-law and a daughter. The *puja* is done in the morning. The materials required for the *baya* are four *kachoris*, four *puris*, two *antharse-ki-golis*, and two fruits. These are placed on a *thaali* at the place of *puja*, where a *chowk* has been decorated, and Gaur Mata (an idol or a picture of Parvati) seated on a *patta*. *Puja* is done just as on Sindhara or Karva Chouth. The auspicious *chunri* is worn and a *chonp* (or *chomp*) is put on the forehead, in addition to the other make-up. Chanting is done by an elderly lady and the same words are repeated as on Sindhara, but the word Teej is used instead of Sindhara. The tith is also corrected accordingly. Whatever is put in the *baya* is given to an elderly lady (preferably to the mother-in-law) after the *puja*. The feet of all elders are touched by the daughters-in-law – the former happily give their blessings. This day – like Sindhara – is meant for fun and frolic. Lunches, dinners, and a lot of dancing and singing are arranged. One can make it a happy occasion by taking the young girls out for shopping and buying them *chaat* during the day and keeping the evening aside for singing and dancing.

15

Raksha Bandhan

RAKSHA BANDHAN FALLS DURING THE MONTH OF SAWAN ON Purnima, i.e., the day of the full moon according to the Vikram calendar. As per the English calendar, this festival comes sometime in July or August. It heralds the arrival of the monsoon.

Raksha Bandhan or Saluno represents one of the most sentimental festivals of India. It is based on the emotional ties that bind a brother and sister in a very close bond – the most sacred relationship of life, without any ulterior motive or demand of any kind – that nature has bestowed on mankind. A brother and a sister have shared similar joys and sorrows in the home and react in ways easily understood by each other. The sharing can be so complete that no other relationship can compare with it, making Raksha Bandhan a day of festivity and pure joy.

Woman, having been regarded as the weaker sex for ages past, had been dependent on one or the other male member of her family, and who else could she depend on for unstinted support but her brother? To symbolise this profound relationship, the sister ties a *rakhi* on the right-hand wrist of all her brothers on this day and they acknowledge this relationship by accepting it with grace and love. With this *rakhi*, she bestows deep affection and blessings on her brothers so as to guard them against all harm, and prays to the Almighty to give the very best to them. These feelings are the ones that symbolise Raksha Bandhan. Gifts of money and/or other presents in kind given to a sister on this occasion are not of any consequence, but only a symbolic gesture. Still it is good to give such gifts.

Now we come to the celebrations at home, so as to bring about an atmosphere in keeping with the occasion. As is the custom for all festivals and *pujas*, the lady of the house dresses up early in the morning in fine clothes. All girls, whether married or not, wear clothes with a touch of *zari* and put a *chonp* on their foreheads. The lady of the house cleans and bathes the gods and the goddesses. The *puja* room is swept and cleaned with a wet cloth, and a *chowk* is laid out on the floor. (If the room is carpeted, one need not do this.) The puja *thaal* – with water, *roli*, *aipun*, rice, flowers, coconut, *kalava*, *batashas*, *paans* and *rakhis* which have been received by post or brought in as *teeka* by sisters living in the same town – is placed before the gods. A *rakhi* should be tied onto or placed before the chief deity of the family. A daughter of the house must apply the *teeka* and tie the *rakhis* on the wrists of the menfolk, if a sister is not present but has sent the *rakhi* and *teeka* to the brother's house.

The unmarried daughter can perform the ceremony in the absence of her aunts or elder married sisters. The *teeka* is applied by the thumb on the forehead, along with *roli*, and then a little rice is stuck onto the *roli*. A small *thaal* should be arranged separately from the *teeka thaal*, with water, *roli*, *aipun* and rice, and passed around for everyone's convenience to do the individual *pujan* — first with water, then with *aipun*, then with *roli* and lastly with rice and flowers. This is done by dipping the third finger of the right hand in the liquids, and with the help of the thumb, sprinkling the contents onto the gods from afar — three times for each liquid. The dipping of the finger can be done once in each liquid but the spraying is done thrice, by holding the third finger by the thumb and then letting it go with a jerk. The rice is picked up and showered onto the gods. From the *teeka thaal* the sisters again put a *teeka* on the forehead of their brother, and then tie the *rakhi*. They also put some *mithai* in his mouth and bless him silently. However, if a brother is not present, a coconut is taken in the left hand and a symbolic *teeka* put on its broader side.

The *puja* of Raksha Bandhan is performed in the morning as the family members disperse early for their places of work or study, it normally being a working day. The men hurry away with the *rakhi* and *teeka* intact, as it is a matter of pride to show that one is loved and cared for at home. If for some reason the *puja* cannot be arranged in the morning, then it can be done in the evening. Most of the boys really feel bad if no *rakhi* is tied onto their wrists, while others display half an armful! Little kids going to school especially feel a sense of fulfilment and happiness if such attention has been paid to them. So, even if the *puja* has not been done in the morning, the *rakhis* should be tied to the male members in any case.

The ones left behind sit down to hear the story told on the occasion of Raksha Bandhan, which is usually narrated by the eldest lady of the house, and runs as follows:

Once upon a time there was a couple who wanted a child very much, and prayed to God to give them a son. Since they were both very pious and good in deed and word, God listened to them, and soon they were blessed with a baby boy. They were full of joy and named him Shravan Kumar. The boy grew up to be a very dutiful son, and fulfilled all the hopes and aspirations of his parents. The parents slowly grew old and feeble, and both of them lost their eyesight. They realised one day that they had not undertaken any pilgrimage, and asked their son, who was by now a strong young man, to take them to a holy place where the Ganga flowed, so that they could take a dip in its cool waters and wash away their sins. Gangaji is so pure and good of heart that she takes away the sins of mortals who come to bathe in her. The son wanted to fulfil his parents' last wish, and so he built a *baingi* (a long pole with two baskets hanging on both ends, one basket for carrying his father and one for his mother for they were feeble and could not walk far). So, it came about that Shravan carried his parents on his shoulders all the way. Soon it was time to rest and the parents felt thirsty, and asked their son for water. Shravan could hear a stream gurgling nearby, so he took a small pitcher and left his parents under a tree.

At this very moment, Raja Dashrath was out hunting. At that stage of life he was a very sad man as he had no children, although he had three wives. The king was also near the stream when Shravan went to fetch water. Dashrath heard some rustling in the bushes. He felt sure that it was a deer which had come to drink water, and did not wait to confirm this, but shot an arrow into the thicket. It was poor Shravan whom the arrow pierced near the heart. Shravan cried out in pain, and King Dashrath realised that he had shot a man. He quickly ran to the man and saw him in the throes of death, with a *lota* lying nearby. Slowly and gently, he lifted Shravan and made his head rest on his knee. Shravan could hardly speak, but somehow managed to tell the king about his blind mother and father waiting for him to give them water to quench their thirst. The king offered to take the water to them, but Shravan was apprehensive as once they knew it was not their son, they would not drink the water. So he told the king not to speak to them but to give them the water first, and then only tell them about their son's death. And Shravan Kumar soon died on the lap of the king.

The king took the *lota* and filled it with water, and made his way towards the tree where the blind couple were sitting in their baskets. As the king approached them, they asked with one voice if it was Shravan who had come to give them water, and why he was so late? The king did not reply but still they persisted. The king handed them the pitcher filled with water, but they would not take it, and insisted on knowing who it was, for they knew that it was not their son Shravan. King Dashrath slowly told them what had happened. On hearing this terrible news, they pushed the pitcher from the hands of the king and cursed him thus: 'May your death also be due to agony of the heart while waiting for your son, so that you may know one day the pain that you have brought upon us.' Saying this they both fell down dead. King Dashrath was very sad because the words from such pure hearts always come true. On returning home he lay down on a couch as he was very upset about what had happened and was constantly thinking of the curse that the couple had cast on him. His wives came running to him on hearing that he was in such anguish. They called the royal astrologers and wise men, and told them the full story. All of them shared the king's sorrow over the tragic incident that had taken place, but smiled when they were told about the curse, for it would surely bring children to the king – which was the greatest wish of the whole kingdom and not just that of the king. The king was very happy now and did not mind the prospect of agony at the last moment of his life. So it happened that Ram, Lakshman, Bharat, and Shatrughan were soon born as sons of Dashrath. Ram and Lakshman later went into exile for fourteen years and that brought about the fulfilment of the curse, and Dashrath died of a broken heart.

The crux of the story is that Shravan did not have a sister and no one had ever tied a *rakhi* to protect him in time of danger. Therefore, everyone should have a *rakhi* tied, even by an adopted sister, for the truest protection comes from the truest prayers.

At the end of the story narration the *puja* is completed and everyone sits down to eat and drink with joy in their hearts. Usually, it is lunchtime and *karhi-chawal* is made in addition to other dishes. As it is normally not a holiday, the celebrations can take place in the evening, and so ends another day of festivity.

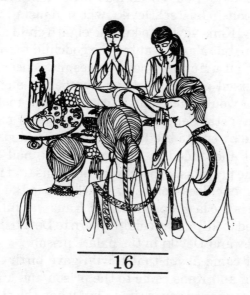

16

Janam Ashtami

LORD KRISHNA, THE EIGHTH *AVTAR* OF VISHNU WAS BORN IN the Duapar Yug which came just before Kal Yug (the yug in which we find ourselves today). His birthday falls on the Ashtami of Krishna Paksh or the 8th day of the dark fortnight in the month of Bhadon (eight days after Raksha Bandhan), some time in July or August, according to the English calendar. This is during the rainy season and is known as Janam Ashtami.

This festival is celebrated on two days, once on the actual day of his birth in prison at Mathura, and then on the very next day on his being discovered in the house of Nand and Yashoda at Gokul.

According to Hindu mythology, Naradmuni, had told Kans, the cruel king of Mathura and maternal uncle of

Krishna, that he would be killed by the eighth child of his favourite cousin (sister) Deviki, who had just got married to Vasudev. Kans vowed to kill the eighth child as soon as it was born, but Narad wanted the godchild to come soon. It is said that a nursing mother does not conceive, and if Deviki nursed each child for a number of months, the eighth one would take long to come. Narad took a lotus with eight petals and began counting from one of the petals, one by one to the last, and then counted from the next petal and ended at the one that he had taken as number one previously, thereby telling Kans that in certain situations, one does not know which one is the first and which one is the last. Consequently, Kans was full of anger and decided to kill all the children born to Deviki. He locked up Vasudev and Deviki in the palace prison.

So it came about that Deviki gave birth to a child every year, and Kans came to the prison and killed each one. This happened seven times, but when the eighth was born, a miracle happened. All the guards went to sleep, the doors of the prison flew open, and the shackles of Vasudev and Deviki burst open. The child was a beautiful boy beyond compare, and very dark in complexion. There was a voice from the sky (*akashvani*): 'Take this child O Vasudev, to your friend's house at Gokul – Nand and Yashoda. They have had a little girl just born to them, bring her here in place of this little boy, they will not know about the exchange. Go now, or else Kans will destroy this one, born to get rid of evil from this world.'

Gokul, where Nand and Yashoda lived, was across the river Yamuna, which flowed near the city of Mathura. Vasudev found a *chhaaj* (reed contraption by which all foreign matter is removed from any lentil, rice, wheat, etc.) in which he put little Krishna and took him to the banks of the great river Yamuna. It being the rainy season, the river was in full spate, and it was still raining. On stepping into the river, poor Vasudev tried to save the baby from the rising river by holding him higher and higher. He was getting very frightened and anxious, but then he remembered the *akashvani*, which is the voice of angels, and he was reassured. Little Krishna knew of the dilemma facing his father, and quietly put one foot out and touched the water, and behold, the water after touching the foot of the Lord, started to subside and soon the river split up making a dry path for Vasudev to walk upon.

At Gokul, Vasudev entered the house of his friend Nand, who was asleep and so was his wife Yashoda, and so were all the attendants. He saw a sweet baby near Yashoda and quickly exchanged the babies and carried away the little girl. Back at Mathura, he placed her beside his wife. Soon the shackles were back in place, the doors shut and the guards woke up. The attendants on seeing the baby, rushed up to their master Kans, to give him the news. Kans came in a great hurry, because it was the eighth child. He picked up the baby and threw it against the wall, but the little girl flew up into the sky, and a voice was heard: 'O Kans, your destroyer has already been born, and is elsewhere', and, along with laughter, the child suddenly turned into lightning and vanished. This little girl has come to be worshipped as Deviji ever since, taking various names like Durga, Tara, Ishani, and Mandakini.

Janam Ashtami is celebrated with great pomp and show in temples and homes. Krishna is the one who has given us the life-enduring message of the great *Bhagavad Gita*.

Incidents of his childhood are depicted through cribs and other decorations made in homes and temples. Such items display his childhood antics and sober moments, and can be arranged with dolls dressed up as kids, men and women, with *lehangas*, *chunnis*, *dhotis* and *kurtas*. The flute of Krishna can be made out of reed. Radha, his childhood sweetheart, or the Gopis going for water to the river or carrying butter and milk in small earthen pots, one on top of another, can be depicted. *Raas leelas* of every type are arranged. Vishnu and Shiv (with the river Ganga

flowing from his head) also present an attractive feature.
The layout looks very nice with freshly mowed green grass
spread out, and pathways created in the midst, with red
gravel. It is great fun planning and executing the
decoration, as the whole family is occupied for the entire
day. Little children get very much involved in cutting the
grass, bringing the mud, gravel, leaves and plants, and
watch, bright-eyed, as elders dress up the dolls with *zari*,
gota and other shining material.

It is best to decorate the crib in a room where it can
be displayed for a few days, as people can admire the effort
and the beauty.

Most families keep a fast on this day, but one meal
is allowed. This is known as *phalar*, and consists of fruit,
mithai, curd, *kuttu singhare-ki-puri* or *pakori*. This
phalar is taken in the afternoon (around 2-3 p.m.). Tea
and coffee are not forbidden, and can be taken at any
time of the day.

In the afternoon the *prasad* is prepared for
distribution in the evening. This *prasad* consists of the
same eatables that a new mother used to be given after
childbirth, and is still given in traditional homes. This is
known as *paggi-hui-meva*. Fruits like banana, guava and
apple, cut in pieces or slices, can be added to the *prasad*.
Of course, *kasaar* and *charnamrit* are a must. A piece of
fruit or only *kasaar* can also be given as *prasad*, if too
much workload is not desired. It is not essential to distribute *prasad*, even if a crib has been decorated and *bhajan*
singing has been arranged.

However, if one does not have the resources or time
to decorate a crib or even otherwise cannot undertake too
much of decoration, only the pictures and idols of all gods
and goddesses can be brought out of the *puja* room and
put on a big *chowki* or table placed against a wall, leaving
plenty of space in front for people to sit down. Krishna
is the main deity of the day and his idol or picture is

placed in the centre, and should be garlanded. *Teeka* should be applied on all pictures or idols except perhaps on Lord Krishna on whom it could be applied at midnight, welcoming him at the exact time of his birth, but only if possible. A lamp (*jyot*) should be lit in front of the gods as soon as it starts getting dark. Another table for keeping the *prasad* is placed in front of the main *chowki*. There should be place also for a small *thaali* containing the *roli*, *aipun*, water, rice and flowers, a small bell and the *arti*. These items should be kept handy to be used at the time the birth of Krishna is welcomed at midnight by the gentleman or the lady of the house by applying the *teeka* and then doing *pujan* by sprinkling first water and then *aipun* and *roli* and, lastly, showering some rice.

In the evening, the family members gather together and sit down in the room where all the decoration has been done, and sing *bhajans* in praise of the good Lord Krishna. Children are greatly encouraged to bring their talent to the fore. Musical instruments like harmonium, *tabla*, *khartal* and cymbals are brought out to accompany the *bhajans*. People who drop in also take part in the singing with gaiety. Since Krishna was born at the stroke of midnight, the singing should commence with a view to ending it at midnight. 'Om Jai Jagdish Hare...' is sung on this night as *arti*. Everyone should stand up for the *arti*, after which flowers are showered on the main idol or picture of Lord Krishna. *Prasad* and *charnamrit* are then distributed to all present. The *prasad* can be easily distributed on pieces of paper or in *thonas* available in the market. *Charnamrit* can be served in cups or in *matkenas* (or *kullars* as some people call them). All this saves washing up. Now one can settle down to a hearty meal consisting of the usual vegetables, *puris*, *chutneys*, and *achars* – one can eat anything vegetarian during the night meal.

RECIPES FOR THE *PRASAD*

PAGGI MEVA

Makhanas

Ingredients and other items	
Makhanas	50 gm
Sugar (ground)	2 dessertspoons (*bura* is available in the Indian market)
Water	2 dessertspoons
Ghee (or any other good, non-odorous cooking medium)	1 teaspoon
Karahi (heavy-bottomed or a deep frying pan)	1
Kalchi (flat ladle)	1

Method

Cut or break the *makhanas* into two or three pieces and remove any part of the black hard husk that may still remain on them. Take the *karahi* or the frying pan and put it on a medium fire. Next, put the oil or *ghee* into it and add the *makhanas*, constantly sautéing them with a *kalchi* (ladle), and letting them roast. *Do not* let them get brown; adjust the fire to hot and reduce it when desired. This process will take about three or four minutes. Add the ground sugar, and mix it with the *makhanas* quickly. Next, add the water and mix it with the sugar and *makhanas*. Do not let the sugar and *makhanas* get brown; the sugar should be such that it provides a slight coating. *Makhanas* need not stick together but should remain white and round. The cooking time is five to six minutes. Take them out and put them on one corner of a *thaal*. Clean the frying pan before using it for the next item.

Kharbuja Beej

Ingredients and other items	
Kharbuja beej	50 gm
Sugar	2 dessertspoons (finely ground – it's better to use *bura* available in the market)
Water	2 dessertspoons
Ghee (or any other good cooking medium)	1 teaspoon
Karahi	1
Kalchi	1

Method

Clean the *beej* (seeds) and take out any small stones or other foreign material from them. Do not wash the *beej*; they must be dry. Take the frying pan or *karahi*, put it on a medium fire, and add one teaspoonful of oil or *ghee*. Next, drop the *beej* into it, all the time sautéing them with a *kalchi*; let them roast. The *beej* will splutter while being sautéd; so be careful and do not let them hit you (especially in the eyes) when some of them pop out of the frying pan! The colour of the *beej* should be just light brown; they will puff up and become rounded. Cook for about three to four, minutes, adjusting the fire according to the need. Add the sugar and then the water, which will form a sticky sweet binding for the *beej* when taken out, and set next to the *makhanas* in the *thaal*. Be careful that you buy *kharbuja beej* and not *beej* of any other melon. Clean the frying pan before using it for the next item.

Paggi Gari (Coconut gratings)

Ingredients and other items

Gari	100 gm
Ground sugar (or *bura*)	2 dessertspoons
Water	2 dessertspoons
Ghee (or any other cooking medium)	1 teaspoon
Karahi	1
Kalchi	1

Method

Put the melted cooking medium into the frying pan and add the *gari*; sauté it for three to four minutes, adjusting the fire according to your requirement. Do not let the *gari* become brown or mushy; it should remain a bit loose even after adding the sugar. Now add the water, which will become an invisible syrup and will bind the *gari* together to a certain extent. Cook for another two minutes or so and then take it out and set next to the *makhanas* and *beej* in the *thaal*. Cooking time is five to six minutes.

Charonji

Ingredients

Charonji	50 gm
Ground sugar (or *bura*)	2 dessertspoons
Water	2 dessertspoons
Ghee (or any other good, non-odorous cooking medium)	1 teaspoon

Method

After cleaning the *charonji*, keep it ready for use. Place the frying pan on a medium fire and put the cooking medium into it. Next, put the *charonji* in and sauté it for three to four minutes, controlling the fire as required. The *charonji,* which is brick-red in colour, should retain its hue but must be nicely roasted and should not remain raw from inside. Now, add the sugar and stir it thoroughly, adding water immediately after adding the sugar. The sticky syrup will bind the *charonji,* and after another two minutes, the mixture will be ready and can be put in the *thaal* along with the rest of the *meva.* Time taken is again five to six minutes. Clean the frying pan before frying the next item. Since the pan is always hot, it can be put under the tap and wiped dry with a cloth – everything is thus easily removed from the pan.

Gond

Ingredients	
Gond	50 gm (white variety meant for eating)
Ground sugar	2 dessertspoons
Oil	1 cup (or to be determined according to the size of the pan)

Method

Gond or gum crystals are available in small pieces, clean and white, especially meant for eating after being cooked. The brownish variety does not cook so well, so be a little fussy in your choice. This way of consuming *gond* is supposed to be very good for backaches and is highly recommended for the mother after childbirth. For frying the *gond,* one must heat the cooking medium beforehand and then put the crystals in. The pan should be half filled with oil so that the crystals can be more or less deep fried. They will puff up beautifully into small shapes; turn them over and see that both sides are evenly puffed. *No water should be added*, and the sugar added only when the crystals have been brought out of the pan, but are still very hot. Sprinkle the sugar evenly on them, and set the final product beside the other *paggi meva*.

Kasaar

Ingredients	
Rawa	1/2 kg
Asli ghee (pure *ghee* or saltless butter) or any other good cooking medium	1 level teaspoon
Ground sugar	3 level dessertspoons
Gari, *makhanas* and *beej* (from the *paggi meva*)	Small quantities

Method

Place a *karahi* on a medium fire, put the *asli ghee* and sauté the *rawa* in it, working it all the time. When slightly brown (more whitish), add the sugar and continue sautéing it until the correct shade of very light brown is attained. On adding the sugar, the *rawa* will turn white again. Take the *karahi* off the fire. After cooling, add a little of the *beej*, *makhanas* and very little *gari* to it; the entire *meva* should not be more than one or one-and-a-half dessert spoons, and that too should be decorated on top of the *kasaar*, which is mixed while serving.

Charnamrit

Ingredients	
Milk (cold)	3/4 kg (750 ml)
Cold water	500 ml (3 glasses)
Asli ghee	2 drops
Dahi (curd)	2½ dessertspoons
Ground sugar	6 dessertspoons
Pure honey	1/2 dessertspoon
Tulsi leaves	8 (broken into pieces)
Makhanas	8
Gari	1 teaspoon (grated)
Ganga *jal*	1 dessertspoon

Method

Take the *dahi* in a container along with a few dessert-spoons of the cold milk, and slowly beat it so that it mixes very well into the milk; then add it to the rest of the milk. Add all the other ingredients now leaving the *tulsi* leaves, *makhanas* and *gari* for the end. Slowly stir the mixture with a spoon. Keep in the refrigerator, and take out at the time of *puja*. Serve in small *matkenas* or small cups. A little *dahi* can be kept aside.

The foregoing recipes for *prasad* are meant for 12 to 15 persons. Add a piece of banana and a slice of apple to the servings, if so desired.

Since no one is allowed to taste the *meva, kasaar* or *charnamrit* before the *puja* is finished, the housewife has to be sure the proportions are absolutely correct. The foregoing recipes have been tried out with great success, and if followed carefully, they should give very good results!

RECIPES FOR THE PHALAR

Kuttu singhare-ki-pakori or puri

Ingredients and other items	
Kuttu ka atta	100 gm
Singhare ka atta	100 gm
Arvi (Colocasia)	1/2 kg
Salt	1 teaspoon
Water	1 cup
Oil or *ghee*	sufficient quantity for deep frying
Karahi	1
Ladle with a sieve	1

Method

Boil the *arvis* so that they become very soft. Peel off their skin and keep them aside. Now, mix both the *attas* and the *arvi*, squashing the *arvis* and mixing them well with the *atta* and salt, while slowly adding the cup of water. The mixture forms a sticky dough. Set the *karahi* on full flame and put enough oil or *ghee* so as to deep fry the medium-sized *pakoris* that are dropped into it. The *pakoris* are just broken from the dough which is held in the hand and dropped into the hot oil; they take their own shape. If one desires to make *puris* then they have to be rolled out on a board with a rolling pin with a little dry *atta* of *kuttu* or *singhara* spread on the board and the rolling pin so as not to let the dough stick on. These *puris* are also deep fried.

Makhane-ki-kheer

Ingredients

Milk	1 kg
Makhanas	2 cups (cut into pieces)
Ground sugar	2 dessertspoons
Paggi gari	2 level dessertspoons
Almonds	1 level dessertspoon (cut into bits)

Method

In a suitable vessel, mix the *makhanas* with the milk and keep on the fire. After about half an hour, the *makhanas* will have been cooked. Now add the sugar and take the vessel off the heat and let it cool. Add the *paggi gari* (coconut) and cut almonds. The *kheer* is not thick enough and will be more watery than the *kheer* made with rice. It should be cooled in the refrigerator.

Barfi: This can be bought from the market.

Curds and potato curry without onion or garlic form a filling item for the *phalar*. Potatoes can be made into a *chaat*, adding cucumber and tomato as required, if a curry is not necessary. Tea, coffee or milk can be taken at the time of *phalar*. The *phalar* is the only meal during the day and is usually taken between 3 and 4 p.m. Water and other drinks can be taken at will.

17

Onam

KERALA, WITH ITS LUSH VEGETATION AND THE WAVES OF THE Arabian Sea lashing its coastline, is one of the most beautiful states of India. Its landscape is unlike that of any other state of our country. The sea makes inroads into the mainland in several places and fishermen with their catamarans and sailboats dot the horizon. The sea overflows onto low-lying areas when the tide is high, forming lakes and backwaters. There are also many freshwater lakes which are rich in seafood. Coconut palms growing straight or arched, some touching the earth in a deep curve trying to reach the sunlight, grow in abundance.

This land was home to the king Mahabali, who was
the grandson of Prahlad and son of Valchana, both great
kings. Onam is celebrated for three days in memory of
that time, the golden age of Kerala. The people believe
that Mahabali comes to Kerala to see his people once a
year because of a boon granted to him by Vishnu in his
Vaman *avtar*.

Onam falls on Daadshi of Bhadrapad or the 12th
day of the waxing moon in Bhadon (in August-
September), when the rice fields have been harvested.
It is two days before Anant Choudesh, when the
immersion ceremony of Lord Ganesh is being celebrated
in Maharashtra and some of the other states of India.

The people of Kerala count the days of a month
according to the moon cycle; each day is dedicated to a
star and has a distinct name. The stars, like the *tith*,
may overlap or vanish altogether, thereby sometimes
resulting in two days dedicated to the same star, or not
having one particular star at all in a given month
(depending on whether the star is at the position which
determines the day). The calculation tallies with the
lunar calendar. The date of course changes every year
according to the English calendar. It is best ascertained
by using an almanac (*jantri* or *panchang*).

Onam has become the festival for everyone in
Kerala and has been declared a national festival by the
government. It is celebrated with great fervour
irrespective of caste or creed. It is, of course, a harvest
festival but during this time, after the harvest, everyone
rejoices with thoughts of the time of Bali, who brought
great peace to this land.

The people of Kerala are 100 per cent educated,
but are very simple in their habits and dress. The women
mostly wear off-white *saris* made of cotton, although
terrycot and pastel shades are becoming popular. On
festive days the *sari* worn has a *zari* in the centre.
Glaring designs are shunned.

All women wear flowers – jasmine in single or double strands decorate the hair, falling alongside single plaits of hair. On festive occasions flowers are woven into intricate designs and put on the base of the head. A strand of jasmine or any small seasonal flower is a temptation to which most women, old or young, succumb. Women in South India do not cover their heads as they do in the north.

The men wear *lungis* with *zari* for occasions, otherwise too the *lungi* is the common dress for men. The upper part of the body has a cloth known as *utthariyeem* hanging on the shoulder and reaching to the waist or a little higher. This is also off-white, with *zari* for occasions. Nowadays, shirts or *kurtas* are worn as upper garments and the *lungi* or *dhoti* still worn around the waist and legs. The Keralites often pick up their long *lungi* from the lower ends and tuck it into the waist, thus making it into a half *lungi* and allowing the legs free movement in water.

The story of Mahabali or 'Bali' is told in the *Bhagwat Purana*. Bali was a noble, generous righteous and powerful king who ruled with justice, wisdom and generosity. Although he was an *asur*, no *devta* was as noble, in thought or action, as him. He never refused anyone who asked for a boon. He did the *Viswajit Yagna* under the guidance of Guru Sukre (who is the guru of all *asurs*). This bestowed on him the strength of the three worlds. No one could stand against Bali. The people loved him and he glowed like a jewel. He looked so handsome that Indra (the king of the *devtas* who was always afraid that his throne would be taken by someone who became too noble) got very jealous.

Indra had, time and again, foiled the divinity reached by several sages who had by their actions or *tap* (great meditation) nearly reached his stature. This time the *devtas* approached Vishnu to come to their aid. Narayan (Vishnu) was aware that an *asur* dynasty would not in the end be good for the earth and so took the Vaman *avtar* as the son of Aditi and Kashyap, and remained in the form of a small boy with an umbrella and a *kamandal*, even in adulthood.

    Mahabali was, at this time, about to perform the *Ashvamedha Yagna* so that he be proclaimed the most powerful king in the three worlds. He decided to do it on the banks of the river Narbada. He was proceeding with the rituals, when he saw a great glow coming towards the *yagshala*. He found a small boy, glowing like the sun, with a *kamandal* in one hand and an umbrella in the other, coming towards them. Bali knew it was no ordinary child and in all humility asked him to sit down. He asked him to demand anything he desired as his glory and sanctified the *yagshala*. The child demanded three paces of the ground, measured by his own foot. Bali thought that three paces of a child's foot was not enough and told the child to ask for something more. The child Vaman insisted on three paces. Guru Sukre saw through the game and told Bali not to accede to this demand as he was being cheated and that in such a case there was no sin in going back on his word (so the Vedas say). Sukre knew that it was Vishnu in the guise of Vaman, but Bali did not budge; he had given his word. Sukre left the gathering in disgust, thus giving permission to his pupil to do as he wished. Vaman took the first step and became Lord Narayan, one pace took the world and the second took the heavens. Then there was no land left and Narayan became Vaman again and asked where he should take the third step. Bali asked him to step on his head as he would be blessed by the feet of Narayan, and so he was sent to *satalalok (pathal lok)* with one foot on his head, but was blessed with the words that even after losing everything on this earth he would gain eternal wisdom and the personal love and care of Lord Narayan.

    Bali asked for one favour: that he be allowed to visit his people on earth once a year. It is believed that he comes to see his people on Onam. The people rejoice to know that he is with them and want to show him that they are as happy as they were when he was their ruler so as not to cause him pain and unhappiness.

The celebrations start exactly ten days before Doadshi, i.e., from the Dooj of the waxing moon to Doadshi of the waxing moon and as in Ganesh Chaturthi, Durga *puja* and Pongal, everyone is out to have fun.

The houses in Kerala are usually kept so clean that there is no need to do any sort of spring-cleaning before Onam. The furnishing is minimal but the kitchen has a lot of pots and pans which are kept shining all the year round. The weather here is not like in North India, where it becomes very hot during the summer, with hot dusty winds depositing dust on the walls and every nook and corner, and it becomes incumbent to whitewash and clean the houses just after summer (before Diwali being an ideal time). Tamil Nadu is also very hot and sultry during summer. The winter is not so cold, hence Pongal is chosen for spring-cleaning when everyone is bursting with enthusiasm.

In homes, the celebrations for Onam start with decorating the gate or the main door as well as the inside of the house. Branches full of coconut (red coconuts are used for this purpose), banana leaves, along with coconut fronds decorate the corners and walls of the house. There is no deity associated with Onam and there is no special *puja*; still the housewife performs daily rituals with a little extra piety.

The first day of Onam is known as Attam. On this day the formal functions start with the housewife and the other ladies and girls of the house waking up early in the morning, taking a bath and dressing in clean (usually new) clothes. They wear jewellery, generally of gold.

Children also get up very early and, after bathing, go to the parks and market to pluck or buy the flowers and flower petals which will decorate the home. The women of the house prepare the ground on the east side of their house, making it smooth and then spreading cowdung evenly on which the petals or flowers are placed in a manner which is beautiful to behold. If the cowdung becomes dry, a little water is sprinkled on it so that it can hold the flowers in place; wet cowdung acts as a light glue. The *attam* is usually round in shape and the artistry of the young comes to the fore. A lump of cowdung is put in the centre, symbolising Ganesh. Once the *attam* is completed the women gather round it and dance and sing special songs, in praise of Mahabali. Clapping of hands is with the person on either side, much like the Danda dances of Rajasthan or Maharashtra.

Every day the flower decorations are renewed; the old one is not scraped but water is sprinkled on top and a thin layer of cowdung added and a new design carefully patterned on it. This is done right up to the main day of Onam and every day everyone dances around it.

Community *attam* is becoming popular now and common grounds are used for singing and dancing around beautiful flower decorations which are guarded day and night; in fact, people keep guard, turn by turn, to see that no one takes away the fresh flowers brought in for decoration every morning or even an evening before.

For ten to fifteen days, something or the other in the name of social or cultural activity takes place in homes and at the state level.

On the third day of Onam, feasts are arranged by families at lunchtime and everyone is invited in one home or another. The food is vegetarian; the main dish is rice with many types of curd, vegetables and *kheer*.

Food in Kerala is served on banana leaves; each one is about two feet in length, and on the left of the leaf a little pickle is placed along with banana chips (a favourite with Keralites), *papadom* and different types of curd, either mixed with cucumber (*pachei*), or fried ladies fingers (*khistry*) and coconut chutney. Rice, the main dish, is served with many types of vegetable curry. A different curry is served with each helping of rice. The first course is usually with *sambhar* and pure *ghee*. Then comes *rasam* and *aviyal* (a large number of vegetables cooked in a curry, again a speciality), *thuvasan* (string beans cooked dry in a little mustard oil, mustard seeds and grated coconut; cabbage can also be prepared like this), *kalan* (dahi with some vegetables), and *oalan* (a type of yam cooked like a vegetable).

The *kheer* can also be of many kinds. These include :

(1) *Ada* (rice or wheat made into *chappatis* and cut into small bits with milk and sugar added and cooked.

(2) *Parippu* (made with milk and lentils).

(3) *Seviya* (milk, vermicelli and sugar).

(4) *Payasam* (dry rice, brown in colour).

Presents are given to anyone one wants to. What is to be given to whom is carefully worked out before the festival begins.

The government celebrates Onam with boat races and pageants. On the Onam day the government takes out floats as it does on Republic Day, with each competitor vying with the other for the prize. School children, and the police and other organisations form a parade. Elephants from nearby temples are decorated and paraded on the main road as they are considered auspicious. The parade goes onto the main roads and the Governor takes a salute. There may be some illuminations in shops, but houses are not illuminated at night, as this is a daytime festival.

People are tired, yet joyous, after the ten to fifteen days of activity and slowly return to their chores, looking forward to the celebration next year.

RECIPE

Kheer (Payasam)

Ingredients and other items	
Milk	2 kg
Sugar	4 tablespoons
Rice	3 fistfuls
Almonds	10 (sliced lengthwise)
Raisins	2 teaspoons or more as required
Kevra essence	2 teaspoons
Chandi ka varak	(Silver beaten into very thin paper) for decoration (optional)
Karahi	

Method

Soak the rice in water for half an hour, then drain it. Wash again and drain until absolutely clean. Put the milk on a slow fire, add the rice to it and cook, stirring all the time, until it thickens to the required consistency (setting will make it thicker so do not let it become very thick). Add sugar and cook for another five to seven minutes. Take it off and add the *kevra* essence. Now pour it into a large bowl, and arrange the silver paper by holding the paper on which the *varak* is (or else the silver *varak* will get stuck to your fingers). Set it on the *kheer* by manoeuvring the plain base paper and decorate the almond slices and raisins. Put in the refrigerator and serve when required.

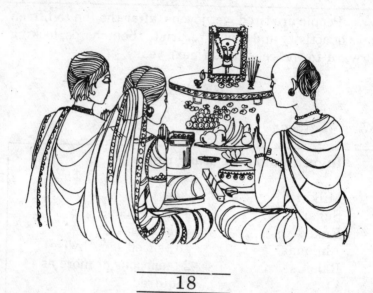

18

Shraadhs

LIFE IS MEANT TO BE A COMPLETE STORY WITH ITS SHARE OF joy, sorrow, ambition and achievements. After going through childhood, middle age, and old age, all people have to leave this world one day. Whatever be the age of a person, he or she is missed the most by the family. Irrespective of the contribution of each person towards family and society, that person's life leaves an indelible mark on the lives of those who came in contact with him or her. The family forms a sort of a cocoon from where an individual contributes his share to the external world. The family also gains from it, and each member builds from the spiritual and material endowment left behind by the father, mother, brother, sister, grandfather, grandmother, uncle and aunt so as to take hold of and anchor one's life.

One should be proud of one's ancestors for one has gained from them in one way or another.

Amongst all the gay and happy occasions, like festivals, marriages and engagements, one should not bring forth too much the memory of those who have left this world, for a sense of gloom may descend on the gathering. Life must go on with a joyful note; but those who have gone, having given so much to us, must not be allowed to fade away, and should be remembered with reverence and dignity, creating an atmosphere of happy memories.

On a special day, we invite those who have departed, to be a part of the family. In their honour, a feast befitting the sanctity of their abode in the heavens is given once a year.

The Hindus set aside sixteen days in a year which are known as 'Shraadhs', 'Pitrapaksh' or 'Kanaagath'. The Tith, or the date (according to the Hindu calendar) of death is considered as the Shraadh of that particular person. The waning period of the moon during the month of Kwar, plus the Purnima of the previous fortnight, form the period of Shraadhs. They fall somewhere in August or September. The sixteen days include the Tith of death, irrespective of the waxing or waning of the moon. We have Purnima, Parva, Dooj, Teej, Chauth, Panchami, Chat, Saptami, Ashtami, Navami, Dashmi, Ekadashi, Dwadashi, Treodashi, Chaturdashi, and Amavas. One can find out from the *jantri* (almanac) or from the panditji, the corresponding dates according to the English calendar and note them down against the name of each individual who is to be honoured. Individually, on the Tith of each person, the ceremony can be performed. There may be a common date for two or three persons.

On the appointed day a pandit or panditani — as the case may be — is invited as a special guest, and he or she personifies the departed soul. The pandit or panditani is chosen because he or she is supposed to belong to the learned class and does not fall in the material category. Such persons are supposed to be away from monetary and other worldly desires. They are supposed to keep erring society in a 'spiritual sphere' by their teaching and guidance. Hence, they are to be honoured, and looked after, by society itself. They supposedly are the people fit to represent those who have gone away from this world.

Let us now come to the actual ceremony, which is done on the day of Kanaagath, or Shraadh of the person to be remembered. This ceremony is not performed in the *puja* room, but in any other room arranged for this purpose. The chosen room is cleaned properly, and sponged with water. No one should be allowed to wear any footwear inside this room. A low table or *chowki* is placed against the wall, on which the photograph(s) of the departed person(s) is (are) made to stand. The table should be covered by a clean tablecloth, and flowers arranged on it. *Agarbatti* or *dhoop* is lighted near the photograph(s) and a small *thaali* containing *roli* and rice is kept nearby. There is no need of *aipun* or water since only *teeka* is put on the photograph(s), which has (have) been cleaned with a wet cloth and garlanded. A carpet or *durrie* is spread in front. A place for the panditji is made by placing a clean rug on one side; on the other side, two rugs are placed for the couple performing the Shraadh. The others can sit on the *durrie*. Custom has it that the eldest male member does the Shraadh, and the lady of the house runs around collecting the items required during the ceremony, but this author has seen at Badrinath that both the husband and wife do the Shraadh together. The relatives of the wife are also to be honoured similarly, even in the husband's house (on their respective Tiths). The woman along with her husband does the *turpun* (offering of water), for both sides of the family. One *turpun* is also done for Bhishma

Pitamah, who died without getting married and had no children. To honour him, and to remember him, is the duty of every Indian, for he lived for the betterment of the people, without caring for himself. Any childhood friend is also remembered. In fact, at Badrinath, each one has to make twenty-two rice balls in memory of at least three generations on both sides of the husband's family, and three generations on both sides of the wife's family. There is no clearer proof of equality of both partners in a household. Badrinath is one of the four great pilgrimage *dhaams* set up by Adi Shankaracharya. Visiting the four *dhaams* during one's lifetime leads to *moksha*. Badrinath is the abode of Vishnu the preserver.

The kitchen is also cleaned properly, and the person cooking should bathe early, and wear clean clothes. On this day, no onion, garlic or turmeric (*haldi*) is used. All vegetables are allowed. The vegetable, *mithai* or fruit most liked by the person who is being honoured should be served to the panditji. The food cooked and other items required for the ceremony are as follows:

(i)   Potato with a little gravy.

(ii)   Ladies' fingers (*bhindi*), *arvi*, white radish with its leaves (*mooli saag*), brinjal (*baingan*), gourd (*kaddu*). Two or three vegetables need to be cooked.

(iii) White radish (*mooli ki churri)* is a must. Grate the white radish and mix with salt, red chilli powder and lime. Green chillies cut in bits can be used instead of red chilli powder.

(iv)   Ginger (*adrak*) cut in pieces.

(v)   Lemon (*nimbu*).

(vi)   Curd (*dahi*) mixed with sugar.

(vii) *Mithai* according to the choice of the departed soul.

(viii) *Kheer* made from cereal or *makhanas* (rice cooked with milk and sugar and thickened or *makhanas* done likewise is known as *kheer*).

(ix) Fruit according to the choice of the departed soul.

(x) *Puri* and *kachori* made from wheat *atta* (Indian style pancakes).

(xi) *Roli*, rice (*chawal*) and flowers.

(xii) Banana leaves cut in four portions.

(xiii) Pitcher (*lota*) of water.

(xiv) A saucepan for *turpun*.

(xv) *Dhoop* and *agarbatti*.

(xvi) Oil for lamp.

The quantity of food should be enough for the whole family, as this food is taken as *prasad* by everyone, and it comprises the afternoon meal.

The panditji is taken to the room where the ceremony is to be performed. Here he asks for items such as banana leaves, *roli*, rice and flowers, a saucepan, one pitcher or jug (preferably of metal) filled with water, *agarbatti*, *dhoop* and oil for the lamp. The *thaal*, with all the cooked items neatly served in *katoris,* is placed as *prasad*. The panditji applies the *teeka* on the photograph, and garlands it. Then he applies *teeka* on the foreheads of those who are doing the Shraadh. He chants the *mantras* and asks the gods, Navgrahas and the departed soul, to come and grace the occasion. Chanting of *mantras* is the job of the panditji, and he should be one who knows the job. If a pandit is not available, then one may close one's eyes in remembrance of the person, whose Shraadh is being performed, and pray for his/her soul. Water is offered to the departed soul by pouring it onto the right hand and letting it fall into the saucepan amidst the chanting of Sanskrit *slokas* if a pandit is available, otherwise by just concentrating on the well-being of the departed soul. This is known as *turpun*. From the cooked food, four shares are apportioned on four different banana leaves. Each part consists of half a *puri* with a bit of other eatables – one

is for the cow, one for the crow, one for the dog and one
for the ants. This concept embraces the idea of all living
beings being partners in this world, and shareholders
in the realm of man.

The panditji then eats whatever he wants. He
should be looked after very well. He should feel very
welcome, and be content with the food. When he has
finished, fruit and money (as one desires) can be given.
Now he chants some more *slokas* asking the souls to
return to their abode in heaven. The leftovers and a little
extra food are sent along with the panditji to his house.
The rest of the family now sits for their meal, which is
not in the room of the ceremony, but in the dining room.
The photograph, etc., are left in the ceremony room to
enable the children and others coming back from their
places of study or occupation to do *pranam* and pay their
respects.

It may be difficult to set individual dates for each
person to be so honoured. Hence on Amavas, the last
day of the Shraadhs, or on the Tith of the most revered
member of the family, the ceremony can be done at one
time for all departed souls. Even if one has forgotten to
do it on the actual Tith, or one does not remember the
Tith, then again on Amavas, the ceremony can be
performed.

If, however, there is no way of conducting the
ceremony, then one can send to the *mandir*, or to any
pandit, what is called *seedha*, i.e., uncooked food like
potatoes, green vegetables, white radish, curd, lemon,
ginger, wheat *atta* along with oil, *mithai* and money. This
can be done for every one individually on their Tith. In
case one desires to do it all at once, then, again, on
Amavas the *seedha* can be given.

Finally, one should remember that in societies all
over the world, there are always ways and means and
occasions to honour the dead in some manner or the
other. Do not make this a sad occasion, but a soul-
cleansing one and a day of remembrance for the whole

family. Sisters and brothers are invited along with their families on such a day. However, no money is given to sisters.

So ends a day in memory of those who have given us life. During the year of a death no 'Sharaad' is observed during the 'Sharaad period' for the recently dead, but every month a pandit or panditani — as the case may be — is fed and respected as is done during the yearly 'Sharaads' on the 'Tith' of the departed. This is a private affair of the immediate family, but a 'Havan' is performed on the 'Tith' of the eleventh month, when the extended family members are also invited. A Sharaad lunch is organised for everyone. After the first year the 'Sharaad' is designated to the 'Sharaad period' for future observance. For any individual whose date of death has not been determined i.e. in case of war etc. the 'Tith' is observed as it is on the day the news is received.

Ganesh Chaturthi

GANESH IS THE FOREMOST GOD OF THE HINDU PANTHEON.
The god with the elephant head is the second
son of Shiv and Parvati (in south India he is
regarded as the first son). He was born on Sukul Paksh
Chouth in the month of Bhadon (which falls sometimes
in September of the European calendar) and is known
as Ganesh Chaturthi. He was born in Kashi in the home
of his maternal grandparents Himachal and Maina while
Lord Shiv had gone to Mount Kailash for *tapasya*.

Ganesh is worshipped first on all auspicious
occasions, whether it is a marriage or a religious
function. His image is prayed to first and is there even
in a temple dedicated to other deities. Ganeshji is also

invoked and worshipped before any festival, or a new project or venture that a Hindu undertakes. The housewife utters his name before even starting a small chore like putting a new vessel on the fire; he is the remover of all *sankat* (obstacles) and is an extremely benevolent god, fulfilling the wishes of those who pray to him sincerely.

Ganesh is usually shown with four hands, each one has a special symbolic object in it. One has an *ankush* (a goad), the second has a *trishul* (a three-pronged weapon) or an axe made from his own broken tooth, the third has a lotus flower, and the fourth has a rosary. He has many faces; he is sometimes shown with two hands in a dance pose (*abhaya* and *varda mudra*). Gajamukh (elephant face), Baraganapati and Tarunaganapati depict him as a child and a young man. Vinayak has the four arms in which he holds his symbols. In this stance he sometimes holds a pot of *moodak* in one hand instead of the rosary, or holds it in his trunk and retains the rosary. In his form as Herambeganapati he has five heads and ten hands, three eyes in each face and rides on a lion. The extra eye in each face is between his eyebrows. As Viranvighnesa, he exhibits a martial spirit with several weapons held in his ten hands. Shaktiganapati is shown with his 'Shakti' or his consorts Riddhi and Siddhi (success and prosperity) or Buddhi (knowledge) or even Lakshmi sitting on his thigh. Worship of this aspect of Ganesh is supposed to grant you wishes very quickly. Then there is the Nattaganapati, a beautiful form, showing him in a graceful dance pose; Ganesh is supposed to have taken this stance when the Creator bowed to him and he was so happy that he started to dance and thus earned the title of the master of the arts of music and dance.

Varasiddhi Vinayak is the aspect worshipped during Ganesh Chaturthi. He is shown standing on a demon named Vighnasura whom he destroyed. The swastika is accepted as the graphic symbol of Ganesh and is therefore found at every auspicious place or occasion.

Lakshmi, the consort of Vishnu, is always placed along with Ganeshji. Because we love Lakshmi (wealth) and are ever worried about annoying her, to be on the safe side we worship her along with Ganesh. Since she cannot precede him, she sits next to him; she is never neglected. She is always placed to the right of him as she is like a mother to him.

Ganesh Chaturthi is celebrated all over India, but the people of Maharashtra have made Lord Ganesh their patron. Lokmanya Tilak realised that community celebrations would bring people together and he started the Ganesh Chaturthi celebrations in a big way, making it into a community affair – Ganesh became the beloved of the people of Maharashtra. The Maharashtrians celebrate this festival like the Bengalis do Durga *puja* and the Oriyas Rath Yatra.

Since the festival is a community affair, everyone in the locality contributes towards the making of the idol, the upkeep of the *pandal*, as well as the expenses of keeping a pandit and the cost of the offerings of *prasad* every day. A special pandit is appointed for each locality and each locality vies with the other in beautifying their idols and decorating the *pandal*. The devotees gather in groups and sing songs in praise of Lord Ganesh. Singing is done mostly in the evenings, while during the morning and the daytime, individuals and families come and offer *prasad*.

A beautiful *chowk* in front of the deity is decorated with flowers and with powder of different colours; it can be changed everyday if one so desires. Two oil-lamps stand on either side of the idol and a *thaal* with *kumkum* and *haldi* and another *thaal* and some *katoris* for serving the food cooked for the family are placed nearby. This is first offered to the deity and then eaten for lunch- and dinner. Special *prasad* is made only on the first day (rice and *arhar dal* are usually made). Any seasonal vegetable is cooked without onion and garlic. A special sweet is made every day to make the ten days especially festive. Some people keep a fast for just the day, but the *vrat* is not a tough one. *Til* and *gur* (jaggery), in the form of *gazak*, *revri* or *til ke laddoo*, are taken along with other *mithai*. Tea and coffee and water are allowed throughout the day.

The installation of the idol in a community centre is done amidst the chanting of Sanskrit *slokas* by learned pandits with the people of the locality gathering to salute Ganeshji. The decoration is fabulous and the idols surpass each other in their craftsmanship and beauty. *Arti* is done twice a day after the installation, but the evening *arti*, done when people have returned from their work becomes very important and there is always a large crowd singing till late in the night.

The people offer *prasad* of *moodak* (a special type of *laddoo*) or *peras* at the *pandal*, at least one red flower – preferably hibiscus – a bunch of three sheaves of grass, collected and tied together or many sheaves forming a bigger bunch, *kumkum* and *haldi* and rice along with the *mithai*. This *prasad* is easily available near the *pandals* or at special *puja* shops. Those who can made *prasad* at home make the special preparations known as *moodak* (the recipe is given at the end of this chapter). Generally *moodak* is offered as *prasad* to the household deity and *peras* are taken to the community centre.

In certain cases there is a tradition of getting an idol of Lord Ganesh installed in a home and the community can come there to pray. Some, however, instal an idol only for the family and have the *puja* done by a pandit. If a pandit is not available then, of course, the eldest member of the family does the rituals after installing a small *murti*. This is done with great sanctity. Everyone present in the house bathes and wears clean lothes. A table or *chowki* is placed against a wall in the uja room or any room which can be cordoned off for he duration of the *puja*.

Ganesh is worshipped in Maharashtra in his nature form. His idols are not dressed with actual lothes, but clothes are painted onto idols. The clothes re painted in red. The torso has an *angavastra*, ewellery covers the neck and reaches right up to the tomach, and the lower part has a yellow or red *dhoti*. aneshji's stomach protrudes as he loves good food.

There is a story connected to Lord Ganesh's eating abits. Long ago, he cursed the moon for making fun of im for eating too many sweets and that is why the moon annot maintain its full form all the time; it waxes and anes making it less beautiful and at times it vanishes ltogether. The story teaches us not to make fun of nyone.

Ganeshji always wears a tiara or a crown on his ead and a belt round his stomach to keep the garments om slipping off. The belt is in the form of a snake which e inherited from his father, Lord Shiv, who has serpents anging all over him. The trunk of Ganesh can point ither to the right or left. Nowadays, it is also made traight. It is said that a trunk to the left is made for the lol which is not worshipped. The trunk points to the ight in idols that are made of stone and are installed in emples. Now, however, you will find idols made from laster, metal or stone with trunks pointing to wherever he artist fancies.

uja in Other Parts of India

anesh *puja* on Ganesh Chaturthi is done at home in ost parts of India. The *puja* room is cleaned and the nage or picture of Ganesh is set in the centre. The image s not dressed with garments as it is already well ecorated. It is cleaned so that it is shining on this day

particularly. A garland of red flowers is put round th
neck of the image or picture, and floral or chalk design
decorate the floor of the *puja* room. Lord Ganesh i
seated on a decorated table or *chowki*, and a lamp is l
in front. The head of the family performs the ritual afte
bathing and wearing clean clothes; new clothes are nc
required on this day but all members should bathe befor
the *puja*. School children can do the *pujan* on their retur
from school but the children should be told abou
Ganeshji being the first among all gods, and the one t
be worshipped at all festivals before the main deity c
the day.

A *thaal* with red flowers, *roli*, rice and *aipun*, an
rice along with a coconut, preferably with the husk or
a bowl of *laddoos* of any type, some *batashas* and five o
seven *paans* and a small *lota* of water must be kept read
by the housewife and placed near the deity. A *teeka* i
put with *roli* on the forehead of Lord Ganesh and a fe
grains of rice are stuck onto it. Then *teeka* is put o
everyone present. Everyone does the *pujan* with wate
first, then *aipun* and last *roli*, then rice and red flower
are showered on him. 'Ganesh Asthuthi' (a song in prais
of Lord Ganesh) is sung. Arti (*Om Jai Jagdish Hare*
can be sung by everyone; if one does not have the specia
arti of Ganeshji, red flowers and rice are kept in th
hand while singing the *arti* and *Karpur Gauram* an
Tum Mev Mata; everyone then showers the flowers. Th
arti is done by everyone in turn around the deity onc
or twice with small circular movements and handed t
the next person. The *prasad* of *laddoo*, a few *batasha*
nariyal and one *paan* is handed to each person; th
person takes a *laddoo* and puts back the rest onto th
thaal. A lady or male member of the house takes th
small *lota* and, pouring some water in the hand
sprinkles it on the gathering saying, *Chittan para nee
ka, dukh gaya shareer ka* (a sprinking of water and a
the ailments of the body disappear). Everyone joins i

this chant and the *puja* is finished. Everyone goes back to their different occupations.

There are no dinner invitations or giving of presents on this festival. Fasts or *vrats* are kept by the very pious, with sweets, *gazak* and *rewri* as the main *phalar*. Tea and coffee is taken several times. No garlic or onions are used even for making ordinary food during these days. In North India, some of the *pandas* and *chaubas* (members of a community of pandits who have earned the title of Chaube) do not keep a fast on this day; they feel that a birthday should be celebrated with eating and merry-making and should not be an austere occasion, so they eat a lot of sweets, especially *laddoos* and *peras* which Ganeshji is supposed to love. The *pandas* of Mathura love sweets also and the *peras* of Mathura are very famous.

In Rajasthan, on Ganesh Chaturthi, an image of Ganesh bathed in red *kumkum* with a garland of red flowers is installed by many households right outside their entrances. A small *thaal* with *haldi* and *kumkum* is also placed at the entrance so that people who come visiting take a pinch of each and put it on their foreheads and throat. A kilo of *laddoos* are usually kept in the house and after offering them to Ganeshji they are offered as *prasad* to whoever visits.

The annual celebration comes to an end on Anand Choudas when all the idols used for the community and private celebrations go for *visarjan* in the sea in Maharashtra or the nearest river or tank in the other towns of India.

There is a procession of all the locality devotees as they take the idols with great fanfare, to the waterfront. There is usually a lot of *bandobust* by the authorities to keep the traffic running smoothly. In Maharashtra people take the idols, shouting *Ganpati Bappa Maurya, Pudchya Varsha Luvkarya*. There are fireworks all the way and the procession stops now and then for people to have their last *darshan* of the year.

In all the towns, there is always a great crowd and shouts of *Ganpati Bappa Maurya* rent the air as the idols are taken into the depth of the water, facing the direction of the locality or home from which they have come. Slowly, they are submerged into the sea, river or tank, and as dusk settles in, people return to their homes and wait for the next year's festival of the first god of the Hindu pantheon. The artists start deliberating on their efforts for next year, for Lord Ganesh provides a lot of people with a livelihood.

Visarjan for household idols can be done after one and a half, seven or ten days.

There are many stories about how Ganesh got an elephant's head, why he is worshipped first, and about how he got a broken tooth.

Ganesh seems to have been born at a time when Shivji was not with Parvati; he had gone for *tapasya* to Mount Kailash, and Parvati was with her parents at Kashi. Parvati had not informed Shankar Bhagwan about the birth of their second son. She did not even tell her son the identity of his father. Shivji also did not seem to know that a child was born to Parvati who after his birth threw Ganesh in the Ganga in sheer anger – but Gangaji saved him and gave him back alive to Parvati. Ever since then he is known to be a *devta* with two mothers.

Without knowing Shiviji, Ganesh grew up into a lovely little boy. One day, when Parvati went for a bath, little Ganesh was asked to stand at the entrance of the *baori* and not let anyone enter while she was bathing. At that very moment Shivji came back from his *tapasya* and, finding out where his wife was, made straight for the *baori* and decided to go down to the water. Ganesh, little as he was, stopped him and stopped right in front of him. This annoyed Shivji very much; he ordered

Ganesh to step aside. Ganeshji did not budge and Shivji's anger got the better of him. He chopped off Ganesh's head. The noise and commotion brought Parvati out of her bath and she hurried to where the noise came from and saw, to her great anguish, what Shivji had done. She was very angry, and told Shivji in no uncertain terms that he had killed his own son. Shivji was horrified and promised to set things right at once. In the meantime, one of his *doots* had run off with his son's head and it could not be located. Shivji then promised Parvati that he would put the head of the first living thing that came his way on the shoulders of his son. As luck would have it, it was an elephant that found his way there. Shivji cut off its head and put it on Ganesh's shoulders. Ganesh came alive but it was a very strange Ganesh! Parvati was all the more angry and she set up a lament. No one would pay attention to her little son and no one would even worship him as a *devta*, she said. Shankarji declared then and there that Ganesh would be worshipped first, before all the other gods. No *puja*, festival or marriage would be celebrated in future without invoking the name of Ganesh in all the three worlds. Lord Shiv is himself the 'Supreme' and his word is law; therefore, Ganesh *pujan* is to be done first, even on Shivratri. The other gods didn't appreciate this so they went to Brahmaji and asked for his help, as they felt that justice demanded that the most intelligent and clever amongst them should be worshipped first. Brahmaji told them that since Lord Shiv is one of the holy trinity and that each of the trinity (Brahma, Vishnu and Mahesh) holds another of the trinity as equal, he could not alter the verdict: only Shivji could do so. All of them then went to Shivji and asked him to test their intelligence before deciding on such an important issue. Shivji was fair-minded and he asked them to go round the world on their *vahans* (vehicles) and whoever came first would be the one to be worshipped first. Everyone,

including Ganesh, and Kartikeya (Skand), the elder son
of Shiv and Parvati, started on their fast *vahans*, fully
confident that Ganesh on his *musak* (rat) would never
be able to compete with them. Ganeshji is reputed to be
highly intelligent, and this became apparent; he just went
around his parents on his slow *musak* and declared that
as they were the Supreme they were the real world. No
one could dispute that; hence he was chosen to be the
first to be worshipped by all the gods and men without
argument.

Ganesh is worshipped as a mature god in
Maharashtra but in most parts of North India he is
worshipped as a child. He is full of intelligence and is
the giver of *buddhi* and knowledge. *Buddhi* is even shown
sometimes as his consort although he was married to
two damsels, Riddhi and Siddhi (success and prosperity).

Children are initiated into study by praying to
Ganesh. In Maharashtra, when children start school
their first lesson is on Ganesh Chaturthi. Although
Saraswati is the goddess of learning, she is prayed to
after Ganesh.

Ganesh was chosen by Narad to be the
stenographer to write down the *Mahabharata* for
posterity, while Vyasji related the tale of his grandsons
to him. He chose his broken tusk to write. He told Vyas
that he would only write if Vyasji gave the dictation
continuously and did not stop or hesitate and waste
time. His mother Bhagwati (Parvati) asked Ganesh to
use his *buddhi* while writing also and explain certain
points so that the generations to come would understand
the great epic as it was meant to be understood.

There is a story explaining why Ganesh has one
tusk. Ganesh had two tusks as is usual with elephants,
but he had a great fight with Parshuram, when Ganesh
laid claims to immortality. There are only seven who
are immortal – Hanumanji, Vibhishan, Kripacharya,
Parshuram, Ashwathama, Bali, and Ved Vyas (Markande

also joined their ranks later). These great men do not die and even when the world dissolves and a new world takes birth they will be here. They are not born again and again. They live on the mighty Himalayas and it is said that some great souls do come across them. Anyway, Ganeshji declared that he was eligible for such a position, but Parshuram was not satisfied and wanted to test him. Parshuram loses his temper at the drop of a hat (as the saying goes), so he declared he would fight with Ganesh; if Ganesh won, only then he would be immortal. There ensued a terrible battle. Parshuram became very ferocious in the heat of the moment and in the process he broke one of Ganeshji's teeth; Ganeshji gave up the idea of being immortal. Therefore, he is born like us but the difference is that he is born at the beginning when the world is formed and only dies when *pralay* or the end of world comes.

Ganeshji is the remover of all obstacles, and there is a story connected with this aspect of Ganesh. All the gods and *devtas* were married and those that were not, were getting ready offers because of their position and good looks. No one was, however, ready to marry his daughter to Ganesh although he was the first amongst all the gods and *devtas*. His elephantine looks dismayed everyone and no one was ready to give his daughter to him in marriage. So Ganeshji decided to create problems for the other gods and *devtas* who had the audacity to make fun of him. He asked all the rats and mice to go and make burrows in the path of all those getting married and make it impossible for them to tread the path, thus creating so much confusion in the way that no one could move without falling into one pothole or another. All the gods then rushed off to Brahma and asked him to do something. Brahma went to Ganeshji and asked him to stop creating so much chaos. Ganeshji was adamant and declared that until he got married, he would not let anyone else get married either. Brahmaji in consultation

with his wife Saraswati, then created two lovely
maidens, Riddhi and Siddhi (success and prosperity),
and gave them in marriage to Ganesh. He did the
kanyadaan along with his wife. He and Saraswati
thereby became the father-in-law and mother-in-law of
Ganesh. Ganeshji became very fond of them and did as
Brahma had asked him and stopped the rats from
creating havoc. He gave the rats the honour of becoming
his *vahan*, the vehicle on which he rides. He thus won
the name of Vigneshwara or Vighnaraja (the Lord of
obstacles). He always has a rat under him in all his idols
and pictures.

Moodak

Ingredients for dough

Rice flour	2 cups (grind rice in a mixie)
Water	4 cups (double of rice)
Oil	1 or $1^{1/2}$ teaspoonful

Ingredients for filling

Fresh coconut gratings	2 cups
Sugar	1 cup
Dry fruits	4 tablespoons or according to taste
Milk	1/2 *katori* or 1/4 cup
or	
Khoya	2 tablespoons

Other items

A pressure cooker or a vessel for steaming the
moodak.

A steel gauze on which the *moodaks* have to be steamed. or a gauze made especially for the *moodak*.

There are special cooker attachments available for cooking *moodak*.

Method

Boil the water along with the oil and take it off the heat. Add rice flour, cover the dough for some time and allow it to cool. Take it off the vessel and knead it well, then put it aside.

Filling

Mix the grated coconut, sugar and the dry fruit. Put them in a frying pan or a vessel and cook, stirring all the time. Add the milk or *khoya,* mixing it well – it should be dry. Take it off the heat when cooked satisfactorily.

Make small holes in the dough and fill them with the dry filling, closing the hole firmly in each *moodak*. Shape it like a whole garlic with a little point on top. Make lines on the *moodak* shaping it just as a garlic. Put them on the net gauze on top of a vessel with water and steam for 10 minutes. Cooking is like *idli* cooking. Take it off and keep in an airtight box for use later.

20

Durga Puja

THE POWER OF THE MOTHER GODDESS IS PERHAPS GREATER than that of any other god. She is even worshipped by all the gods themselves. She is Shakti — the power of Brahma, Vishnu, and Mahesh. She takes the form of their consorts, without whom, none of the gods can achieve anything. She is worshipped all over India with the same ardour under different names and manifestations — the most benign face of the goddess is Durga. Durga *puja* is performed twice in a year — for nine days each time — once at the beginning of summer, some time in March or April, and again at the beginning of winter, some time in September or October. In summer, the month according to the Hindu calendar when Durga *puja* is performed is Chait. The festival is celebrated during the moonlit fortnight of the month, the first day being Parva. Chait Devi *puja* is done for eight days, the ninth day being Ram Navami. In winter, the month of celebration is Kartik and, again, the *puja* starts on Parva of the moonlit fortnight. During Kartik the *puja* goes on for nine days and the tenth day is Dussehra.

The Hindu month is marked by fifteen days of a waxing moon and fifteen days of a waning moon, thus comprising thirty days. The name given to each day, or Tith as it is called, is the same during both the periods, but the moonlit period is known as Sukul Paksh, and the dark period is known as Krishna Paksh. The time scheduled for Durga *puja* on both the occasions is nine days (actually nine nights) during the moonlit fortnight, and these are known as Navratris.

The *puja* during Chait is mostly observed as a private, homely affair, but the one heralding the winter is celebrated with great pomp and show, especially in Bengal, from where it has spread to all parts of India.

During the Kartik festival, huge *pandals* (tents) are erected and beautifully decorated with images of Durga Ma in her many moods. In each locality, almost everyone contributes towards the event and every evening *kirtans* and *bhajans* are sung in every *pandal*. Making of the images or idols of Durga Ma is an art in itself and brings forth the best in the craftsmen. They start the process many weeks prior to the festival and really try to outdo each other in their skill. Clothes and jewellery of the images or idols are magnificent as the images are larger than life and can be seen from afar. On seeing the decorated idol, one automatically bows one's head and does *namaskar* and the children seeing the elders bowing so humbly before the image, also develop a feeling of faith and goodness, which are very essential for a human being. Now let us leave the public celebrations to those who can arrange such affairs. Let us instead concentrate on the celebrations at home.

On the first day of the *puja*, the *puja* room is thoroughly cleaned, silver and brass items are polished, all images made of metal cleaned likewise, and new clothes like *lehanga* and *chunni* with *gota* and *kinari* (made earlier) are draped on the image of the goddess and the other deities like Ganesh, who is to be worshipped before any other god. All other deities should also be freshly dressed, and old covers of the *puja* table removed and new ones used in their place.

Everyone who performs the *puja* must bathe in the morning. Some like to fast, but it is not compulsory and, in any case, *phalar* is allowed once a day and liquids can be taken any time. Some persons observe the fast only on the first day and the last day, but some even observe it for the full nine days. During the day, *puja* can normally be· done only by the women as the men and children would have gone to their places of work and schools, respectively. The day *puja* is shorter in duration as compared to the evening *puja*. The *prasad* distributed in the morning can be some *elaichidana* (cardamom seeds) only. The worship of the deity is done by sprinkling water, *aipun*, *roli*, rice and flowers as in all *pujas*. The *bhog* sung while offering *prasad* to the goddess is given at the end of this chapter.

A story is narrated each day, to whosoever is present during *puja* time. Basically, four main stories exist, which are repeated to fill the nine-day period. (The stories have been given later in this chapter.) During the morning *puja*, when one is alone with just a few members of the family, the *arti* sung is a shorter one (also given at the end of this chapter), whereas in the evening, the longer *arti*, namely, 'Jai Ambe Gauri...', should be sung. The *arti* is sung at the end of the *puja*, but before it begins, everyone is given some flowers or rice to hold in their hands. The youngest member of the family is given the *puja* bell and keeps ringing it throughout the *arti*. If any one possesses the breath capacity, a conch shell can also be sounded. The sound effect of everything together is so good, that most children remember it right up to their old age as one of the most pleasant and unifying experiences of their lives. After lighting the camphor and reciting the Sanskrit couplet

> *Karpur gauram, karuna astharam*
>   *sansar sarum, bhuj gendra haaram,*
> *sada vasantam, hriday arvinde,*
>   *bhawan Bhawani, sahitam namami*

everyone showers flowers or rice on Durga Ma, chanting together:

> *Sada Bhawani dahiney, sanmukh rahen Ganesh,*
>   *panchon Dev raksha karen, Brahma,*
> *Vishnu, Mahesh, Bolo atal chhattra ki jai.*

The head of the house then takes a little water from the *puja lota*, and sprinkles it on all gathered with everyone chanting again: '*Chittan para neer ka, dukh gaya shareer ka*'.

The much awaited *prasad*, consisting of *puri*, black *chana* (fried in a very little oil with just a small quantity of salt) and a sweet, like *jalebi* or *halwa*, is distributed to everyone. If, however, one does not like to make too many items, *halwa* and *chana* will suffice. To add some excitement to the occasion a little money is given along with the *prasad* to the children. This *puja* is done every day for eight days, commencing from the first day (Parva) to the eighth day (Ashtami), but in some households, the *puja* is also performed on the ninth day. Most of the people like to fast on Ashtami, even if they do not fast on any other day, but of course, as in all Hindu fasts, one can consume food without cereals in the afternoon.

Little girls are regarded as a form of Durga Devi (*devi ka roop*) as they are supposed to be pure and innocent. Little boys are regarded as the '*roop* of *langooras*', supposed to be the servers of the Devi in her celestial abode. They are invited for lunch on Ashtami and can turn up in any number, but must be under twelve years of age. Usually, the household children do not sit for the *bhoj* (feast), but it is not a rule. The *prasad* that is served as lunch consists of *puri*, potatoes, ladies' fingers, sweet gourd, colocasia (*arvi*) and radish – grated radish mixed with a little salt and chilli powder is greatly relished. Sweet curd and sliced ginger, marinated with lime, are also much appreciated. No item should contain onion or garlic. In the plate of every girl, two small rolls of *mehndi* (moistened *henna* made into two small rolls) and a string of *kalava* are placed along with some cash according to one's desire. Sometimes garments or even a length of material (cloth) are given to both the girls and the boys. Some prefer giving a utensil, or the plate which the child has used for eating. In fact, anything can be given in the name of Durga Ma. In inviting the children one symbolically invites the goddess herself. Generally, only girls are invited and boys feel very sorry for themselves and tend to quarrel with their sisters.

Before serving the food to the little ones, the elders performing the *puja* wash the little ones' feet, and welcome them by serving with their own hands. When the children finish eating, the elders touch their feet and bid them farewell.

Those who worship the Mother Goddess as their chief deity sometimes go in for what is known as a *bhandara*. This means that a lot of little girls and boys are invited (forty or even hundred in number) and a big lunch is arranged, with catering done by a *halwai*. Something substantial is given to the *kanyas* (little girls) and to the *langooras*. The gifts can be given in the form

of jewellery as well. These *bhandaras* are very common
in North India, and can even be arranged in temples
where catering facilities are available.

Durga *puja* as celebrated in Bengal is during *Sarat*
or autumn, between September and October. Though
Durga as Annapurna is also celebrated in *Basant*, it is
the former that has come to stay. It is said that although
Lord Ram had invoked Ma Durga during this time, it
was considered untimely and was therefore known as
akal bodhan. Perhaps the pleasant climate, marked by
clear blue skies after the rainy season, came to be
deemed more suitable for this great festival of Bengal.

Durga *puja* is a nine-day celebration starting from
the day after Mahalaya which is on the last day of the
waning moon or new moon of *Sarat* (Amavas) in
September-October sometime.

On Mahalaya radio and television broadcast Ma's
agamoni or arrival to the accompaniment of songs,
narrating the story of Durga who was created by the
gods to fight the *asuras* or demons. The story reinforces
the concept of the triumph of good over evil.

On the sixth day or *sashthi*, the images of Durga,
along with her four children, Lakshmi, Saraswati,
Ganesh and Kartikeya (regarded as her children in
Bengal) are installed in the various *puja pandals* erected
for the festival in the state and outside it. For Bengalis,
the advent of the goddess Durga assumes a special
significance for it is believed that Ma Durga as a
daughter, along with her children, comes visiting her
mother during these four days from her icy abode in
Kailash in the Himalayas, where she lives with her
consort Shiv. Every year, legend has it, she comes in a
special transport – the boat – because there are floods
in the eastern parts of India.

Durga *puja* has become as much a social event as
it is a religious one. It is unique in the sense that the
entire community pays homage to Ma Durga in the

different community *pujas* that are held. Only a handful of households, mostly with zamindari backgrounds, celebrate the festival at home.

The main function begins on Sasthi – the unofficial first day of the Durga *pujas* – when the priest does a sort of *puja* which is *bodhan*, whereby the deity is unveiled. Women keep *vrat* for the welfare of their families; the fast is broken by partaking of fruits and food products made from *maida* (flour). Usually the whole family conforms to the traditional routine on that day and meals are of *luchis/puris* and *sabji*.

The rest of the *pujas* are organised on a mass scale at the *puja pandal*; the expenses are taken care of through subscriptions. There is little an individual need do besides being present at the actual *puja* which is during the evening. On Mahapanchami the *kolabau* (the wife of Ganesh made from the banana plant) is installed. The origin of this practice can be traced to the agrarian society of Bengal.

On Mahaashtami day, people offer *anjali* to the goddess and a priest chants *mantras* over the loudspeaker; on this day young girls have *kumari puja* performed on them and they are presented with red *saris*, bangles and money. Vegetarian food is eaten on this day, especially in homes that are Vaishnavite. The worshippers of Kali or those known as Shaktas, however, eat meat. A special *bhuni khichri* is made on this day (recipe is included). *Luchis* with a vegetable preparation known as *chhokka* (recipe at the end of the chapter) followed by *payesh* comprises dinner. *Anjali* is offered during a certain time in the morning. Many take this opportunity to offer a *dela* (bucket or tray) to the goddess which consists of five different seasonal fruits, *mishti* (sweets) and sometimes a red-bordered *sari*. In the evening, *arti* is performed when the priest breathes life into the idols by reciting special *slokas*. Many watch this spectacular ritual where the drumbeats, and the sound of cymbals and dancing accompany, *dhoop and dhuns*, in front of the goddess.

On Mahanavami, meat is eaten as part of great feasting and friends and relatives meet. A mutton preparation, cooked without garlic and onions, is a great favourite among many.

The last day coincides with Dussehra. Idols are taken away in large processions for immersion in water. Before Ma leaves, married women of all age groups visit the nearby *pandal* to take part in an emotional ritual where vermilion (*sindhoor khela*), is applied to the parting of each other's hair. The *loha* (the metal and gold bracelet given to the bride by the mother-in-law) and *pala/sannbha* (the red and white bangles worn by many married Bengali women) are also touched up. *Sindhoor* is applied by the women and the priest on the forehead of the goddess.

A mother-in-law gives an iron bangle interlaced with gold or silver (for decoration) to a new bride as the first gift, a token of *suhag*, which the daughter-in-law wears all her life. During Durga *puja*, when idols are being taken away for immersion, *sindhoor* is taken from in front of the idols and applied to the parting in the hair by married women. What is left on the fingers is applied to this iron and gold (silver) bangle, and is known as touching the *loha*.

The ritual of applying *sindhoor* can also take place at home when Bijoya Dashami is celebrated with family members. The younger members do *pronam* (touching the feet) to the elders while the men do *kolakuli* (embrace). Sweets are prepared at home but today most make do with sweets brought from the market. Savouries like *nimki* are often made at home to be distributed to friends, relatives and well-wishers.

On all these days of the *puja*, it is advisable to wake up early, and bathe and wear fresh clothes. Most of the time the clothes are new as clothes and gifts are exchanged during this time. The children must have new outfits each day. In many homes, the cooking of meals comes to a standstill as food is available on a small scale in the *pandals*. Rich households always have meals organised for the poor.

On Durga *puja*, the goddess Durga is worshipped first; Saraswati and Lakshmi are not worshipped individually as such. On Diwali, which comes about twenty days after Dussehra (Vijaya), the Bengalis of East Bengali origin worship the goddess Lakshmi. Otherwise Kali, who is another *roop* of Durga is worshipped – again through the community *pujas*.

STORIES RELATED TO DURGA PUJA

The stories included here are, for some reason, only told during the morning *puja* – perhaps because the men being regarded as 'serious minded and intelligent' need not listen to childish and silly stories! These stories were mainly meant for the superstitious women and kids left at home. In days gone by, some children did not attend school till quite late, and, in any case, most of the girls did not attend school at all. If they did, they dropped out very early. In fact, in joint families, there were always many who just 'stayed at home'. It was usual in such families that one person earned, becoming the pride of the household, while the rest just loitered around the house. They were all accepted, married off, and had children. There was no such concept as getting a job before getting married. Life was much more easy and less complicated. So, for our morning *puja*, there were plenty of people around! So, here begin the stories!

1. GORAJARI BAHU

A long time ago, there was a household comprising a mother with three married sons. Two of the sons were

working but the youngest was not able to, since he was
not as bright as the others. He was, in fact, a little
mentally retarded. Since marriages were arranged in
childhood itself, and as luck would have it, he got the
most beautiful and talented wife! Her name was
Gorajari. As the couple had no money, they had a difficult
time in getting food and clothing. This situation hurt
Gorajari very much, but women could not go out and
work in those days, so she had to be content with eating
the leftovers of her sisters-in-law. Her husband tried to
go out and earn something, but people just threw him
out even before he could do a day's work. Poor young
things! They had a very hard time, and everyone was
nasty to them, except, of course, the old mother. As she
was under the watchful eyes of the two elder daughters-
in-law, she could not even give a *sari* or blouse to
Gorajari, or a *kurta-pyjama* set to her son. To add to
their woes, Gorajari and her husband did not have any
children. So their days were very miserable and unhappy.
Sometimes, the mother, when she found something very
tasty, served to her during a meal, would hide it in her
sari and when no one was looking, she would slyly take
it for her youngest son and his wife. Sometimes, the elder
daughters-in-law would get suspicious, but the mother
would keep them content by saying: 'No *bahu*, I only
wanted to sit out and eat these delicious preparations
that you have made for me', and she would try to gulp
down each morsel in front of them.

It was a very bad situation indeed. It got so bad
that the young people decided to live separately in a
hut outside the main house, so as not to see the lovely
goings-on, of which they could not be a part.

Soon Durga *puja* arrived, and everyone in the family
began preparing for the festivities. Everyone performed
the *puja* with great pomp and show, but our poor little
young wife just did the *puja* with whatever she was able
to obtain by begging. This annoyed her so much that she

decided to go and sit in a *dharna* (sit-in) in the temple
of the goddess. She went and lay down at the back of the
temple, and did not eat or drink for the whole day. Durga
Ma soon became aware of somebody's presence in the
back, so she called her *langoora* and asked him to go
and have a look and find out why her hair felt heavy as
if somebody was sitting on them. The *langoora* went to
check and came back to state that a very poor woman
with torn clothes, who looked thin and miserable, was
lying there, and was adamant that she would not budge
until Deviji herself spoke with her. Durga Ma asked him
to bring Gorajari to her. When Gorajari arrived, Durga
Ma asked her why she was so distressed. Soon Gorajari
related all her woes to Durga Ma. Durga Ma then asked
her *langoora* to give Gorajari the leftovers of the food
from the *bhandaras*. This annoyed Gorajari
tremendously, and with tears in her eyes, she said, 'I
always get leftovers at home and even in Devi's temple,
I am being given leftovers'! (*Ghar jhooth bahar jhooth,
Devi ke dwar bhi jhooth*). She started to cry, uttering
heartbreaking sobs. Deviji then said, 'O girl, there is a
lot of difference in the leftovers of others, and mine; go
home, and share it with your husband, and enjoy this
food to your heart's content.' Gorajari thought to herself
that since it was Durgaji saying so, she would take the
leftovers. Moreover, she had had nothing to eat for two
days, and was extremely hungry and knew that her
husband would also be as hungry as herself. So she picked
up the food in her *jholi* (a part of the *sari*), and went to
her *jhopari* (hut). There her husband was waiting for
her, not knowing where she had disappeared for so long.

Both of them started to eat the food, none too happily.
But lo behold! As they ate they noticed that the food turned
delicious and fresh as if it had just come from the kitchen.
The ordinary utensils became gold and silver, and their
own clothes changed to fabulously rich garments. Both
looked at each other and then at themselves, and stood up
in amazement. As their gaze went to their hut, it had

become the most beautiful palace one could imagine. They were overcome and fell prostrate, and thanked Durga Ma again and again for the bountiful *prasad* she had given to them.

Not able to contain herself, Gorajari rushed over to her mother-in-law to tell her about her good fortune, but before she could do so, her sisters-in-law saw her in all her finery. They came out with stunned and angry looks, and asked: 'Whom have you stolen from? Whom have you snatched from? How could you get these grand clothes and jewellery, O Gorajari?' The mother-in-law came out running as well. Seeing her youngest daughter-in-law so radiant, she was very happy, but could not say anything because of fear of the elder daughters-in-law. Touching her feet, Gorajari declared: 'I have robbed no one, I have snatched nothing from anyone. It is Devi Bhawani who has showered all these good things on me.' One sister-in-law declared: 'We pray with pomp and show, and spend so much for Devi Bhawani, but she has not shown such generosity to us. Then how could you, who has nothing but dust to eat and dust to offer, be the recipient of such generosity? You are a liar, O Gorajari.' 'Not so, not so,' cried Gorajari. 'Let us go to the *darbar* of Devi Ma and you can ask her yourself.' So they all went to the main temple of the town, and Gorajari fell prostrate before the Devi, and asked her: 'Tell them the truth, O Great Mother, for they do not believe me. Come to my rescue, or else everyone will think me a thief.'

Durga Ma spoke to all of them and said: 'She speaks the truth – this Gorajari, whom you have all ill-treated. She is pure of heart and action, therefore I have given her this treasure.' The daughters-in-law said: 'We have prayed to you for eight days, and kept the fasts and also done the "Ashtami *pujan*" with grandeur.' Deviji replied: 'You have done my *pujan* with great grandeur, but not sincerity, and you have not been kind to the poor and the needy, and most of all to your kith and kin. You have been nasty and cruel. How could I bestow, on such people, my blessings? Go and be good and kind to all, specially the needy and those close to you, and see my kindness then. Just now you are arrogant, and it is mercy on my part not to take away the wealth you possess.' The two sisters-in-law got the fright of their lives, and realised in their heart of hearts that what Durga Ma said was very true, and they were ashamed and filled with regret. Durga Ma forgave them and told them to mend their ways and thoughts, and then blessed them all. The other brothers and their mother also arrived, and bowed in shame before the goddess. They were also blessed likewise. All the three brothers and their wives, along with their mother, went home happily and vowed to be good to each other, and tell no lies, nor have any jealousy towards each other, and so they lived happily ever after!

2. THE POOR BRAHMIN AND THE *TOMARI*

Once upon a time there was a very poor Brahmin. He was a religious man and prayed to the goddess Durga every day. He decided one day that he would go to the temple of the goddess Durga during Navratri. As the time came near, he tried his best to gather something valuable to offer to the Devi. He could not find anything worthwhile to take with him, and could only think of his scythe and sieve, with which he used to work on his small piece of land. Since he could not find anything else, he just put these two tools in the bundle with some clothes and food, and went along with the *yatris* (pilgrims) to the temple.

For nine days he prayed in the temple like everyone else, and when other people offered their cash and jewellery, he offered his scythe and sieve and placed them on the altar. Soon, the *puja* was over and everyone left for home, but the poor Brahmin stayed behind, and sat behind the altar of the goddess. The idol of the goddess

was decorated in full glory. Now, the Devi felt a great
heaviness on her back, so she called one of her *langooras*
and said to him: 'O lad, go and see who is sitting at the
back door of the temple?' The boy went running and
quickly came back to report: 'O Great Mother, a very
poor and thin Brahmin is sitting there. He seems too
weak and hungry to even move.' The goddess then said:
'Go and fetch him here, and let me see as to why he is
tarrying, when all else have gone.' The Brahmin was
brought into the presence of the goddess, and she asked
him: 'Good Brahmin, why haven't you gone? The *puja*
festival is over, and there is no one left but my *pujari*.
Moreover, why are you so thin, O Brahmin?' He replied
with tears in his eyes: 'Mother, O Mother, I am a poor
Brahmin, and I am thin because I hardly have anything
to eat, and now that I have given my scythe and sieve to
you, I have nothing left with which to earn myself a single
meal for even a day.' The Devi Ma was touched by his
plight, and said: 'Here, take this *tomari* (basket made
out of a dry pumpkin) with you, and whenever you ask
for food or anything else, it will be there before you. You
will never go hungry, as you can ask for any amount of
the choicest food.'

The Brahmin was very happy, and after taking the
tomari, he made his way to his little thatched hut in the
village. He soon asked the *tomari* to get him some good
things to eat, and would you believe it, the eatables
appeared there right in front of him! He ate with relish,
and was so delighted that he thought of inviting the whole
village for a feast. Not content with that, he decided to
invite the king as well. Soon he went around the whole
kingdom, and announced that he wanted all the people to
have the afternoon meal with him on the very next day,
and that he would also be inviting the king! The people
were very puzzled and curious as to how this impoverished
man would provide for so many, and even for the king!
However, they all agreed to attend.

The next day they set out for the lunch, but some prudent ones left some food cooked at home, as they were quite sure that they would come back home hungry. They were surprised when they saw the king along with his men making his way towards the house of the Brahmin. All the persons sat on the grass with a *pattal* (dry leaf used as a plate) kept in front of them. The Brahmin brought out his *tomari*, and said: 'Dear *tomari*, spread the choicest dishes, fit for our king.' No sooner had the words been uttered than such a sumptuous meal was laid out on golden plates, that the eyes of everyone nearly popped out in surprise! They all ate to their heart's content, and the king was very impressed. He asked the Brahmin the secret of it all, and said: 'O Brahmin, you cannot have come into such riches by any known means.' The Brahmin revealed the whole story, and said: 'See this is the *tomari* that the Great Mother has given to me,' and showed it to all gathered there. The king's men quickly seized it, saying that such a thing should belong to the king, and no one else. They marched off with the *tomari* leaving the poor Brahmin in a very sad state. He decided to go back to the temple of the goddess, and narrate to her the tale of the cruel king, who wanted everything for himself.

He joined a group that was going to the temple, and went along with them. He did the same thing as before, and stayed behind even after all had left. Again, the Brahmin was summoned in front of the Devi and she asked him why he had come again, for she had already given him a gift that none else in the world had ever seen or possessed. Now, the Brahmin told her the entire story. On hearing this, she became very angry with the selfish king and his men. She asked her *langoora* to go and fetch the *tomari's* sister *mogari* and she gave it to the Brahmin and told him to again invite the whole village along with the king and ask the *mogari* to do as the *tomari* had done.

So it happened that there was again a great feast where everyone arrived eagerly, along with the king, to have lunch at the Brahmin's house. They were curious to know if the Brahmin could manage a grand meal again without his *tomari*. The king was also anxious to come, since the *tomari* (which his men had forcibly taken) when asked to produce food, would just produce bitter seeds, which made the king very unhappy.

.Everything was arranged at the Brahmin's house with great pomp and show, just as it had been before. Everyone sat down with great enthusiasm as they could hardly wait for the meal to begin. The Brahmin brought out the *mogari* and said: 'O great *mogari*, given to me by Great Mother Goddess, do justice to this gathering for they have come with great expectations.' The *mogari* picked itself up, and started beating the entire gathering, including the king, who got really scared and asked the Brahmin to stop it. The *mogari* would not stop, and only when everyone had been thrashed soundly did the Brahmin ask it in the name of the Mother Goddess to stop. Now it did so, and said: 'This is for the selfish and unkind things you have done to this man of God. Give him back the *tomari*, otherwise I will beat you black and blue.' All of them agreed at once, and since in any case the *tomari* was giving nothing but bitter seeds to eat, the king agreed to give it back and save himself and the rest from this terrible beating.

The Brahmin explained that the Mother Goddess had told him to do all this, and he did not really mean to harm or insult anyone. The king then understood that a person who has enough should not be greedy and snatch away other people's belongings, and that the Mother Goddess looks after everyone who worships her and is faithful to her. So the king asked all who were gathered there to worship Durga Ma every six months and thank her for whatever she had given them, and only ask her for whatever they needed, and surely they would be rewarded like the Brahmin.

3. THE KING AND THE MAIDEN

Once upon a time, there was a young king who was very fond of hunting and he liked to go into the jungle as often as he could. So, whenever he was free he would take along his best young men and go off looking for something to hunt.

One day, while he was looking for something to hunt, he saw a beautiful maiden sitting under a tree and singing in a melodious voice. She was wearing ornaments made of flowers and leaves, and was looking so lovely that the king decided to marry her. He soon brought her to his kingdom. A grand wedding was arranged and the maiden became a very beautiful queen. But the maiden, in reality, was the daughter of a farmer, who earned his living from the fields, and brought wheat and millet into his home, and his children would even eat them raw. The children grew to like their food that way. So, one day when our queen saw some fields, she asked for some sheaves of millet and wheat. She was happily chewing them when the king saw her from a distance. He was very curious, but could not come to her at once, since he was busy doing the rounds of his kingdom and looking after the welfare of his subjects. However, in the evening, when he met the queen he asked her what she had been eating. As our queen had been telling everyone that she was a princess from a very rich kingdom, and thus was used to a grand way of life, she could not tell the king the truth. So, she told the king that she had been chewing pearls and rubies, which she had brought from her home. The king was very impressed, and asked her to show him the pearls and rubies. The queen managed to make some excuses for that day and quickly ran to the temple of the Mother Goddess. There she lay down flat before the deity. The goddess was disturbed, and asked her *langoora* to go and find out what was the problem with the woman. The queen, with tears in her eyes, told the *langoora* to take her to Durga Ma. The queen was taken to the Devi, who asked her: 'What is troubling you, my child, that you have been sitting here without food and water for so long?' The queen replied, 'O Mother, please help me as I have been lying to the king to whom I am married that I am the daughter of a very rich king, who has a great palace in which I used to live, and that I ate pearls and rubies as snacks. Now what do I do? Please, please help me!' The goddess looked sternly at her, and told her that lying always landed people in trouble, but since she had already done penance by staying at the temple for so long without food and water, and had also prayed with a true heart, she would be rewarded, and said, 'Go my child, and take your husband to the very tree in the jungle under which he saw you for the very first time.'

The queen did just that, and a few days later, she, along with the king, started on the visit to the kingdom of her father. On reaching there, they all looked stunned at the grand palaces, houses, roads, wells, gardens, and fountains – even the king was dazzled! The whole convoy stayed there for a long time. They were entertained and fed with the choicest of foods that one could imagine. Soon they had to leave for their own kingdom. With a heavy heart, the king bade farewell to all the grand people of that kingdom.

They had travelled a little distance when the king realised that he had left behind his *dhoti* (a loose type of lower garment worn by men in India) drying out in the backyard of the palace. Since the *dhoti* was an expensive one, he sent his horsemen to fetch it. The horsemen obeyed the command and went back to the place where the kingdom was. But they could not find anything except an old tree amidst a big dense jungle. They peered inside the jungle and thought that they must have missed the place, as they could find no palace, no houses, no roads, no fountains! So they came back to their king and with bewildered expressions told him that there was nothing there except an old tree. The queen heard of this and came running to the king, and said: 'My lord, I must confess that I have committed a great sin in telling you a lie when I said that I belonged to a great kingdom.' The king was surprised and asked her: 'Then tell me, who entertained us, and provided us with such luxury to live in.' She replied: 'All that you saw, my lord, was conjured up by Deviji, to whom I had prayed after having lied to you.' The king then asked: 'Really, my queen, does Deviji bestow such abundance on those who pray to her?' The queen said: 'Sire, I am merely a villager, who lived near the tree where you first saw me. I was only eating millet and wheat when you saw me in the fields. But as I was afraid that you would throw me out if you found out the truth, I had to lie to you.' 'You, my queen, whom Deviji has blessed, really are a very pure person for she only listens to those who are good at heart,' the king said. 'Now, let me order all my subjects to pray to Deviji every six months for nine days, before the commencement of every winter and summer.'

4. THE KING WHO WANTED A CHILD

In days gone by, there lived a very great and powerful king, who had a noble and beautiful wife. They were very happy together, and the people of their kingdom were also very happy with them. The royal couple paid special attention to all the needs of their subjects, and heard their woes and alleviated them to the best of their abilities. However, the king and queen had one sorrow that saddened them immensely – they had no children and as such their palace was bereft of any sound or chatter of little ones. Even one little child would have made the palace echo with the patter of little feet running here and there.

Soon the queen, who could think of nothing else, suggested to the king that he marry her own sister, as, then, perhaps her sister could beget a child. The king was stunned, but all his ministers and courtiers thought it was a good idea, and advised him to marry his wife's sister. They all felt strongly that there should be an heir to the throne, and although it was against the wishes of the monarch himself, they were able to persuade him in the larger interest of the kingdom.

Soon, another splendid and grand marriage took place and everyone rejoiced because the older queen did not feel jealous at all. She made a great occasion of the day. The younger queen was also very beautiful and always listened to her elder sister. In fact, now they both consulted each other in the affairs of the palace, and lived happily together.

Alas, there was still no news of a baby's arrival, and the king became very worried and sad again. So, the two queens thought up a scheme in which they made the younger queen tie a small cushion around her waist beneath her garments, and told the king that she was expecting a baby. They also told him that the astrologers of the court had forbidden the king from going anywhere near the 'pregnant' queen until the baby was born. The king was very happy and agreed to do as he was told.

Every month a bigger cushion was tied round the younger queen's waist, and she was shown to the king from afar. This state of affairs went on for nine months, and the time for the birth of the baby arrived. The queens were now in a state of panic, and were frightened as they did not know what to do. They decided to pray to Deviji, and told the king that since Deviji had been so very kind to them, they would like to visit the great temple, situated far away, to offer their gratitude. The king also decided to go along with them and no one could persuade him not to do so. He declared: 'Deviji has been kind to me and my queens and so I must accompany them to the great temple.' The queens were flabbergasted and said: 'Sire, you have so much work in the capital, that your going with us may not be the right thing to do.' The king replied, 'What will Deviji think of me! She has so blessed us, O queens, that I must also thank her.' Then he made arrangements for his prime minister to look after the kingdom, while he went to the temple to worship. Fruits, flowers, jewels, and gold coins were taken along to be offered at the altar of Durga Ma. Amidst all this grandeur, the caravan of the king and both the queens started, the younger one with a big cushion tied to her waist. As they neared the temple, the elder queen said to the king: 'O Lord, we have forgotten to bring the silver *chhattra* (canopy) that we were to offer to Durga Ma, and without that all our offerings would be at naught.' The king was very anxious to please the goddess, so he quickly made up his mind to go himself, and said: 'You, O queens, proceed and reach the temple. I will go quickly and return with the *chhattra*.' He went very fast, but as he was travelling on foot (and that too barefooted!) he took quite some time to reach his capital and return.

Well, now the queens made the entourage travel very fast and reached the temple a day earlier than scheduled. They went straight to the altar of the goddess without taking any food or water, and lay prostrate before her, with tears of bewilderment streaking down their faces. Deviji asked her *langoora* to find out what ailed these two ladies, who came in their finery and riches. The *langoora* asked them: 'Why have you come, O women, with such sad looks. You do not look as if you have come to thank the goddess, but instead you look as if you have come to ask her for something.' The elder queen replied:'O *langooraji*, we are in great trouble. We lied to the king – a great mistake! Now we have come to the Mother Goddess for help. We told the king that the younger queen was expecting a child when she really is not, as the king wants an heir to the throne. O *langooraji*, do help us.'

The *langoora* went and told the Mother Goddess the exact situation. Deviji, in all her kindness, asked the *langoora* to fetch a coconut. Then she asked the younger queen to sit cross-legged before the altar. The *langoora* then put the coconut in her lap, and lo behold, a beautiful little baby started to cry in her lap! Everyone was so thrilled that they danced with joy and sang in praise of the great goddess.

In the meantime, the king arrived, and seeing the commotion, asked everyone what the matter was. People said: 'The queen was not actually expecting a baby, but the goddess made it happen, and now there is a real baby in the younger queen's lap.' The king was overjoyed and rushed up to the altar and lay face down before the goddess.

Now, the elder queen felt jealous, and demanded to know why the Mother Goddess had not given the baby to her, since she had also prayed so much to Deviji. 'Why, O Mother, did you choose the younger queen and not myself? I also came barefoot to your temple and prayed with a pure heart. It should be my baby and not my sister's!' she pleaded. 'Woman, O woman, I will just solve this problem. Both of you wear blouses made out of jute, and whoever gets milk in her breast to feed the baby, can claim him,' said the Mother Goddess. Both women did likewise, and held the baby to their breasts, but only the younger one produced the milk. 'Why this partiality?' cried the elder queen. Deviji replied: 'Because the younger one had to put up with the inconvenience of a cushion tied to her waist, and did not come out of her palace for nine months, so that none could find out the real situation. Therefore, she deserves the right to feed, but both of you are mothers and as such, both of you should look after the baby sincerely.'

The queen realised that being the elder one she should be more understanding and give the credit of bearing the child to the younger one. So they returned to the capital in a joyous mood. All the people of the kingdom rejoiced, and the king declared that henceforth

Devi *puja* must be celebrated twice a year in his kingdom – once before the coming of winter and once before the coming of summer – for nine days each time. And so continues the tradition to our day.

Chhokka

Ingredients

Potato	250 gm (cubed into small pieces)
Red pumpkin	250 gm
Tejpatta	2
*Panchphoran**	1 teaspoon
Ginger	1/2" (scraped)
Red chillies	2 (cut into two pieces)
Green chillies	2 (slit)
Dhania-jeera powder (dry roasted)	1 tablespoon
Salt and sugar to taste	

* This includes *kala zeera* (onion seeds), methi (fenugreek), saunf (aniseed), sarson (mustard)

Method

Lightly fry the potatoes and red pumpkin pieces with a little *haldi* and salt. Do not deep fry. Put 2 tablespoons cooking oil. Put in *tejpatta, panch phoran* and red chillies. When the good smell comes put in the vegetables, about half a cup of hot water and the ginger scrapings. Cover and simmer till soft. Sprinkle some powdered masala on the top after taking off fire.

Bhuni Khichri

Ingredients

Rice	1 cup
Chana dal	1 cup
Ginger	1" piece
Tejpatta	2
Dalchini	2" piece
Elaichi	4 - 6
Cloves	6
Salt and sugar	

Method

Wash and strain the rice and *dal*. Keep them separate. In a big thick-bottomed pot pour 3 tablespoons of good *ghee*. Put in the *tejpatta, dalchini, elaichi* and cloves. Do not let it burn. Now put the *dal* and fry a little; then put the rice and fry some more -- if it sticks put in a little more *ghee*. Put in the ginger scrapings and add enough hot water to cook the rice and *dal* but Bhuni Khichri has to be dry. Cover and simmer. Look now and then see that it does not get burnt. Put in salt and a little sugar; a few green chillies may also be added. Remove from the fire when done. Sprinkle a little *dalchini* powder and cover.

DAY ARTI FOR DURGA *PUJA*

Maole ki arti — ya vid ki jai —
    Sone ka diya kapur ki baati
Surai ka girat bale dui rate
    Made ki arti — ya vid ki ja
Nagar kot Devi Agre Bhawani
    Langur bermiya agwani
Ya Vid ki Jai
    Maole ki arti sab jug sowe devi jage

Deviji ke age pathur nanche
Maole ki arti – ya vid ki jai –
    Nagar kot Devi Agre Bhawani
Langur agwani
    Maole ki arti – ya vid ki jai

BHOG

Bhogon hi bhogon, Ambe bhogon hi bhogon
    meri abla maiye, cholewali ma
Thaan mera mun younhin patiya
    A ma bhogon hi bhogon Ambe bhogon hi bhogon
Aye ma sone ka Garva Ganga jal paani
    ma thanda thanda paani ma mithra mithra paani
Ma piyo piyo piyo meri ad Bhawani
    Ma nagar kot ki rani – ma dholagarh ki rani –
Ma Kalka Bhawani
    Ma joogmaya rani – annapurna devi rani –
Ma Vaishnov devi rani – ma achman le durge achman
    le – thaan mera mun youhi patiya
Ma bhogon hi bhogon Ambe bhogon hi bhogon
    Aye ma mugmeva pakwan mithai,
ma bathua ki bhaggi maiya
    saras banaye – ma kheer khand deva or
metheyai – ma sunton ka dana
    sant piyaron ka dana –
Baali bholo ka dana – nipat garibo ka dana
    mere abla maiye cholewali ma
Thaan mera mun yohi patiya – ma bhogon hi bhogon
    Ambe bhogon hi bhogon
Ma Bhola bhagat tera haar le aya
    Ma Dhan bhagat teri beera le aya
Ma gajra pheno gajre pardesan ma
    Aye ma beera lo beera
Jag tharan ma, devi tharan ma
    Thaan mera mun yo hi patiyan
A ma bhogon hi bhogon, Ambe bhogon hi bhogon

DEVIJI KI ARTI

Jai Dev Jai Dev Jai Ambe Gauri
    Maiya Jai Ambe Gauri
Maiya Har Mangal Karnee
Thum Ko Nis Din Dhyaven
    Devaji Ko Sada Manave
Brahma Har Shivri
    Jai Dev Jai Dev
Maang Sidoor Birajat Teeko Mrithmathko
    Maiya Teeko Mrithmathko
Ujwal Se Do Naina Chandra Badenni Ko
    Jai Dev Maha Dev

Kanan Kundal Shobit Nasha Grah Moti
    Maiya Nasha Grah Moti
Kotik Chandra Diwakar 2 Raajat Sum Jyoti
    Jai Dev Maha Dev

Kanak Saman Kalewar Rakthambar Raje
    Maiya Rakthambar Raje
Rakt Pushp Jai Mala Rakt Pusph Jai Mala
    Kanchan Per Saaje
Jai Dev Jai Dev

Kehar Vahan Durge Kharak Khaper Dhaari
    Maiya Kharak Khaper Dhaari
    Surnar Munijan Seven
Tin Ke Dukh Taari
    Jai Dev Jai Dev

Shumb Nishumn Pachare Mahishasur Ghaati
    Maiya Mahishasur Ghaati
Dhroom Vilochan Naana (2)
    Nis Din Muth Maati
Jai Dev Jai Dev

Chonsath Yogini Gaawat Neerat Karat Bhairon
    Maiya Neerat Karat Bhairon
Bajat Taal Mridungum (2)
    Bajat Sankh Mridungum
aur Baja Dumru
    Jai Dev Jai Dev
Tum Brahmani Tum Rudrani
    Tum Kamlarani Maiya Tum Kamlarani
Aagum Nigam Bahkani Aagam Ved Bakhani
    Taa Per Shiv Rani
Jai Dev Jai Dev Brahmadik, Rudradik,
    Sankadik Dhyaven
Maiya Sankadik Dhyaven
    Jo Nar Tum Ko Seven
Jo Nar Mataji Ko Seven
    Echcha Phal Paaven
Jai Dev Maha Dev

Kanchan Thaal Birajat Agar Kapur Baati
    Maiya Agar Kapur Baati
Maal Ketu Mein Raajat Kot Ratan Jyoti
    Jai Dev Jai Dev

Kashi Mein Arti Prem Sahit Gaave
    Maiya Prem Sahit Gaave
Kahat Shivanand Swami Vanat Shivanand Swami
    Sukh Sampati Paave
Jai Dev Jai Dev, Jai Ambe Gauri
    Maiya Jai Shama Gauri Maiya
Har Mangal Karni........
Tum Ko Nis Din Diyave
    Devaji Ko Sada Manave
Brahma Har Shivji Jai Dev Jai Dev

Karpur Gauram Karuna Astharman
  Sansar Sarum Bhuj Gendra Haaram
Sada Vasantam Hriday
  Bhawan Bhawan Sahitam Namami
Sada Bhawani Dahncy, Samukh Sehen Ganesh
  Pancho Dev Raksha Brahma
Vishnu Mahesh
  Bolo atal Chatre Ki Jai

21

Dussehra

THE DUSSEHRA FESTIVAL FALLS DURING THE MOONLIT fortnight, i.e., on the 10th day of the waxing moon in the month of Kwar. Thus, this festival comes some time in September or October, depending on the Tith (as determined by the Hindu calendar). The dates according to the Christian calendar can be ascertained from the *panchang* (almanac).

On this day in the Treta (or Trita) Yug, Ram (the 7th incarnation of Vishnu), killed the great demon Ravan, who had abducted Ram's wife Sita to his kingdom of Lanka. Ram, along with his brother Lakshman and devoted follower Hanuman, and an army of monkeys fought a great battle to rescue his lovely wife Sita. The war against Ravan lasted for ten days and the story of Ram and Sita is recounted with affection and love in the great epic *Ramayana*. To this day the whole of *Ramayana* is enacted in dramas staged in huge *pandals* and maidans, in cities, towns and villages. Beautiful tableaux of actors in costumes of ancient times are taken around the city before they culminate at the venue where the action takes place. After the drama is over the actors of that day's episode return in a procession to the place from where the *yatra* (journey) had begun. Thus, virtually the entire city can then have the *darshan* before and after the enactment of each day's drama. These tableaux and enactments are known as Ram Leelas. The whole spectacle is a big *mela* (fair) and is greatly enjoyed by young and old alike.

Ram was a great believer in the powers of goddess Durga, and he prayed to her for nine days before he himself entered the battlefield on the tenth day. On this day he killed Ravan, Meghnad and Kumbhakaran, and people proclaimed it as the greatest victory of good over evil. The day became known as Dussehra and we still celebrate it with gusto, connecting us with the important events of the distant past.

Huge effigies of Ravan, his brother Kumbhakaran and his son Meghnad are made, and filled with large quantities of crackers and fireworks. At just about sunset, an actor depicting Ram shoots an arrow from his bow, which hits the Ravan effigy in his navel (where a pot of nectar – the reason for Ravan's invincibility – was stored, and none could kill him unless he knew the secret of drying this nectar by shooting straight into the navel). This was revealed to Ram by Ravan's own brother Vibhishan, who had changed sides and had become the great adviser to Ram on the affairs of Lanka. Similarly, the other two effigies are set alight. The effigies become a huge display of fireworks for the children and elders to feast their eyes on, and to bring delight to their hearts. A great deal of noise is made as the crackers burst and this provides joy and happiness. Children are given full liberty to buy bows,

arrows and all the other items which abound in the *mela*.
In North India, the grounds where Ram Leelas are held
are known as *baaras* and amateur actors get a chance to
exhibit their talent to the full.

In Bengal the occasion is celebrated as the day on
which Durga Ma killed the terrible demon Mahishasur.
The essence is the same – this festival is celebrated all
over India as a symbol of victory of good over evil.

The celebration at home begins ten days earlier, on
the first day of Durga *puja*, in the month of Kwar. A few
seeds of *jowar* (millet) are usually planted on the first day
of the *puja* and watered so that the millet sprouts up into
long sheaves by the tenth day and is ready for Dussehra.

Dussehra *puja* is done in the morning. Everyone
wears good clothes with *zari* and *gota* as on all festive
occasions. It is said that if one wears a set of new clothes
on this day, one shall get ten sets of new clothes in the
coming year. There is no compulsory wearing of the *chunri*,
but there is no taboo on donning it either. As always, *chonp*
on the forehead is a must. The *puja* is done in the *puja*
room and no specific decoration is required, but if one likes,
one can make a *chowk* on the floor. On this day, all
weapons, tools, instruments, pens and pencils are
worshipped, because they are the means of fighting
injustice, ignorance and evil. These items are placed in
front of the gods. A foolscap paper is decorated all around
the edges with *aipun* and a swastik is placed on the top
of this paper to remind us of the Aryan origin of the
inhabitants of India. The eldest member of the family then
writes on this paper:

> *Uttar ka ghora, Dakshin ka neer*
> *Paschim ka varda, Purav ka cheer*

The foregoing couplet is about the famous things obtained
from the four corners of India and it focusses children's
attention onto them. The names of all those assembled
are then added onto the paper. It would be better if
everyone present signed it, as it is a record of the people
present during the *puja* that year. The month, date and

year are added to the paper and it is glued on with *atta* (dough) near the gods.

A *puja thaali* (plate), containing the *roli*, *aipun* and rice in their respective *katoris*, some *batashas*, seven *paans*, some *mithai*, fruits and a coconut, is tastefully decorated. In some cases, this *thaali* also has a glass full of wine, whisky or rum placed along with the rest of the *prasad*. (Dussehra is a feast celebrating victory in war, and so alcohol is allowed even in the *puja*.) First of all, a *teeka* is put on the forehead of all the gods and goddesses, and then the youngest girl of the house applies the *teeka* on the forehead of all the members present. She uses her right-hand thumb, and puts an oblong *teeka* with a little rice on it for the men, and a small *bindi*, using the tip of her third finger, on the forehead of the women. Everyone then worships the gods and the weapons, etc., as usual – first with water, then with *aipun* and *roli* and, lastly, with rice. If flowers are available, their petals are also showered. The eldest lady member present then picks up the *nariyal* (coconut) along with some sheaves of millet, some *batashas*, a fruit, a little *mithai*, one *paan*, a pencil or a pen (usually belonging to the individual to whom the *prasad* is being given). The receiver holds the two hands together and accepts the *prasad*. It could be practically difficult to hand over the *prasad* all at once, so it is best to give it in two instalments. Those receiving it touch the *prasad* to their forehead; they then take some sheaves of the *jowar* and put them on top of one ear. They can then place the *prasad* back onto the *thaali* – a little piece of *mithai* or a *batasha* should be taken and eaten there and then. Each person then picks up his or her own pen or pencil and individually dips it seven times into the alcohol and then into an inkpot, saying:

Hey Prabhu meri kalam mein aisi tezi ho, jaisi ki is sharaab mein hai.
(O God let my pen gain as much sharpness, as is in this alcohol.)

On Dussehra, usually a big lunch or dinner is arranged for the sons-in-law and the daughters of the family. The daughter brings a *teeka*, just as is done on Raksha Bandhan or Bhai Dooj but there is no presentation of money by the brothers. This is a day of family get-togethers and feasting. There is no restriction on serving meat and hard drinks. One can enjoy oneself to the fullest extent.

On Dussehra, since all articles that are used for progress and prosperity of mankind are worshipped, all vehicles like cars, trucks, and buses are also worshipped by the individuals using them. A sign of the swastik is made with *roli*, *aipun*, and rice on the vehicle which has been cleaned and polished earlier. In all army, police and paramilitary organisations, the drivers clean and polish their vehicles with great solemnity and patience, and then perform the *puja* of the vehicles.

The Dussehra festival is one of the greatest and most important festivals in India and with it comes winter.

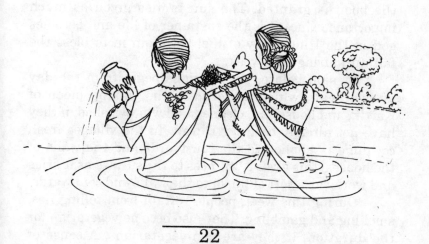

22

Chhat

THERE IS NO *VRAT* AS SEVERE AS CHHAT. THE PEOPLE OF BIHAR have made it their special celebration. The eastern parts of Uttar Pradesh and some parts of Madhya Pradesh also give great importance to this fast, and all of them celebrate it as a festival for six days, beginning from the day after Diwali (which is in Kartik and culminates on the 6th day of the waxing moon of the same month). The Tith is Chhat, hence the name. It falls somewhere in October-November.

Chhat is considered to be one of the most rewarding fasts and *pujas*. Lord Kartikeya or Skanda – the first son of Shiv and Parvati – is prayed to on this occasion along with the sun. Kartikeya is all-benevolent and said to have the power to fulfil all desires. Therefore, people undertake this fast for children, or for their own health or wealth. They continue doing it year after year until the boon is granted. The sun is also given as much importance since it is the sustainer of life and becomes god in the Hindu way of life; both join in to bless the faithful during this week.

As said before, preparations begin from the day after Diwali, which is *Parva* of the waxing moon of Kartik, and houses are cleaned and whitewashed, if they have not already been for Diwali. In the villages fresh cowdung is applied to the courtyards and the walls of the houses; this gives a stiffness to the surface as it dries and works as a sort of finish to the walls and courtyards.

During this week people refrain from telling lies, smoking and gambling. They also become vegetarian for the duration, if they are non-vegetarians. A sense of purity and piousness becomes the order of the day, especially for those who keep the fast. But even those not keeping the fast, but living in the same house as people who are, should be able to feel the impact of the occasion. The main activities on the third day, known as Nahan Khan (literally eating after a bath), are cleaning the body thoroughly, cutting nails and washing the hair, wearing absolutely clean clothes, washing and cleaning the *puja* and putting fresh tablecloths on the tables and *chowkis*, and dressing up the deities. The ladies of the house, who usually keep this fast, leave the men to pursue their usual occupations outside the home without the austerity. Some men, however, do keep *vrats*.

From the first day of Chhat onwards, the food is without garlic or onions and it must be vegetarian. There is no restriction as to the number of times one can eat. Coffee and tea are allowed all through the day. This day is more in preparation for the actual days of *vrat*.

The next day is the day of fasting and is known as Kharna. On this day, the fast is an absolute fast without water or anything to eat, not even in the early morning;

hence the food and liquids taken on the day of the Nahan Khan are the ones that will sustain one right up to the evening, thus making it a 24-hour fast in its first phase. The whole day is spent in cleaning and making arrangements for the food to be cooked for the evening. The food is usually cooked away from the main kitchen, preferably in a courtyard where a *chulha* is made out of bricks; some cowdung is applied onto it and the surrounding area, since cowdung is supposedly very clean and pure. No one is allowed near the *chulha* with shoes on and no one can cook until they have bathed and worn absolutely clean clothes. The utensils used for cooking should be new; if they are not, then they are washed with *gobar* (cowdung) or *mitti* (dry mud) to make them pure. The fire lit in the *chulha* is of wood. A stack of wood is required to feed the fire and keep the heat even. This practice, however, is for the very orthodox, or those who live in houses with grounds or courtyards. When one lives in a flat with limited space for cooking, it is best to cook in the kitchen after cleaning the stove and the kitchen thoroughly to give a sense of cleanliness and sanctity. If you require a utensil for your kitchen, buying it during this period gives a sense of doing the right thing and gives the family something to think and talk about. The food cooked for the evening is *kheer* and *puri*. The wheat for the *puri* could be freshly ground from wheat bought specially for the *vrat*; otherwise buy a new packet of wheat flour if you want to go along with conventions. In Bihar such rules still catch the imagination of the people, and as long as it does not make for tension and unpleasantness, there is no harm in treating the festival in this special manner.

In the evening the *puja* to Kartik Bhagwan is performed in the *puja* room which has been duly decorated with a new *chowki* and flowers or *kharia matti* decorations on the floor. Fresh flowers and garlands decorate the deities. Lord Ganesh, the younger brother

of Kartikeya, is always to be honoured first; therefore
the first *teeka* is applied on his forehead, after which it
is applied on the other gods. The youngest girl of the
house applies the *teeka* of *roli* and rice to all those
present – she applies it on the forehead with her thumb,
elongating the *teeka* a little, from between the eyebrows
up to the forehead, with a little rice stuck to the wet
roli of the *teeka*. A round *teeka* is applied to women with
the third finger of the right hand between the eyebrows
without rice stuck on. *Pujan* is done first with water,
then with *aipun* and *roli*, and last with rice; flowers are
showered on all the deities by everyone, turn by turn.
Bhog (*prasad*) is offered to Lord Kartikeya and the other
gods. The food that is to be eaten in the evening is offered
as *prasad* (*puri* and *kheer*). A coconut and seven *paans*
and *batashas* are placed in a *thaal* alongside a bowl of
kheer and some *puris* and is then put back into the main
food which is in the kitchen. Any special song in praise
of Lord Kartikeya or a *bhog* song is appropriate to sing
before the *arti* which can be a special one for Lord
Kartikeya or the universal *arti*, 'Om Jai Jagdish Hare'.
The *puja* is completed with the usual chants of *Karpur*
gauram and *Tvmev Mata* and the showering of water
on the assembly with 'Chittan para neer ka, dukh gaya
shareer ka' (these drops of water drive away all the
illnesses of my body). The *puja* finishes and all those
who have kept the *vrat* gather together in a room where
there is no noise and, without speaking, they serve
themselves the *kheer* and *puri* either from the dishes
placed in the middle, or straight from the kitchen.
Bananas, water and tea can also be taken, but they must
be eaten without speaking. No one should call another;
even outsiders must not call anyone's name during the
process of eating. If someone does call out by mistake
the person who has been called or the person who
unwittingly says something must stop eating at once.
This is a very serious matter since another fast for the

next 36 hours will have to be kept to complete the ritual of Chhat. This is the only meal between the 24-hour fast and the 36-hour fast which commences at once. Tea and coffee are also allowed to be taken at this time but in continued silence. Therefore it is best to close the area and no one other than the ones observing the ritual should be allowed anywhere near. Getting up and moving around is also not allowed. It is difficult but people adhere to it with great devotion. No one with a weak constitution should undertake the fast in all its severity since the next day is even more demanding and extremely arduous, to say the least.

From the morning of the third day those who are observing the fast start preparing for the evening when each one offers *argh* to the sun god along with the *soop*, a reed contraption used for cleaning lentils, wheat, rice or anything with husk or small stones mixed in it. The item is put in the *soop* and thrown up rhythmically, thus leaving the rubbish in the front from where it can pushed off with very little effort. Each *soop* must be filled with any of the following items:

(1) *Alta* (a red piece of paper)
(2) Coconut (dry)
(3) Sugarcane
(4) Radish (white)
(5) 1 *mithai*
(6) Flowers
(7) Sprouted grain
(8) *Khajurees* (*gujias*) (recipe at the end of the chapter)

These are in the count of one, seven, nine or even eleven, depending on the desire of the person. A double number of *soops* have to be prepared because the number of *soops* offered in the evening to the setting sun have to be offered the next morning to the rising sun. This *aajal* to the sun god is done while standing in water; therefore,

one has to go to the river-bank or to a tank. If there is no
natural water near the town or village, a ditch is dug at
an appropriate place in the house, and fresh water filled
in it. People go to the water with a feeling of great
devotion wearing clean or new clothes and either
walking bare feet all the way or doing the *Dhaud
Pranam,* which means lying down on the ground, face
down and hands joined in prayer over the head, then
getting up and again lying down at the spot where the
hands were, and very slowly proceeding towards the
river or tank. Many people take it upon themselves to
clean the path where the devotees would proceed
towards the waterfronts, and one can see people
sweeping and washing roads and lanes, removing
garbage from the houses on the way to the waters. Some
people whose wish has been fulfilled can be seen going
with full-fledged bands playing happy tunes.

The festivities become a community affair from
now on. On reaching the *ghat,* everyone gets into the
water and takes a dip or just sprinkles some water on
the body before offering the *argh* to the setting sun, while
standing in knee-deep water. *Argh* is offered from a *lota*
full of water held in both hands and raised high; water
is poured gently into the main stream, then, one by one,
the *soops* are raised likewise and offered to the sun god
with a prayer on the lips. *Agarbatti, dhoop* and flowers
are thus raised and presented to the sun. Prayers are
performed silently. Everyone remains in the water until
the sun has set completely. Since the next morning the
same ritual is to be done to the rising sun, none of the
vratis can eat or drink anything until the morning prayer
has been completed. People prefer to remain at the *ghat,*
singing songs in praise of the sun god or interacting with
acquaintances and generally socialising.

As soon as the sun's rays announce the rising sun
in the morning, the same devotion is shown as on the
previous evening, with the same amount of *soops* kept

aside for the morning *puja*. The contents of the *soops* are the *prasad* for this day and everyone breaks the long fast by partaking from the *soops* right at the river - bank itself. The *prasad* is distributed to everyone, known or unknown; some, of course, is kept for the family and for distribution among relatives and neighbours. Rest becomes the order of the day. One can eat and drink now, although it becomes difficult to eat a normal meal; it takes some time for the juices of the body to start functioning normally, therefore light food is taken. People are quite sure of the effectiveness of this *vrat*. It is a great discipline and hats off to those who abide by it – they deserve to be rewarded by the Almighty!

RECIPE

Khajurees

Ingredients	
Maida	1/2 kg
Sugar	1/4 kg
Dry coconut	1 tablespoon
Cardamom	4
Cloves	2
Dry fruits like cashewnut and *kismis*	

Method

Mix the *maida* with a little *ghee* and sugar and warm water. Put all ground cloves, cardamom and small pieces of cashewnut and *kismis*, and coconut. Mix the dough properly so that it becomes of binding consistency. Take small quantities of the dough and flatten on the palm like small pancakes. Heat the *ghee* in a *karahi* and fry a few at a time on medium heat until golden in colour. Cool and keep in a container.

23

Karva Chouth

KARVA CHOUTH FALLS ABOUT NINE DAYS BEFORE DIWALI ON the Kartik ki Chouth (fourth day of the waning moon or the dark fortnight) some time in October or November. It is the most important fast observed by the women of North India. A woman keeps such a fast for the well-being of her husband, who becomes her protector after she leaves her parents' home. Her husband provides her with food, shelter, clothing, respectability, comfort and happiness. In times gone by, a widow became a burden to the household and was best got rid of by burning her on the funeral pyre of her husband. This was glorified by attributing great virtue to the woman concerned, having brainwashed her enough so that she herself would decide to become what was known as a Sati. So it became

198

exceedingly important that her husband remain alive. Hence, the great importance of this fast.

In the olden times, the elders of the family were also keen to discipline the young wife, who sometimes arrived at the tender age of seven or eight years. Great care was taken on the day of this fast to ensure that she took neither food nor water unwittingly. An older woman would accompany the young girl even to the bathroom, or the toilet, to ensure that she did not drink any water.

This is indeed a very tough fast to observe as it starts before sunrise and ends after worshipping the moon, which usually rises at about 8.45 p.m. No food or water is to be taken after 4 a.m. or after sunrise. Nowadays, this fast is kept even in modern educated homes, becoming a symbol of the sentiment that a woman has for her husband. Many women do not adhere to the strictness of the fast, and many do not keep it at all, without causing any ripples in the Hindu society or any damage to their dear husbands! Actually, such a fast is not bad at all, since it is good for the digestive system, and does teach one to complete an assignment, however difficult it may be. Still, if it is inconvenient, and causes one to fall sick, it should be abandoned or the severity curtailed, by taking water, tea or coffee during the day.

There is great festivity on this day, and the day preceding it, as the mother-in-law of a newly wed makes much ado about sending the stuff for *sargai* (eating before sunrise on the day of the fast). Women whose husbands are alive join together and eat before sunrise. The food they take is thirst-quenching and keeps the body liquids in proper shape – milk, fruits like *singhara* and oranges, *sherbet*, tea or coffee must be taken and, of course, *puri* and *aloo*, cooked fresh in the morning, and *pheni* dipped in milk and anything else one may fancy. All these items, except the liquids, are sent to the girl's house by the mother-in-law a day prior to the actual *vrat* (fast), as the girls spend the night in their mothers' house but come to their in-laws' place during the day. This is the custom for a newly wed, otherwise both *sargai* and *puja* are done in one's own house. On the day of the *vrat*, the women rise early, have their bath, and dress up in finery, with *gota* and *kinari*. Those who have the *chunri* wear it even for the *sargai*. The newly married girls wear their *lehanga* and *chunni*, which is very much in fashion again. Heavy jewellery can be worn, but one has to be careful these days.

On Karva Chouth the young women are not supposed to do any work of the household, or any stitching or knitting either. So, these free young ladies generally crowd around a *mehndiwali* and a *churiwali* (bangle-seller), wherever they can find them, getting their palms and feet decorated with *henna* and filling their arms with bangles. It is fascinating to watch *henna* coming out of the container and forming the beautiful patterns on the palm, as the *mehndiwali* decorates it with great artistic precision, quite like icing a cake. Really, one has to see for oneself to believe the variety and the beauty of their designs. Buying bangles, *bindis* and *kajal* all for oneself, without anyone putting a spoke in the wheel for once, makes the occasion so very enjoyable. It's a day to fuss over oneself. Going to a movie or playing cards is the order of the day and keeps the women busy and happy. Of course, too much excitement must be avoided as it leads to one becoming thirsty, and maybe, a little sick.

The *halwais* do brisk business on this day since mothers send the *baya* for their daughters. This *baya* normally consists of ten big *mathris*, ten *puas* (sugar mixed with *atta* and kneaded with water and made into medium size *pakoras*), *halwa*, along with some cash and clothes, if one desires. The cash amount need not be too much; it can be anything from Rs. 5 to Rs. 50. A *karva* is a must – a *karva* is a *lota* (small pitcher) made out of *matti* (round earthen pot with an outlet on the side, and open from the top with a lid). It should not be too big, but should be the size of an ordinary bath *lota*. If a *karva* is not easily available, then any utensil resembling a *lota* can be used by making a little round spout (*taunti*) with a piece of kneaded *atta*. A *sari* (in the *baya*) is a must for the first Karva Chouth of a girl. One thing to be taken care of is that the *baya* reaches the girl's in-laws' home, where the girl has gone during the course of the day, before the evening. The *baya* is given to the mother-in-law after the *manasna*. If the mother-in-law is not present, then the eldest lady in the house is presented with the *baya*. Sometimes, the elder one chooses to take only the perishable items, and leaves cash and clothes for the mother-in-law. The *baya* can be accepted by widows also.

The preparation for the *puja* should be started at about 4 or 5 p.m. Someone older, who is willing, or the housewife herself as the situation demands, prepares a suitable place in the *puja* room, in case it is a big room which can accommodate all the women who have been invited for the *baya*; otherwise the best place is a verandah or the open courtyard, since generally the weather is not cold during this season. The *puja* place is decorated with *kharia matti*, which has been soaked in water two to three hours earlier, and takes a semi-liquid form. A *chowk* – like in any other *puja* – is decorated on the floor (*chowk* is described in the glossary). On top of the *chowk*, the *seep chowk* is decorated with *aipun*. This whole *chowk* should be placed against a wall on one side, where a similarly decorated *patta* is kept, on which the Gaur Mata is seated. Since the drawing of the *chowk* takes some time, it should be done much earlier. The Gaur Mata used to be made with cowdung in the shape of a human figure, just about two inches tall. Nowadays, a picture or an idol of Parvati is placed on the *patta*.

Just about an hour or so before moonrise, those who have observed the *vrat*, dress up again in their *chunris* or in red or pink clothes with *chonp* and *bindi* on their foreheads. Everyone now gathers around the *puja* place, where a carpet or *durrie* is spread over the *chowk*, leaving space for the *puja* items. The *baya* for each individual is kept on a *thaali*, over the *karva*, which has a little water and seven pieces of *pua* in it (seven pieces broken from one big *pua*). The *karva* itself is decorated with *kharia*, *aipun* and a little *roli*. A strand of *kalava* (red thread) of any thickness is tied around the narrow part of the *karva*. The top cover is also decorated and the *thaali* is placed on the cover, but if the cover comes in its way, it should be set aside. The *thaali* should be small so as to balance on the *karva* where the ten *mathris* or *puris* with ten *puas*, *halwa*, and cash are placed. If a set of clothes is to be given, it need not be placed on top of the *karva* but near it. The women sit facing the gods, and one elder member (there is no taboo on widows) of the family narrates the story and does the chanting for each woman doing the *puja*. This is known as *manasna*, which means to give away and never take back. First of all, *roli teeka* is applied on the forehead of Gaur Mata before the start of the *puja*. All the women doing the *puja* also apply *roli teeka* on their foreheads and hair parting (known as *maang*). Everyone does *pujan* by first dipping the third finger of the right hand in water and sprinkling it with the help of the thumb three times on the deity; the same procedure has to be repeated with *aipun* and *roli* and, lastly, the rice is showered. This depicts the bathing of the deity, decoration with *aipun*, putting of the *teeka* with *roli* and, lastly, worshipping the deity with rice. Then, taking a little rice in the hand everyone sits down to listen to the story, which is as follows:

Once upon a time, there was a very young girl about seven years old, who was married and had to come for the first Karva Chouth to her father's house. She was the only daughter with seven elder married brothers. Their wives and this young girl kept the fast of Karva Chouth with great devotion. Now, this little girl's brothers could not get used to the idea of their darling sister remaining hungry and thirsty for hours on end. Their patience had nearly run out by evening; and they could not bear to see the pale face of their sister. So, they asked her to take tea or even drink a little water, but she refused as she was very anxious to follow her sisters-in-law. The brothers could not bear it, and even as twilight fell, and no moon was seen, they went out of the house and lit a fire in the forest. They then came home excitedly, and told the little sister that the moon had come out. They gave her a round sieve and asked her to look through it. She ran to each of her sisters-in-law, and asked them to come and see the moon. Each one refused, saying: 'Bibi rani, it is not our moon, but your moon which has come out.' She was very puzzled but took the sieve, and ran out. Looking through it, she saw a bright ball and decided that her brothers were right and sisters-in-law were very wrong. After doing *puja* to the moon she consumed some water and food and, lo and behold, her husband fell down in a great swoon! She was petrified and ran helter-skelter, crying and demanding to know what had happened? When she would not stop, and kept pestering everyone, one of her sisters-in-law told her the truth. She was very shocked and resolved that since she was not at fault she would demand the return of her husband to consciousness from Gaur Mata herself. Keeping her husband's head on her lap she just sat down near the image of Gaur Mata. Very soon Gaur Mata came and exchanged *karvas* with all her sisters-in-law saying: 'Take O *suhagan* this *karva*, and give me O *suhagan* your *karva*', seven times to each sister-in-law. Then came the turn of the little girl. Gaur Mata refused to exchange *karvas* with her, but the little one insisted, and finally Gaur Mata turned towards her and said: 'O you, who cannot remain hungry, take this *karva*. O you, who cannot

remain thirsty take this *karva*.' The young girl pleaded:
'No, no. Please say, take O *suhagan* this *karva*, and give
O *suhagan* your *karva*, just as you have said to my sisters-
in-law.' Gaur Mata replied: 'This I cannot say, but next
year my sister will come and perhaps she may say it to
you.' So this little girl sat with her husband's head on her
lap for another year, without eating or drinking. She
refused to budge from the place of worship and, on the
appointed day, when the second Gaur Mata came, in a
great cloud of wind and dust, looking really fearsome, this
young bride did not move and insisted that the Gaur Mata
stay and exchange the *karva* with her seven times. The
fearsome lady refused, saying: 'Next year my older sister
will come, perhaps she may have the power to restore your
husband.' This event went on for six years, and each time
a more fearsome aspect of Gaur Mata came and went,
without doing anything for this young girl, but the girl
loved her husband so much that she was ready to go to
any extent to get him back and restore his health and
happiness.

Then came the seventh Karva Chouth of this bride,
who had been sitting without water or food all this while,
and had not complained even once. Her husband neither
stirred nor opened his eyes. Yet, she had put her faith in
the goddess and did not flinch. Her brothers and her
sisters-in-law came to her and tried their best to convince
her that those who have gone from this world can never
be brought back to life again (as it seemed that her
husband was totally dead now). But she would hear none
of it and, so, on the appointed day of Karva Chouth she
was not afraid of the coming of the goddess, even after
having experienced terrifying apparitions each year.

The moment came at last – the moon of the fourth
day after full moon in Kartik arrived. She saw all the
women of the household, dressed in their best, perform
the *puja* and exchange the *karvas*. Then there blew a great
storm, dark clouds covered the sky, the moon vanished,
and a great roll of thunder rumbled and a flash of

lightning streaked the sky. The trees bent double under the wind, and the rain came down in torrents. All rushed in and shut themselves indoors, but she would not move, and in the lightning she saw a huge figure of frightening dimensions and terrifying aspect, too terrible for any human to behold. And yet, she did not blink her eyes, but smiled a welcome, and implored the goddess to exchange the *karva* with her. The goddess roared and told her that as she had not been able to abide by the laws of the fast, it was not correct to ask for such a boon.

Now, the girl told the goddess about the trick that her loving brothers had played on her. Since the goddess was Parvati, she could not retain her awful aspect for long and started to shed tears of love for this little girl. She assumed the shape of a very beautiful woman, and the terrible storm, rain and thunder stopped. The moon came out in all its beauty, and there, alone in the courtyard, the goddess brought her *karva* towards that of the little girl, and said: 'Take O *suhagan* this *karva*, give me O *suhagan* your *karva*', just once, and the body, which was lying still on the girl's lap, came alive and the young husband rubbed his eyes and looked at his wife. It was a wonderful sight of happiness. The bride then took her *karva* and exchanged it seven times with Gaur Mata, who herself looked very pleased. There was an aura around them and thus rose the husband after seven years. Soon Gaur Mata left, and the young couple entered the house. There was no mark or strain of the seven years on her or her husband, and they looked radiant and full of life and vigour. Thus was rewarded the young bride's perseverance and faith. May everyone be so blessed!

At the end of the story, when Gaur Mata exchanges her *karva* with the young bride, each woman doing the *puja* exchanges her *karva* with the lady next to her, seven times, saying: 'Take O *suhagan* my *karva*', with a *karva* in her two hands slightly raised, along with the *thaali* on top carrying all the goodies, and the other woman says: 'Give O *suhagan* your *karva*', bringing the *karva* towards herself. Everyone present takes a partner and does the same. Then these partners do likewise, but with the roles reversed. Now one by one, each woman does the *baya manasna*, individually, by taking a little rice in the cup of the left hand and adding a little water to it, then taking the edge of the *pallu* in the right hand, the index finger is kept dipped in the cup of the left hand, while someone chants the relevant couplet. Then both hands are taken round the *karva* once and then the water is poured on the side of the *karva*, the chanting being done by an elder lady. The whole process is repeated a second time without the chant.

The chant is as follows: '*Addey-addey Krishna pakshe var* (whatsoever day it is) *Tith Karva Chouth* (name of the member) *manse hain apne suhag ke liye yeh karva, mattri, halwa, sari, nagdi, aur* (name any other item on the *thaali*), *apne suhag ke liye rani ka sa raj dena, Gaur ka sa suhag, dena Shri Krishna nimant.*'

After getting up, one must touch the feet of all the elders and take their blessings. Each woman gives her *baya* to an elder member of the family.

The *puja* now ends and one of the women takes the *puja thaali* with a lighted *diya* (lamp) and a small utensil of water (hopefully the moon has been sighted by now). One by one they perform *pujan* of the moon. Each woman offers water to the moon by holding the lamp in the left hand and with the right hand pours the water on the ground seven times, also throwing seven pieces of freshly broken *puas*. She herself chants: '*Char peher ka deevla, char peher ki raat, bale chandrama arak doon, Karva Chouth ki raat.*'

This chant is repeated seven times by each one. The woman does not touch the feet of either of her parents or people from her own family (as opposed to her husband's family), if she is doing the *puja* in her mother's house, since she is regarded as '*devi roop*' in her own household.

Those who have kept the fast break a *pua* into ten pieces (each person individually) and each piece is eaten one by one with a little water drunk in between. This is done in total silence.

Now the family dinner is served. Festive items cooked for the occasion are placed on the table, like *puri*, *dahi-vada*, with four vegetables, *sounth ki pakori* (this is made by soaking *sounth* in water and making a thin liquid more or less drinkable, mixed with sugar, salt and red chilli powder, all to one's own taste, and adding small round *pakoris* of *besan* to this mixture). This dish tastes very good and is also very good for digestion. Rice and *dal* are not cooked on the days of any fast. The food is made without any onion or garlic. Thus, the great fast of Karva Chouth comes to an end.

24

Diwali

DIWALI MARKS ONE OF THE BIGGEST AND GRANDEST celebrations in India. Diwali is also known as the 'festival of lights.' On this day, Lord Ram (the incarnation of Lord Vishnu in the Treta Yug) returned to his capital Ayodhya after the exile of fourteen years thrust upon him by his stepmother Kaikeyi in jealousy, because Ram would become the king and not her own son Bharat. Thousands of years have passed, and yet so ideal is the kingdom of Ram (Ram Rajya) that it is remembered to this day.

Diwali comes exactly 20 days after Dussehra on Amavas (new moon), during the dark fortnight of Kartik some time in October or November. The exact date is taken from the Hindu calendar and since that calculation is

208

different from the European calendar, we cannot give the exact date according to the Western system.

As we have already mentioned (under Dussehra) the evil-doer Ravan has been eliminated – along with most of his *rakshasas* – by Lord Ram and his brother Lakshman, and their army of monkeys. Sita has been returned to her husband Ram, and they now make their way to Ayodhya in triumph and glory. Kaikeyi, meanwhile, has done enough penance for the misery caused to the family and the kingdom. Bharat had refused to sit on the throne, and has kept vigil as a regent, and had told Ram that if he did not return on the last day of the fourteen years' exile, he would immolate himself. Consequently, to commemorate the return of Ram, Sita and Lakshman to Ayodhya people celebrate Diwali with the bursting of crackers and by lighting up their houses with earthen *diyas* or other lamps in the grandest style, year after year.

The thirteenth day of the dark fortnight, i.e., two days before Diwali is known as Dhan Teras. On this day a new utensil is bought for the house. The house has to be cleaned, washed and whitewashed. On this day, the children are taken out to buy crackers, candles, earthen *diyas* and a *hatri* (a small house-like structure made of mud, where a small idol of Lakshmiji sits in the middle). A pair of earthen Lakshmiji and Ganeshji are a must for Diwali *pujan*. (Ganeshji is to be worshipped in all *pujas* before any other god or goddess.) Lakshmiji, the goddess of wealth, is supposed to visit everyone during Diwali; therefore she must also be fussed over. Earthen *katoris* known as *kulris* and *chaugaras*, lots of *kheel* (puffed rice), toys made out of candy (known as *khand ke khilone*), *batashas,* etc., are required for the *puja*. The markets are extremely well decorated and full of items which one can buy for the home.

Special foods like *papri* and *deevlas* are made at home. The day prior to Diwali is known as Chhoti Diwali.

On that day Hanuman (Pavanputra or son of the God of Wind), the great *bhakt* (worshipper) of Lord Ram, had come flying to Ayodhya to inform the family and the kingdom that Ram, Sita and Lakshman, were coming back the following day so that arrangements to welcome them could be made (of course in a great hurry). Today, we have more time at our disposal and so we start the celebrations much earlier. On Chhoti Diwali, *mithai* is displayed by gaily decorated and well-lit shops, and they do very brisk business. Many business houses and individuals distribute *mithai* to their associates, families and friends. A lot of visiting is done on this day. The business community begins its new year from this day.

One word of caution – one must remain within a budget. Almost everything bought during Diwali time is of little use later on, except utensils, and a few other durables, so please do the buying by your own standards and not the neighbours'! One should remember that 21 or 51 *diyas* are bought (although candles are much in use these days). This is just to keep the old tradition alive, and maintain a continuity from time immemorial right up to this very day. In case one is in another country, where one cannot get *diyas*, then one just has to make do with candles. One big *diya* is definitely required for the centre and can be made with *atta* dough. The *diyas* are filled with oil (ordinary mustard oil) and wicks are made from old cottonwool. Please soak the *diyas* in water for a couple of hours and dry them before use, as they will soak up the oil very fast if used absolutely new.

Now let us get to the ceremonial side of Diwali, so as to make it an attractive occasion for the family. Even if no one is invited, it is a busy day in itself. The *puja* starts on Chhoti Diwali itself, when the place of worship is decorated with a small *chowk* made with wet *kharia matti*. Most Indians know how to decorate the floor with colours, but the quickest one is with *kharia matti*. Flowers and leaves can be the motifs of the floor decorations; or else geometrical designs can be made. A *chowki* or a *patta* should also be decorated and placed against the wall of the place of worship to seat the gods, namely, Ganeshji and Lakshmiji along with (idols or pictures of) Ram, Sita, Lakshman, and Hanuman. Empty *diyas* or unlit candles are decorated before the *puja* and everyone then does the *pujan*.

On the main Diwali day, a morning bath is very essential. In South India to bathe before sunrise, after a good oil massage, is considered very auspicious. A bath in starlight, before sunrise, is accepted as a bath in the holy Ganga. In North India, gambling is freely allowed during the festival; usually card games are played. The children are also given money to play and join in the fun. They are even allowed to gamble in front of their parents so that they don't do it in secret. They then understand that there is a time and place even for gambling, but it must have certain limitations. These children seldom grow up to be gamblers. Gambling goes on for about a week or two, in one house or the other, and then it stops until the next Diwali.

Now let us move on to the ceremony itself. During my grandmother's time, we always used to get the whitewashing of the house done before Diwali, specially the place where the *puja* was to be performed. Usually, a more open place than the *puja* room (a covered verandah is ideal) is used for the *puja*. A Madhubani type of painting was made, depicting several episodes of Lord Ram, Sita, Lakshman, Hanuman (and even Krishna *avtar* with its Gopis and *raas leelas*), and the other gods. These depictions were all confined to a square or oblong limited space. A border of flowers was used to frame the painting. The painting was made by attaching cottonwool to small sticks and taking ordinary colours mixed with water in small *katoris*. The women and children all got together and filled the colours into the forms already made by the artist of the family. The drawings of the faces of the gods, Gopis and the animals were always of the side view. This kept everyone busy for a week or two preceding Diwali. At the centre of the painting, Lakshmiji was depicted in the Madhubani style, formed by joining a number of dots together in a manner that a face appeared with a *chunni* on top of it. The dots were all prearranged. Of course, one can draw Lakshmiji or stick a picture of her with glue. Thus, one realises how art was encouraged and taught to the children in this way, when the wall became the canvas and everyone was filling in the colours, producing a beautiful picture. (Such togetherness is rare to find these days.) The joining of dots to form a picture is the basic way of teaching a child to draw.

During the actual Diwali day, people still drop in with sweets and crackers and other presents, and some visit elders of the family and the community out of respect. On this day, business people also give presents to those working for them. The businessmen are very particular about doing Lakshmi *puja* in their shops or offices. There is no fasting on Diwali. The daughters-in-law and girls of the house are given new *saris* and jewellery. A new bride gets a heavier *sari* than the rest. This is not obligatory in North India, but very much so in South India.

Now, in the evening, before dark, the actual *pujan* is done. First the place of the *puja* is decorated with candles, *diyas* and the earthen *hatri*, which is placed in the centre. The pictures of several gods and goddesses – Lakshmi, Ganesh, Ram, Sita, Lakshman, and Hanuman – are placed on the *patta*. The *kulris* and *chaugaras* are filled with *kheel* topped with a toy made out of candy; *papris* and *deevlas* are also kept on top. *Mithai* and fruit are placed on the side of the *puja patta* in a *thaal*. The new utensil, bought for this purpose, is filled with *kheel* and kept on the side. Of course, everyone is dressed very well, in colourful and shining clothes, so that they shimmer in the *diya* or candle-light. The married girls (*suhagans*) can wear their *chunri* with its *gota* and *kinari*, if they so desire.

But a *chonp* (golden *bindi*) is a must on the forehead for the *suhagans*. Now, everyone is ready for the *puja*, which is done first by putting the *teeka* on the gods and everyone present, and then worshipping the gods with water, *aipun*, *roli* and rice. Everyone now takes a little rice in one hand and the story related to Diwali is narrated, which goes as follows:

There was once a king, who loved his queen very very much. One day the king summoned the best jeweller in his kingdom, and asked him to make a magnificent necklace costing rupees nine hundred thousand (nine lakhs) for the queen. When it was made it was so beautiful that the queen wore it all the time and wherever she went. She looked so very beautiful with the *naulakha haar* (nine-lakh necklace) around her neck, that everyone stared at her.

Every morning she would go to the river to bathe with her ladies-in-waiting. She used to take off her jewellery and fancy clothes, and put them on the banks of the river. One day, she did the same and was happily playing and splashing in the river when a kite came flying over the place, and seeing a shining object, it swooped down and took the necklace away. (Kites love to take shining objects to their nests for their young ones to get excited about, and also to decorate their homes with glitter.) The queen came out of the river and found, to her dismay, that her necklace was missing, and she was distressed beyond measure, and no one could console her. She fretted so much that the king heard of it within a few minutes, and came to find out what had happened. He was also very very upset and announced, there and then, that whosoever found the *naulakha haar* would be given anything he or she desired. A man with a *dholak* (drum) went around making the announcement all over the kingdom, and everyone came to know of the great loss suffered by the queen and that the discovery of the

necklace would make the person who found it rich beyond
his or her wildest dreams. So, everyone did nothing but
look for the beautiful *haar* and talk about it at homes and
in marketplaces. The queen could not be consoled. She
gave up eating and drinking, and the king was also very
unhappy and kept inquiring of his servicemen every now
and then as to the progress made in the matter.

Now, there used to be a very old and poor woman,
who lived right outside the town, just where the forest
began. She used to make her livelihood by selling wood
and sticks for lighting fires, which would meet her
meagre daily needs. She had no one else to look after
her as her children were away and she had to do her
own household chores and shopping. In any case, she
could not buy much as she was so poor. As Diwali was
approaching, she was cleaning her hut, which was very
dark and dingy because it was near the forest. She saw
a *patragho* (a large lizard-like animal found in the forest)
in a dark corner of her hut. She killed it, and threw it on
her thatched roof. At this very moment, the kite with
the *naulakha haar* was flying past and its eyes fell on
the dead animal. The kite thought that food was better
than the glittering object that it was carrying. So, it
dropped the *haar* on the thatched roof and made off with
the dead *patragho*. The old woman heard the noise and
on seeing something shining on the roof brought it down
and found, to her amazement, the most beautiful *haar*
that one could imagine. She knew at once that it must
belong to the queen. Soon she heard about the king's
announcement, and the misery in the palace. So she went
and asked for an audience with the king. The king was
surprised, but he was a good and kind person and, so,
she was brought before him. She asked him whether he
would stand by what he had promised through his
announcement. The king looked hopeful and solemnly
declared that he would do as he had promised.

'I have it here,' the old woman said, and took out the *haar* from her torn jute bag, much to the amazement of all the courtiers, who looked startled and wondered what the old woman would ask for. They, as well as the king, expected her to ask for half the kingdom, or any amount of wealth; but she did not. Do you know what she asked for? 'Sire, please order everyone, that on Diwali day no one will light up their houses except me, and the palace shall also be dark.' The king was stunned, but heaved a sigh of relief at the strange request, and he granted it at once. He was afraid that she might change her mind. This was hardly a thing to think twice about. Everyone talked at length about this odd request – in the marketplaces, in the houses, and in the palace. Wise men shook their heads perplexed, not understanding what it would fetch the old woman.

Diwali was near, and soon the day dawned. People were told that not a single light should be seen, or else they would be punished with death – even the king's palace stood in total darkness as the sun went down. There was pitch darkness everywhere, and only one *diya* twinkled in the old woman's house, far away in a corner of the landscape. The old woman just did what she was used to doing all her life during Diwali, and lit only one *diya*, being too poor to afford any more.

At the stroke of midnight, Lakshmiji came down from the heavens in her glittering clothes, so that they would shine all the more in the beautiful lights of the houses and palaces which she would visit. She loved a lot of light and gaiety and so she visited those houses which were bright and shining. Today, she was perplexed for she could hardly move without stumbling against a pillar or post, and nearly fell at several places. She was so miserable, that she scanned the horizon for some light somewhere, and then she saw the little glimmer from the old woman's hut. She made a dash for it, because by now she was completely desperate.

Inside her hut, the old woman had bolted the door and had sat down to do her *puja* with her old broken earthen utensils. Soon she saw a very bewildered and desperate looking tiny little man, who came running to her side in great agitation, shouting: 'Let me out, let me out, old woman. I cannot stand this light, I must get out at once. I am used to darkness and dinginess and dampness. I could stay but for this light.'

The old woman gave him one look and asked, 'Who are you, you funny looking tiny man?'

'I am "Diladdar" ' (absolute down and out one), companion of the very poor, replied the old man. The old woman spoke to him thus: 'You cannot leave me, Diladdar, you have been my constant companion year after year, and I cannot let you go. I will not allow you to go.'

'O woman, have pity on me, I will die in this illuminated house, I am one who can only live in darkness and dirt, and not in light and cleanliness. There is lovely darkness all over the town tonight. Please, please, open the door.'

Outside Lakshmiji was standing at the door and pleading in her lovely soft voice: 'Sweet lady, I am distressed, please show me the light and let me in – yours is the only house in which I can feel comfortable and happy. I cannot see the other houses. I cannot even see my own feet, and I am frightened. Please, please, let me in.' The old woman replied: 'No, no, I will not let you in; you have never bothered about me before, why should I take pity on you?' But Lakshmiji pleaded with her. So the old woman asked her: 'If I let you in, will you promise that you will never leave and will always stay in my house? If you promise me that I will let you in.' Lakshmiji replied: 'Yes, yes, I promise, I will not leave your house ever.'

At the same time Diladdar was shouting himself hoarse to be let out. The old woman told him : 'You promise that you will never come anywhere near my house again, only then will I let you out.' 'I promise, I promise,' cried Diladdar.

Quickly, the old woman opened the door and immediately Lakshmiji entered. Seeing her, Diladdar became more frightened and he just fled into the darkness.

Very soon, the old woman summoned back all her children, who had gone away to other towns in search of food and money, to come and live with her, and they returned and everyone lived happily ever after.

After the story is finished, all members shower the puffed rice that they have been holding in their hands on Lakshmiji and Ganeshji, saying loudly: 'Get out *Diladdar*, Lakshmiji has come' (*Nikal Diladdar Lakshmi aayee*), repeating this thrice.

The lady of the house then takes one *chaugara*, places the *prasad* on top of it, and gives it to each member present. This can be done in two instalments because fruit and *mithai* have also to be given as *prasad* and it is difficult to give everything all at once. Each member then takes a little puffed rice from the *prasad* and puts it inside the *hatri*, in which a silver rupee has already been put. This *hatri* symbolises the home, and the silver coin, the wealth of the house being saved inside it. India, being an agricultural country basically, everyone used to put their share of the produce into the house – so the symbolic gesture of putting in the puffed rice (*kheel*).

The *diyas* from the *puja* are then taken to light the *diyas* or candles already placed around the house and on top of it. These *diyas* are lit only after the *puja*. The first *diya* is placed where one throws the garbage; the belief being that there is prosperity in a house where there is a lot of garbage. *Pujan* should be started at dusk, as the *diyas* or candles are lit afer the *puja*. Fireworks are brought out and the children join in the fun and frolic with all the bang-bang and light from *phuljharis* (flowerpots) and other crackers. It is always nice to distribute the fireworks to the servants and their children, so that there is universal enjoyment. Then start the feast and card games, which are the 'order of the night'. One can carry on for as long as one likes. In some cases, sons-in-law of the house are given some money as a token, along with a peg of whisky. The non-drinkers can just take the money. This is the custom of giving the *pyala*.

Thus, Diwali is celebrated as one of the biggest and grandest festivals of India.

We now present the recipe for a delicious dish prepared during Diwali.

MANDHI

Ingredients and other items	
Karahi	1
Thaali or *parat*	1
Water	¾ cup
Sugar	1 cup
Suji	150 gm (1½ cups)
Maida	250 gm + 50 gm if required for dipping the *rotis*
Ghee or cooking oil	6 dessertspoons for deep frying

Method

Warm the water in a vessel. Then, take it off the heat and mix the sugar with the water. Put it aside. Now sieve the *maida* and *suji* and mix; next add 6 dessertspoons of melted *ghee* or oil and knead into the breadcrumb stage. Sieve the sugar and water through a fine sieve. Mix the sugar and water mixture slowly with the breadcrumb-stage dough and further knead well into a soft dough. Roll out individual flat balls as for *puri*; if they stick, use a little dry *maida*. The thickness should be 1/4" or even a little more.

Pour the *ghee* or oil for deep frying into a *karahi* and let it become very hot; reduce the fire to slow heat and start frying, adjusting the fire. Fry to dark brown, two *mandhis* at a time. The ingredients given here will yield about 14 *mandhis*.

Appendix 1

Bhajans

OM JAI JAGDISH HARE

Om Jai Jagdish Hare
  Swami Jai Jagdish Hare
Bhakt jannu ke sankat (2)
  Shan mein door kare
Om Jai Jagdish Hare

Joe dhyave phal paave
  Thukh bin se munka
Swami thukh bin se munka
  Sukh sampati ghar ave
Kast mite tan ka
  Om Jai Jagdish Hare

Maat pita tum mere
   Sharan gahun mein kiski
Tum bin aur na thuja (2)
   Aas karun mein jiski
Om Jai Jagdish Hare

Tum puran parmatma
   Tum antaryaami, Swami tum antaryaami
Paar Brahma Parmeshwar (2)
   Tum sab ke Swami
Om Jai Jagdish Hare

Tum karuna ke sagar
   Tum palan karta, Swami tum palan karta
Mein murakh khalkami (2)
   Kripa karo bharta
Om Jai Jagdish Hare

Tum ho ek agoochar
   Sub ke pranpati, Swami sab ke pranpati
Kis vid miloon theya mein (2)
   Tum ko mein kumti
Om Jai Jagdish Hare

Dheen Bandhu thuk harta
   Thakur tum mere, Swami thakur tum mere
Apne haath oothao (2)
   Dwar pari (para) tere
Om Jai Jagdish Hare

Vishya vikar Mitavo
   Paap haro deva, Swami pap haro deva
Shradha bhakti baravo (2)
   Santan ki seva
Om Jai Jagdish Hare

TVAMEVA MATA

Tvmeva mata cha pita Tvmeva
   Tvmeva bandhu cha sakha Tvmeva
Tvmeva vidya dravinum Tvmeva
   Tvmeva sarvam mum dev deva

Hey dev pranam dev
   Pranam barum har hey
Phir pranaam barum har hey

HANUMAN CHAALISA

Sri Guru Charan Saroj ji
   Nij manu mukuru sudhaar
Baranhu Raghubar Vimal Jasu
   Jo thayaku phal chaari
Buddhi heen tanu jaanke
   Sumeru pawan kumar
Bal buddhi vidya dehu mohi
   Harhu kalesh bekaar

Chopaee

Jai Hanuman gyan gun sagar
    Jai kapis tehu lok ujaagar
Ram doot atulit bal daamaa
    Anjani putr pawan sut naama
Mahaveer vikram bajrangi
    Kumiti niwaar sumiti ke sangi
Kanchan varan viraj subesa
    Kanan kundal kunchit keesa
Haath brij aur dwaja viraje
    Kaandhe mooch janau saaje
Shankar suven kesari nandan
    Tej pratap maha jag bandan
Vidyavaan guni ati chatur
    Ram kaj karibe ko aatur
Prabhu charitra sunebe ko rasiya
    Ram lakhun sita mun basiya
Suksham roop dhari siyahi theekaawa
    Vikat roop dhari lunk jarawa
Bhim rup dhari asur sanhaare
    Ram Chandra ke kaj sawaare
Laaye sanjeevan Lakhan jeeyaye
    Sri Raghubir harshi ur laye
Raghupati kineeh bahut baraahi
    Tum mum priya Bharat sum bhai
Sahas badan tumhro jas gaaven
    Us kahin sripati kanth laganvan
Sankathik Brahmathik munisaa
    Narad saarad sahit asisaa
Jum Kuber Thigpal jahan te
    Kavi kobith kahi sakae kahan te
Tum upkaar Sugrivhi kinha
    Ram milaaye raj pad deenha
Tumhroo mantr Vibhishan maana
    Lankeshwar bhaye sub jag jana

Jug sahastr jo jun per bhanu
   Lilyo thahi madhur phal jaanun
Prabhu mudrika meli mukh naahi
   Jalthe laandi gaye achraj nahin
Dhurgam kaaj jagat ke jate
   Sugam anugrah tumhre tate
Ram dulare tum rakhware
   Hovt na agya binu paasaare
Sub sukh lahye tumhari sarna
   Tum rakshak kahu ko darna
Apan teaj sumharo aape
   Teeunoh lok haank te kaanpen
Bhut pishach nikat nahi aave
   Mahavir jab naam sunaave
Naasee roog hare sab pira
   Japat niranter Hanumat bira
Sankat se Hanuman churaven
   Mun krm vachan theyhan jo laaven
Sab par Ram thapasvi raja
   Teen ke kaaj sakal tum saaja
Aur manorath jo koye laway
   Soye amit jeevan phal pave
Charoo jug pratap tumhara
   Hay prasidh jagat ujiyara
Sadhu sant ke tum rakhware
   Asur nikandan Ram dhulare
Asht siddhi nau nidhi ke thaata
   Us bur deen Janaki mata
Ram rasayun tumreh paasa
   Sada raho Raghupati ke daasa
Tumhre bhajan Ram ko paave
   Janam janak ke dukh bisrave
Ant kaal Rahgubar pur jaee
   Jahan janam hari bhagat kahaaee
Aur devta chit na dhariya

Hanumat se sab sukh kare
Sankat kate mite sub peera
   Jo sumre Hanumant balbira
Jai jai jai Hanuman gosaain
   Kripa karehu guru dev ki naaee
Jo sut baar paadh kar koee
   Chute bandi maha sukh hoee
Jo yeh padhe Hanuman Chalisa
   Hoove sidh saakhi Gaurisa
Tulsidas sada Hari Chera
   Keeje Nath Hridye muhun daara
Doha

Pawan tanye sankat haran
   Mangal murti roop
Ram Lakhan Sita sahit
   Hyrdiya basahu sur bhoop

Translation of Hanuman Chalisa

Tulsi Das says :
With the dust of Guru's lotus feet
   I first clean the mirror of my heart and
Then I will tell of the great glory
   of Shri Ram,
The son of the dynasty of Raghuwar,
   the one who gave the four great fruits
      of this life.
I am an ignorant person, O Hanuman,
   I beseech you, son of Pawan
to grant me strength, wisdom, knowledge
   and take away all my troubles and miseries
May victory be yours, Hanuman – the ocean
   of knowledge,

Victory to you who is known
in all the three worlds;
  you are the enovy of Ram,
and you have unfathomable strength.
  You are the son of Anjani
and well known as the heir of Pawan.
Mahaveer, you are so strong and full of power,
  you are strong as lightning,
you are the companion of wisdom and
    Your presence dispels darkness and dark
        thoughts.
You are golden in colour, O Hanuman,
    Your ears have earrings and your hair is curly
which makes you look so beautiful.
    In your hand you have the mace of lightning,
in the other hand you have a flag.
    The sacred thread made of munj *grass*
is on your shoulder.
You are the reincarnation of Shiva
    and the son of Kesari.
The light that you emit is glorious
    and is the talk of the whole world.
Listening to the glories of Lord Ram is ever
        dear to your ears
    and you are ever ready to serve Lord Ram.
Ram, Lakshman and Sita dwell
    in your heart forever.
You showed your very small size to Sita
    but you changed into a huge dreadful form
when you burnt the city of Lanka.
    You took the form of Bhim
when you killed all the Rakshas *(demons)*
        and completed the task which Ram gave you.
Bringing the Sanjivini you revived Lakshman
        and Sri Ram embraced you with great joy;

Ram had the highest praise for you
    He said he loved you as he
loved his dear brother Bharat.
    Narayan, the Lord of Lakshmi (in the
      guise of Ram)
hugged you to his heart and said that
      Sheshnaga
(the five-hooded serpent on which Narayan rests)
    always sings your praises.
Brahma, and the sons of Brahma, Narad
    and all the other saints and gods sing your
      praise
Even Yama, Kuber and Digpal
    are not tired of singing of your glory,
You obliged Sugriva and won for him his kingdom
    with the blessing of Ram.
Vibhishan listened to your advice
    and the whole world knows that
he became the king of Lanka.
    Once you just swallowed the sun
which is very very far away
    thinking it to be a lovely sweet fruit.
You held in your mouth the ring
    Lord Ram gave to you
and no one wondered when you
    leapt across the mighty ocean.
Very difficult tasks
    you have overcome in this world.
The gates to the abode of Ram
    are guarded by you
and no one can enter without
    your permission.
Under your care one can enjoy all happiness,
    no one need fear once he is under your
      protection.

You are the only one who can control
your own might.
All the three worlds tremble when you roar.
No evil spirits can trouble or be anywhere
near your devotee
when they hear the name of you, O Mahaveer
one who chants your name all the time
is cured of all disease, sickness and pain.
You keep those that have you
in their heart, action, word and thought
from all the troubles of the world.
Ram, the great ascetic, is the king of all
and yet you helped him fulfil his tasks
Those that came to you for help
always find great success fulfilment in life
All through the four Yugs your greatness
is acknowledged
and the radiance of your glory
spreads through the entire Universe.
You look after all the saints and sadhus
and Ram loves you for it.
Janaki (Sita) has blessed you
so that you can bestow
The eight Siddhis and nine Nidhis
on anyone you so desire
You have the great Ram always with you,
Be always his servant and helper.
One can reach Ram singing your hymns
and lose all the pain of all previous lives
After leaving this world your devotee will
go to
Raghopur (the abode of Ram)
and be known for all times
as the servant of Hari.

Those who do not put their heart in other Gods
      but wholeheartedly pray to you O Hanuman,
will get every joy in life and after.
      From the path of those that pray to you
will be removed O Hanuman all the obstacles
      and pain.
Victory, Victory, Victory to Hanuman, the
      compassionate,
be my great teacher.
He who repeats this lesson seven times
      will be free from all bondage
and he will be the happiest of
      human beings.
He who reads this Hanuman Chaalisa
      will attain Supreme knowledge
like mother Gauri (the wife of Lord Shiva)

I – Tulsi Das – am ever a devotee of thee
Lord Hari
Please reside in my heart forever.

Doha

O the son of Pavan and the embodiment of
      blessings
dwell in my heart along with
Ram, Lakshman and Sita.

Appendix 2

The Calculation of Time

THE EARTH REVOLVES ROUND THE SUN IN 365 1/4 DAYS. THE English calendar, which is in use globally, accounts for 365 days which are divided into 12 months in a year, but to coincide precisely with the cycle of the earth, one day is added every fourth year to February. This year then becomes 'the leap year' and the calculations stand corrected.

In the Hindu method of calculations, although the 365 1/4 days of the revolution of the earth round the sun are recognised, the calculations are done according to the revolution of the moon round the earth, which falls short by approximately 7 days during one year, *vis-à-vis* calculations done according to the solar calendar. The latter calculations are done in India, but are not used for determining the months or the festivals except for Lohri, Makar Sankranti and Baisakhi. The *panchang* based on the lunar calendar, which also has 12 months in a year, comes level with the 'Ayanas' or sun calculation, by adding a month (known as Loonth or Purshottam Maas) after every three years. This month is added in the middle of the year. No festivals are celebrated in this month, but are adjusted earlier or later as the case may be. The calculations of the *panchang* are complicated as the days in each month are not the same and can vary from 27.5 to 29.5, thereby sometimes causing the Tith to overlap the next day or sometimes a Tith vanishes altogether. The calculation is best left to the learned pandits who specialise in this field and issue the *panchang* annually (in booklet form) with all festivals given against the English calendar dates. The *panchang* provides several pieces of other information also, such as the movements of the stars and the planets.

CALCULATION OF TIME

The Hindus had, however, calculated the age of the world and the 'Universe'. But the whole 'Divine Process' is a cycle and creation manifests itself again and again and the cycle never ends. There is a spell of non-existence in between but the 'Creator' is always there.

The ages of the three worlds and the universe, the different types of *pralay* (annihilation of creation) and its different aspects – which have been calculated in accordance with year of Brahma – and the years of the gods and the years of mortals are explained below. The count of a year as regards Brahma is distinct from the count of the year of the gods.

Brahma came out in a lotus from the navel of the ever-present aspect of the Supreme, Narayan. Brahma has a definite age and dissolves into Vishnu (Narayan) with time to appear again and again and create a new

universe (Brahmand). Brahma has an age of 100 years
of God which is equivalent to about 51,10,40,00,00,00,000
years of man, at the end of which the entire creation is
destroyed; this is known as *maha pralay.*

The *yugs* are the first count in time. The *yugs* have
different attributes and different durations. They have
an in-between period known as *sandhya* (twilight) which
is followed by another period, equal to the same length
called *sandhyansh.*

The *yugs* are four in number, and their duration is
computed by the years of gods as well as of man.

Each year of God = 360 years of man

		God years	Man years
1)	Kritayug (Satya Yuga)	4000	
	Sandhya	400	
	Sandhyansh	400	
		4800 x 360	= 17,28,000
2)	Treta Yug	3000	
	Sandhya	300	
	Sandhyansh	300	
		3600 x 360	= 12,96,000
3)	Duapar Yug	2000	
	Sandhya	200	
	Sandhyansh	200	
		2400 x 360	= 8,64,000
4)	Kal Yug	1000	
	Sandhya	100	
	Sandhyansh	100	
		1200 x 360	= 4,32,000 + 43,20,000 yrs of man

Total = 4800 + 3600 + 2400 + 1200 = 12,000 years
                                     of God
                                   = 43,20,000 years
                                     of man
                                   = 1 Maha Yug

Maha Yug

According to the Indian calculation of time, 43,20,000 man years = 1 cycle of 4 *yugs* or one cosmic cycle is 12,000 years of the Gods. It has now been confirmed that a duration of a Maha Yug has been made on particular movements of the earth, i.e., the daily rotation and the annual revolution round the sun at the speed of 66,000 miles per hour in 3,65,246 days.

The basis for calculating each Maha Yug is the following: all the planets occupied the same position at the commencement of each Maha Yug; therefore, this period was fixed by arriving at the lowest common factor of the number of days taken by each planet to make one complete revolution around the zodiac as well as the motion of the earth. This then could be seen to be 43,20,000 years (approx.)

Kalpa

Kalpa is a period of time equivalent to a day of Brahma, or one thousand *yugs* (43,20,00,000 years of a mortal). A month of Brahma is said to contain thirty such *kalpas*. According to the *Mahabharata*, twelve months of Brahma constitute his year, and one hundred such years his lifetime; fifty years of Brahma are supposed to have elapsed, and we are now in the Svetavaraha Kalpa of the fifty-first year. At the end of a *kalpa* the world is annihilated.

Counts of time of Brahma

1000 times the Maha Yug	= 1 Kalpa	= 4320,000,000 years of man
43,20,000 x 1000	= 14 Manvantaras	= 1 day of Brahma
1 day of Brahma = 1 Kalpa	= 4 Yugs x 1000	= 43,20,000000 years of man

1 night of Brahma the same as the day	= 4 Yugs x 1000	= 4320,000000
1 night and 1 day		8640,000000
1 month is of 30 days	= 8640000000 x 30	= 259200,0000000 years of man

1 year of Brahma is of 12 months	= 2,59,20,00,00,000 x 12	= 31,10,40,00,00,00 years of man
100 years of Brahma	= 31,10,40,00,00,00 x 100	
		= 31,104,000,000,000 years of man

Manvantara

Manvantara is a period of age of a Manu (a seer who lays the rules and regulations for that particular *manvantara* according to the conditions and need of that particular time). The Manu changes at every *manvantara* and is nominated by the Almighty according to his merit and enlightenment. A *manvantara* comprises about 71 Maha Yugs which are held equivalent to 12,000 years of the gods or 43,20,000 human years, or 1/14 of a day of Brahma; each of these periods is presided once by its own special Manu. The seventh *manvantara* presided over by Manu Baivasvata is now going on; seven more are to come, making fourteen *manvantaras*, which together make up one day of Brahma, which is equal to one *kalpa*.

Manvantara = 4 Yugs x 71 = 43,20,000 x 71 =	30,67,20,000 years of man	

In between period
of 2 *manvantaras*   = 1 Sat Yug   =   17,28,000
years of man
Total of 14 *manvantaras* = 1 *Kalpa*   =   30,84,48,000
years

Time that has elapsed in the present *Kalpa*.

We are in the reign of the 7 Manu

6 *manvantaras*		=	1,84,03,20,000
7 in between periods	17,28,000 x 7	=	1,20,96,000
27 Maha Yugs	48,20,000 x 27	=	11,66,40,000
1 Sat Yug		=	17,28,000
1 Treta Yug		=	12,96,000
1 Duapar Yug		=	8,64,000
1 part of Kal Yug (Total duration 4,32,000)		=	5095
	Total	=	1,97,29,49,095

Total time for 1 *Kalpa*	=	4,32,00,00,000
Total time elapsed	=	1,97,29,49,095
Time left for 1st *Pralay*	=	2,34,70,50,905 years of man

(The above figures are approximate)

1 Million	=	7 digits
1 Billion	=	10 digits (1000 million = 1 trillion)
1 Trillion	=	13 digits

First *Pralay*

At the end of one day of Brahma the three words (known as *Bhur Bhua Swaha*) – *Swarg Lok, Mrityu Lok* and *Pathal Lok,* i.e., Heaven, the World and the nether regions (or hell) – come to an end. Brahma takes the three worlds (out of the seven which the Hindu believes to exist) unto Himself and then rests for the same amount of time (known as a *kalpa* or the night of Brahma). Then He creates the three worlds again and this goes on for one hundred years of the gods. Then comes the *Maha pralay*.

Second Pralay or Maha Pralay

The second *pralay* is known as Maha Pralaya. This comes after two Parardha or one hundred years of Brahma. In this *pralay*, Brahma is also absorbed in Narayan along with the entire creation. Everything goes within itself. The destruction is complete. Only Narayan remains, within whom the entire creation rests.

The above two *pralays* have a time limit.

Third Pralay

The third *pralay* is known as Aatyantika Pralay. This *pralay* cannot be imprisoned in time. It can come today or it might never come. Time can be adjourned by God at His will. This *pralay* comes if too much confusion reigns and God decides to cancel the 'game' and start again. He has kept the option open since He gives man the right of *karma* (action) and does not hold everything in his own hand; if man gets himself into terrible knots then Narayan has the option of dissolving the world, just as the speaker in Parliament does.

We hear of cult gurus who become god to their followers. They declare a precise date for a 'Pralay' without reasons. They happily declare that they follow the tenets of Hinduism in some form or another. They convince their followers that they have attained godhood and can control the world, yet no Hindu challenges them – they take shelter under this *pralay* for their predictions.

Fourth Pralay

The fourth *pralay* is Nitya Pralay. Every living and non-living being is destroyed after a certain time. Everything has an age in this creation of ours. Everything is born and dies and that death is *pralay* for that particular being.

The year 1996 (according to the European calendar) is 2051-2052 according to the Hindu calendar.

Appendix 3

The Ten Avtars of Vishnu

S. no.	Avtars	Time	Yug	Description
(1)	Matsya	1st quarter	Krita	Fish
(2)	Kurmi		Krita	Tortoise
(3)	Vara		Krita	Boar
(4)	Narsinghe (or Narsimha)		Krita	Half-human and half-lion
(5)	Vaman		Krita	Small man
(6)	Parshuram		Krita	The hot tempered *rishi*
(7)	Ram	2nd quarter	Treta	The perfect man

(contd.)

S. no.	Avtars	Time	Yug	Description
(8)	Balram	3rd quarter	Duapar	Krishna is not counted as an *avtar* as He is considered 'Purna Bhagwan'. His brother Balram is the *avtar*. Balram was Sheshnag; he also came as Lakshman in the Treta Yug.
(9)	Gautam Buddha	4th quarter	Kal (or *Kali*)	
(10)	Kalki			Still to come in Kal Yug – the present Yug. This Yug is made up of 4,32,000 years, beginning from the year 3102 B.C.

Appendix 4

A Bird's Eye View of the Festivals

Solar calendar has 31 days or 30 days, except February 28 days = 365 days; every four years Feb. has 29 days = 365 days.

Lunar calendar has 27.5 or 29.5 days each month (12 months).

Month/s according to English calendar	Name of the festival	*Paksh* (position)	Month/s according to Hindu calendar	Position of the moon
13 January	Lohri	Differs	Magh	Differs
13-14-15 January	Pongal	Differs	Magh	Differs
14 January	Makar Sankranti	Differs	Magh	Differs
January-February	Basant Panchami	Differs	Magh	Fifth day of waxing moon, Paksh fixed Panchmi
January 14 (approx.)	Magh Bihu	Sankranti	Magh	Differs

(contd.)

Month/s according to English calendar	Name of the festival	*Paksh* (position)	Month/s according to Hindu calendar	Position of the moon
January-February	Mahashivvratri	Thretash-Chouthas	Phagun	Thirteenth day of Triodash of the waxing moon of Phagun which falls somewhere in February-March
February-March	Holi	Purnima	Phagun	Full moon
		Parva (Krishna Paksh)	Phagun	First day of waning moon
February-March	Bhai Dooj	Dooj (Krishna Paksh)	Phagun	Second day of waning moon
March-April	Navratri	*Parva* (Sukul Paksh)	Chait	First day of waxing moon
13 April (calculated according to solar calendar)	Baisakhi	*Paksh* differs	Baisak	Position differs; it can be Chait or Baisaakh
March-April	Ram Navami	Navami (Sukul Paksh)	Baisak	9th day of the waxing moon
April 13-14-15	Bihag Bihu	Sankranti	Baisak	Differs
May-June	Nirjala Ekathshi		Jaath	

(contd.)

Month/s according to English calendar	Name of the festival	*Paksh* (position)	Month/s according to Hindu calendar	Position of the moon
June-July	Festival of Jagannathpuri			
May	1) Chandan Yatra	Akash Teej – 3rd day of waxing moon	Baisak	Fixed
June	2) Snan Yatra	Chouth – 4th day of waxing moon	Jaath	Fixed
July	3) Rath Yatra	Doadshi – 12th day of waxing moon	Assar	Fixed
June-July			Ashaad	
July-August	Sindhara	Dooj (Sukul Paksh)	Sawan	Second day of waxing moon
July-August	Teej	Teej (Sukul Paksh)	Sawan	Third day of waxing moon
July-August	Raksha Bandhan	Purnima	Sawan (Sukul Paksh)	Full moon
August-September	Janam Ashtami	Ashtami	Bhadon (Krishna Paksh)	Eighth day of the waxing moon

(contd.)

Month/s according to English calendar	Name of the festival	*Paksh* (position)	Month/s according to Hindu calendar	Position of the moon
August-September	Ganesh Chaturthi	Chouth – 4th day of waxing moon	Bhadon	Fixed
August-September	Onam	Doadshi – 12th day of waxing moon	Bhadon	Fixed
September-October	Durga Puja	*Parva* (Sukul Paksh)	Kwar	First day of waxing moon
September-October	Dussehra	Thesmi or Dashmi (Sukul Paksh) (10 days after Parva)	Kwar	Tenth day of waxing moon
October-November	Chhat	Parva to Chhat 1st to the 6th of waxing moon	Kartik	Fixed
October (about) 14th.	Kati Bihu	Sankranti	Kartik	Differs
October-November	Karva Chouth	Chouth (Krishna Paksh)	Kartik	Fourth day of waning moon
October-November	Diwali	Amavas (Krishna Paksh)	Kartik	New moon

(contd.)

Month/s according to English calendar	Name of the festival	Paksh (position)	Month/s according to Hindu calendar	Position of the moon
October-November	Bhai Dooj	Dooj (Sukul Paksh)	Kartik	Second day of waxing moon
November-December			Aghan (Mausir)	
December-January			Poush	

Glossary

Agarbatti: Joss stick; used extensively by Hindus and Buddhists. Widely available in shops, general stores and in the *puja* shops. Used for all festive occasions or even as a daily freshener for the house. It is a good insect repellent. The flame is put off after lighting the *agarbatti* and aromatic smoke is left to emerge from the joss stick. The burnt portion becomes ash and falls off; so be careful, and put the holder on a plate.

Angavastram: A cotton or silk shawl – white or off white with *zari pallu* hanging down to the waist or even a little lower for men and young boys.

Asur: Opposite of *devta*. Demon or with demon-like qualities.

Bandobust: Arrangement.

Baori: A well with steps leading right up to the water.

Ber: A large berry with a big stone inside. It grows on trees.

Bhagawat Purana: An ancient holy book of the Hindus dealing with a sort of history of mankind in India, with stories of gods, *devtas* and human beings. It contains references to all mythological and supposedly actual events pertaining to India.

Bindi: Same type as *chonp*, but diamond shaped, usually worn above the *chonp*. These are mostly green in colour with a red dot in the middle.

Brahmand: Universe or the entire cosmos.

Batasha: Sugar melted and set into fluffy white round drops the size of a paisa (penny). Available freely at shops that sell grocery.

Baya: Items that are given during *pujas* associated with *vrats* (fasts), such as eatables, clothes and cash sent by a mother for the daughter to be given to her mother-in-law on occasions like Karva Chouth, Sindhara and Teej.

Chaugara: A container made out of mud with four different compartments stuck together and held with a common holder about eight or nine square inches and about four inches high, available during Diwali. During weddings or big sit-down get-togethers, metal ones are also used which are much bigger and can carry four types of foods at one time, making it easier for servers.

Chawal: Plain boiled rice.

Chirva: Flattened boiled and dried rice, available in the market. Can be fried or boiled with other things like vegetables or with *mumphali* (groundnut).

Chonp: A very tiny golden *bindi* with a green or red dot in the centre, worn on all festive occasions and *pujas*. It is sported by married women even before they wear the traditional *chunri*. *Chonp* is available, stuck on very small folded paper, about a dozen in each, and costs very little. Each *chonp* has to be stuck on the forehead by a gluey substance, also available with the *zari* and *gota* merchants.

Chowk: A place in the *puja* room in front of the gods and goddesses, or a place in the verandah or courtyard which has been swept and cleaned with a wet cloth. A decoration with wet *kharia matti* is laid out here with a piece of cottonwool. *Kharia matti* can be easily broken and soaked in a utensil, where it soon dissolves and can be brought to the required consistency. Also, with a piece of cottonwool, flowers and motifs are drawn out on the floor from memory, or from some design already laid out on paper. This will take some time to dry, at least an hour or so and should be done as early as possible so that it becomes dry at the time of *puja*. The length and breadth of the decoration are left to the will of the individual. This is known as *chowk* and should be made so that it can stand against a wall on one side.

Chunri: This is a Rajasthani or Gujarati style of tie-and-dye *sari* in red with green, yellow and white spots in the middle – all over the *sari*. The *sari* is richly decorated with very heavy *gota* and *kinari* all around. The *pallu* has a very broad band of *gota* with all sorts of *kinari* attached along the side to make it artistic and beautiful. *Kiran* (a *kinari* which has been split on one side) gives it the shimmering effect; it is attached on the cloth side of the border after all other things like *beegbaal* and *gota* have been included. This is a traditional auspicious *sari*, and is made for all the daughters, since they must wear it for all the *bayas* and other festive occasions.

It is a tradition guarded mostly because it takes one to one's roots. Those coming from Rajasthan or Gujarat, who do not now wear the tie-and-dye every day, and are settled in different parts of India, treasure it and guard the custom carefully. To follow a custom from generation to generation gives a sense of continuity, belonging and dignity to a household. These customs form what is known as the cultural heritage. The red of the *sari* may differ in shade, or the dots inside may not be there – or even one colour is obligatory – in different households. This is due to a 'tragedy' having taken place while a *suhagan* was wearing a *chunri* and she became a widow suddenly. An elder declares a change in the colour scheme, but it always must be a hue of red (maroon, magenta, mauvish red). A *chonp* is applied on the forehead before a *chunri* is worn. A *suhagan* is supposed to wear the *chunri* even in her funeral pyre – so she is supposed to carry it with her even when she travels outside her town, in case she dies.

Daitya: A non-Aryan — a person of tribal origin.

Dakshinayan: When the Sun moves into the Southern hemisphere on the 14th of July and the last day is 13th January (Lohri) when it leaves the tropics of Cancer towards the equator and towards the tropic of Capricorm.

Darshan: A glimpse or a full view of an object. Usually associated with a deity.

Devta: The shining ones. Beings between the gods and human, they live in *Swarg lok* (heaven).

Dhaam: Place.

Dharamshala: A place where rooms are available with or without food. Usually run by religious trusts or Hindu temples.

Dholak: An oblong drum of India with animal skin stretched on both sides of it. It can be hung around the neck and carried around from place to place while being played.

Doot: A person who attends on a man of position and authority. Lord Shiv has a number of them.

Duapar Yug: During this age mankind loses all sense of proportion, getting lost in the mire of earthly desires and frustrations. Wars between kith and kin occur. Vishnu descends in his *avtar* as Krishna to impart the lesson of the *Bhagavat Gita*. The period for this *yug* is 8,64,000 years of man.

Flowers for Puja: Marigold or red rose petals are generally used, but petals of other flowers can do as well.

Ganesh Puja: Ganesh is the deity worshipped first in every *puja* or festival or on occasions like engagements or marriages. Why this is so is because Lord Shiv had his second son born to him while he was away in the mountains doing *tap* (meditation). Parvati brought up this child alone not letting Shivji know of his existence. He had become a young lad, when one day Parvati was having a bath in a *bauri* (a well which has steps leading down to it). She told this second son, Ganesh, to guard the steps, so that no one came down while she was bathing. Somehow, at that very moment Shiv arrived from his arduous *tap* and made straight for the *bauri* on not finding Parvati at home. Ganesh stopped him at once, and told him that he couldn't enter as his mother was having a bath. This annoyed Shivji very much (it is well known that Shivji gets mad with anger at the drop of a hat, and can even destroy the world if he starts on his Thandav dance) and he took out his sword and cut off the young boy's head. Of course, he had no idea that it was his own son whom he had beheaded. Quickly, Parvatiji heard the commotion and ran up to see what had happened. She started to cry and wail and got very angry with Shivji, who looked bewildered and unhappy on seeing his wife in such a state. She soon told him about how she had kept the birth of their second son a secret from him, because he wasn't around when the child was born. Shivji looked really sorry and told her that he would put the head of the first living being that came that way, and her son would be whole again! It came to pass that an elephant was the first being that came that way. Shivji quickly cut its head off and put it on the shoulders of his son, and the son became alive. This made Parvatiji all the more angry and she told Shivji, that with that head no one will ever count Ganesh as a god, and keep the portion for him during all the *havans* and feasts. But Shivji is one of the Trimurti, the 'Supreme', and he declared then and there that all celebrations in all the *loks* must start with an invocation to Ganesh and only then could any other god or goddess be worshipped. That is why on any auspicious occasion, the first words written or the first invitation written or the first song sung is in the name of Sri Ganesh.

Gaur Mata: Gaur Mata is Goddess Parvati. She is the consort of Mahadev or Shiv. The picture or idol of Parvati can be used as Gaur Mata. In times gone by, a human figurine was made of cow-dung mixed with mud and worshipped as Gaur Mata.

Gazak: Sweet eatables – *Til* mixed with sugar or jaggery and cut into thin, long, broad strips; eaten mostly in winter.

Gita Govind: A well-known epic of Orissa, depicting the eternal love of Sri Krishna and Radha. It is sung at Jagannath temple and other temples of Orissa.

Gota: A shining border made from silver or gold thread. Now it is mostly symbolic. It is very light and thin.

Gugal (OR GOGUL) : This is a black *dhoop* arranged in the form of sticks and kept in boxes available in *puja* shops. It is sweet smelling and burns with a flame. The flame is put off and the smoke aromates the room. It turns to ash when finished and should be put on a stone, even if it is kept in a *katori*, since it burns to the end and may scorch the surface. It comes in various aromas.

Gur: Jaggery – much used in villages instead of sugar; made from sugarcane juice.

Haldi: Turmeric; condiment.

Halwa: A dish made from semolina and is a popular sweet preparation in India.

Immortals: Those that never die. There are seven according to mythology, Asvathama, Bali (Mahabali), Vyas, Hanuman, Kripacharya, Parshuram, Vibhishan and Markanday.

Kachori: A *puri* stuffed with *dal* (lentil) or with potatoes or condiments.

Kalawa: A string of threads coloured intermittently in red, yellow and white with no symmetry. These are available in bundles and have to be made in the form of balls just like wool. They are not strong at all and the strands can be broken with very little effort. Strands are thinned out to the required width, i.e., while tying on a utensil and tying on a person's wrist the thickness required would vary. *Kalawa* can also be used instead of a *rakhi*. The men wear it on their right wrist, whereas the women wear it on their left.

Kalpa: A time period of the Hindus equal to 1000 times the cycle of the four yugs = 43,20,000 x 1000 = 43,20,000,000 years of man.

Kalsa: A vessel made of any metal with a narrow opening and a round body; used for bringing or storing water.

Kal Yug: The worst of times when chaos reigns supreme; killing, hatred, jealousy and selfishness will be the rule. Still, it has a great advantage: whereas in the other three *yugs* one can attain *Moksha* only by several hundred years of *tap* and meditation, in Kal Yug repeating the name of *Narayan* (God) even for twenty-four hours will bring salvation and merger with the Supreme power. Kal Yug is also the smallest of the *yugs*; its duration is 4320,000 years of man. Kal Yug began on the midnight of the 17th-18th February 3102 B.C. according to the European calender.

Kamandal: A bowl made of wood, with a handle, carried by *sadhus*. Used for many purposes.

Kanya: A girl below the age of puberty (about 12 years of age). She is regarded as the symbol of Durga in a home, and is invited for the *kanya jeemna* during Durga *puja* when she is treated as the representative of the goddess.

Karhi-Chawal: A favourite for afternoon meals especially on Sundays. They are two separately cooked dishes. *Karhi*: Broth made with *besan* (gram flour), water and curd. Cooked with small fried balls of *besan* added to it.

Katori: Small round utensil to serve individual portions of liquid items of food.

Karpoor: Camphor. It is available in small squares in bundles. This can be bought from any *puja* shop. It should be stored in a dry place, or in an air-tight box as it absorbs water and becomes liquid. It is also highly inflammable. It is stiff and very brittle and can break off with very little friction and can become powdery. After the *arti* at the end of all *pujas*, a piece of *karpoor* is lighted and left in one of the flames of the *arti*. It burns, releasing an exotic aroma. It burns quickly and more than one piece can be used. If it becomes powdery then it can be put in a small *katori* and lighted separately from the *arti*. The pandits like to burn a lot of *karpoor* while performing *puja*.

Kharia Matti: A yellowish clay available in slabs of small dimensions. It is easily soluble in water and is used for decorating the *chowk*, in the *puja* room, the verandah or the courtyard on all auspicious occasions, or even otherwise.

Kheer: A kind of porridge made by boiling a small quantity of rice in milk with sugar. A favourite sweet dish of India.

Krishna Paksh (waning of the moon): Krishna Paksh or the dark fortnight, when the moon slowly loses its fullness and becomes thinner and thinner until it is not visible in the sky at all for one night – known as 'Amavas'. This cycle takes 15 days – starting from the day following Purnima. The Tiths are the same as in Sukul Paksh.

Laddoos: A round ball of any sweetmeat. Very popular in India.

Langoora: Boys up to the age of 12 are supposed to represent the young lads that serve Goddess Durga in her celestial home.

Lok: The habitable places created by God for different degrees of evolved souls. There are supposedly seven, but the Hindu is familiar with the three known as *Bhur, Bhua, Swaha* (Swarg Lok, Mrityu Lok and Pathal Lok)

Lungi: A cloth tied at the waist and falling right up to the heel, worn both by men and women in different parts of India.

Mahabharata: The first recorded war on Indian soil fought between the children of two brothers for the throne of Hastinapur (near Delhi) on the field of Kurukshetra, a few kilometers from Delhi. The war resulted in the greatest victory of right over wrong.

Manvantara: A period of time of this world ruled by a *manu* (a seer who lays the rules for a particular *manvantara*). There are 14 Manvantaras in a *kalpa* or 71 Maha Yugs = 43,20,000 x 71.

Matka: A round, baked earthen jar with a small (2" to 4") opening at the top.

Matkenas (Kullars): These are baked, round-shaped earthen containers freely available in India. They are easily disposable, like *pattals*. Everyone in India knows about them since curd, milk, water and even cooked vegetables are placed in them by shopkeepers and can be easily carried home. The smell from these *matkenas* is like the smell of the earth, after the first showers of rain during a monsoon.

Mela: A fair.

Moksha: A merging with the Supreme spirit which ends the cycle of births. A state of complete truth, tranquillity and peace.

Mrityu Lok: (Our world) Where one must die. In this world one can reach salvation or *moksha* through *karma* alone and for that one is born again and again. Only from Mrityu Lok can one earn *moksha*. The *devtas* also have to be born here and must leave heaven if they desire *moksha*.

Mumphali: Groundnut.

Murti: An idol.

Musak: A rat.

Nariyal: Coconut. This is a very auspicious fruit and is used for all *pujas* all over India. During launching of ships, a coconut is smashed against its hull. Even

on the commencement of any business or project,
coconuts are distributed as *prasad*; it is akin to
the opening of a champagne bottle as in the Western
culture. Coconut comes in three forms. The fresh
green form. This is not required for any *pujan*, but
is full of sweet water and is widely sold in states
where the coconut is grown. On beaches, it forms a
special attraction. The second type is the one which
has husk on the outer shell and the kernel retains
some water, with a soft white flesh already formed
inside. This is available in states where coconut is
not grown. The third type (called 'copra') is an
absolutely dry variety which has no husk outside,
but looks like a big wooden nut and the kernel is
solid and moves freely within the shell. This can
be kept in the house for as long as one wants and
as such can be even carried abroad. The dry kernel
is grated for making *prasad*, i.e., for Janam
Ashtami and for *kathas*; it is also used for cooking
in some parts of India.

Paan: Betel-nut. The leaf as well as the preparation is
called *paan*.

Paksh: Phases of the moon.

Panditji: A Brahmin. One who knows the scriptures and
is well versed in the Hindu rituals and can conduct
them according to the Vedas.

Pathal Lok: (Nether world) — A place of discomfort
where those who have strayed from the righteous
path go for a period of time. Pathal Lok is earned
by bad actions and those doomed to go there have
to be born again on this earth to redeem
themselves. Human beings have been given the
freedom of action (*karma*) but they must also reap
the results of what they have done. Both destiny
and freedom of action are mixed, like milk with
water, and one is born with both the *sanskar*

(tendencies left from former actions) and the freedom to act on one's own initiative.

Patta: A very low, oblong table or *chowki* which can be decorated for any *puja* with *kharia matti*. When it is dry, a little *aipun* is used to make what is known as a *'seep chowk'*. This resembles a peacock. This is made over the *kharia matti* decoration. If one does not know how to make a *seep chowk* a Swastik can be designed with *aipun*. When dry, this *patta* can be placed against a wall and the deity seated on it.

Pattal: This is a *thaali* (plate) type formation made from the dry leaves of saal or dhaak trees. One leaf is put in the middle and, one by one, other leaves are attached all round in two or three rows, in a circular formation. The attachment is done by sticking small sticks through these dry leaves. The *pattal* can be thrown away after use and, therefore, is very useful during weddings or any large gathering for lunch or dinner.

Piyala (or Pyala): This is a presentation of money given to a son-in-law, after festive occasions, by the father-in-law or the brother-in-law. It used to consist of a token sum of, say, Rs. 5.00 or Rs. 10.00, and is supposed to be in lieu of a peg of whisky. It is given with great respect and delicacy, and the son-in-law should get up to receive it with humility and grace, and perform an *aadaab* (Muslim way of expressing respect and thanks) or a *namaskar* to the elder of the family. In olden times the sons-in-law or sons did not drink in front of their elders, but it was accepted that they took a peg now and then, and the elders condoned a limited use of the beverage and made it apparent that they knew about it. The *pyala* is also given to a son-in-law during his engagement or after the marriage ceremony (only by the in-laws), and, this time, by all the elders who are introduced to the groom in this manner. During the wedding, the wives accompany the husbands, when receiving the *pyala*. The money given at this time is much more; the parents of the girl give at least Rs. 100, and the other relatives diminishing the amount according to their relationship to the girl who is getting married.

Pokri: A natural water pond.

Pralay: The dissolution of the world.

Pujan: This is done by just dipping the third finger of the right hand in water, then by holding this finger by the thumb and letting it go with a jerk, thus sprinkling water with the help of the thumb, three times on the deity. The same procedure is repeated with *aipun* and then with *roli* and, lastly, the rice and flowers are showered, thus depicting the bathing of the deity and then the decoration with *aipun* (in place of sandalwood paste). *Roli* is for symbolising the putting of *teeka* (from far), and lastly the showering of rice and flowers, as a symbol of worship of the deity in all its glory.

Puri: Small *chappatis* but thicker, and deep fried and served in place of *chappatis. Puris* are made with wheat dough.

Purohit: The Brahmin priest (pandit) accepted by a family to perform all the religious rituals in the household. A Brahmin who is well versed in the Vedic rituals.

Rangoli: A decoration deftly designed on the floor or any flat surface by holding white flour in between the thumb and middle finger and changing a design and then filling it with different coloured chalk powders. Used for all auspicious occasions in the western and southern parts of India.

Revri: A round sweet made of jaggery, mixed with *til* and flattened out.

Roli: Red powder available at all *puja* shops. Very little water is added to make it semiliquid.

Roop: Form.

Sapt Rishi: The names of the Sapt Rishis are: (1) Visvamitra (2) Jamadgani (3) Bhardwaj (4) Gautam (5) Atri (6) Kashyap (7) Vasist

Sankranti: Movement of the sun from one *rashi* (zodiac sign) to another. There are 12 *rashis* and the sun takes 30 days in its movement from one to the other. The day it enters the next *rashi* is known as *Sankranti*.

Sat Yug: The time of honesty and truth and long life for mankind and other living beings; it is a period whose duration is 17,28,000 years of man.

Seep Chowk: A decoration made on top of a *kharia matti chowk* after it has dried. *Aipun* is used for making this *chowk* and the formation is that of a peacock in the Madhubani style. This is a small decoration near about the *patta* or on it, on which the deity is seated in the centre, facing the audience.

Singhara: A root fruit grown in ponds, green-black in colour with prickly horns.

Sristi: Creation

Sudershan Chakra: A round disc, the weapon of Sri Krishna.

Suhagan: A married woman whose husband is alive.

Sukul Paksh (waxing of the moon): The Vikram calendar of the Hindus has 15 days denoting the waxing of the moon, i.e., when the moon comes out in the skies as a very thin crescent, after the completely dark night (Amavas) of the previous fortnight. The moon gains (in body shape) each night and, by the 15th day, takes it full round form on Purnima or the full moon night. This is the bright fortnight of a month, and is known as 'Sukul Paksh'. The 15 days are known, respectively, as:

Parva, Dooj, Teej, Chouth, Panchami, Chat, Saptami, Ashtami, Navami, Dashami, Ekadashi, Dwadashi, Treedashi, Chaturdashi and Purnima. These are known as the Tiths.

Swarg Lok: A place where the *devtas* live and where human spirits that have earned their rest in heavenly surrounding go for a limited time; they have earned this rest by their good deeds on earth. They shall be born again on this earth to further their spiritual quest for *moksh* or oneness with the Almighty.

Tapasya: Great hardship.

Thaali (or Thali): A round-shaped metal tray of any size.

Thona: This container is also made from the dry leaves of the dhaak or saal trees. The dry leaves are shaped into a bowl form. The leaves are held together by small even sticks, but unlike a *pattal* which is flat, they are rounded and moulded upwards. The *thona* is, again, disposable. Hawkers and shopkeepers serve eatables in it for immediate use or for taking home. Curd, *methai* and *kachoris* are usually served in them, but all cooked vegetables also appear very inviting in an ethnic way, when served in *thonas*.

Til: Linseed.

Treta Yug: Ram *avtar* descended on to discipline mankind and set an example by rightful behaviour in the family and the state. Its duration is 12,64,000 years of man.

Uplas: Cowdung cakes made by mixing cowdung with pieces of straw. Used for fuel in villages and towns in India.

Uttarayan: When the Sun moves towards the Northern hemisphere into the Tropics of Capricorn -- from the 14th of January (Makar Sankranti, Pongal Goopi etc.) The last date of its remaining in the Tropics of Capricorn is 13th July and then it moves into 'Dakriyan' towards the Equator and on to the Tropics of Cancer.

Visarjan: To put under water.

Vikram Samvat: The Vikram Samvat (or calendar) is the one the Hindus follow for all their festivals. During the reign of Vikramaditya, i.e., 57 years before the Christian calendar, the Hindu calendar came into being. The Hindu year begins always in Chait, and is counted from the Parva of Chait during the Krishna Paksh or the first day of the waning moon.

The months or Jaath according to the Vikram calendar are: Chait, Basak or Baisakh, Jeth, Ashaad, Sawan, Bhadon, Kwar, Kartik, Aghan, Poose (Poush), Magh and Phagun. According to the Christian calendar, Chait falls sometime in March-April.

Vrat: A vow to do a certain thing; usually associated with fasting. On the *vrats* no onion or garlic is eaten in cooked food or otherwise.

Yugs: Period of time of 43,20,000 years of man divided into the following: Sat Yug, Treta Yug, Duapar Yug and Kal Yug.

Zari: Gold thread or work done by gold thread usually on clothes.